RCP New Testament

Reorganized Concise Paraphrased Bible

Book IV-V

By: Obadiah Paulus

ISBN: 978-1-953162-13-7

LCCN: 2020923694

Tigard, OR

Copyright 2020 RCP Bible and Obadiah Paulus

All rights reserved

Dedication:

This paraphrase of the New Testament is dedicated to Jesus Christ and his glory. My prayer is that this book helps you in your faith journey to draw closer to God and make his kingdom great. I wrote this under a pseudonym so that it isn't about me. I want to thank my wife, my children, my mother, and all the other people who have helped make this work possible. I could not have done it without you. Until we all see each other together in heaven.

About the cover image:

The cover image is a dove which is a symbol of the Holy Spirit. The Holy Spirit is the third person of the Trinity and his arrival ushered in the New Covenant that allows us to be reconciled to God.

ABOUT THIS BOOK:

The Bible can be a very intimidating book. This book is an attempt to modernize the language and make the material more accessible. This book is not a translation of the original Greek and I do not claim inspiration. I have written this book by paraphrasing English translations of the original text and expanding when necessary so that the reader can better understand the story. I have also taken out portions that may not be relevant to the modern reader (mainly prophecies that we don't have context for or to nations that no longer exist). This book is not for serious bible study. This is a tool to help introduce people to the biblical narrative and aide in our understanding. I pray that you find this book useful in your pursuit of understanding God and Scripture.

This book is a paraphrase of translations of the original writings, and I have used the ESV, NIV, NASB, and NLT to come up with a readable version of the original text. I have tried to modernize the language by removing passive voice, split infinitives, and other devices that can sometimes make the text harder to understand for the layperson. I've also reorganized the text into chronological order and provided explanatory boxes to help the reader better understand the authors' original intent. If any of these questions spur further interest, I encourage additional study.

This first book is a recreation of Matthew, Mark, Luke, and John, the first four books of the New Testament. This book harmonizes the original Scriptures using the chronology found in the <u>NIV Harmony of the Gospels</u>, making changes where appropriate. These books focus on the life of Jesus of Nazareth, the central figure of the Christian faith. Three of them (Matthew, Mark, and Luke) contain much of the same material, while a fourth (John) is unique. Outside of these four accounts, we have very little information about the life of Jesus.

Each book has its distinctions and each presents a different view of the Son of God. The book of Matthew is written to a primarily Jewish audience and shows that Jesus is the promised Messiah and fulfillment of Jewish expectation. Matthew makes many references to the Old Testament and focuses on Jesus' discourses and sayings.

The book of Mark records the apostle Peter's viewpoint of the life of Christ and he wrote to Roman Christians. Mark presents Jesus as the suffering servant and strong Son of God. It is the shortest and most compact of the Gospels and has a focus on immediate action and his ministry.

The physician Luke's Gospel records the apostle Paul's perspective of Jesus' life. Luke relates Jesus to all of humanity by recording his genealogy back to Adam. This book shows how Jesus reached out to women, children, and the disenfranchised.

The book of John was the last book written about Jesus' life and it presents many events that the other books do not include. John wrote this Gospel to a broad audience so that all people might believe that Jesus was the Son of God.

While each of these Gospels presents a different view, they all speak about one man's life and actions. This text attempts to look at Jesus' life as a single narrative by integrating the text of all four of the gospel records. This is like the process used in a courtroom where lawyers combine eyewitness testimony to paint an accurate picture of what took place. Each of the four Gospels gives a different perspective in the same way that four witnesses of an event will describe it differently.

The second book covers the 23 other books of the New Testament and records the spread of the Christian church. The book of Acts is a historical document of how Jesus' followers shared the gospel with the Jews and Gentiles of the Ancient Near East. The next 21 books are letters from church leaders to local churches dealing with specific issues they faced. The final book, Revelation, is a vision that the apostle John saw that is an unveiling of what was to come.

It is crucial to know that this is a paraphrase and not a translation of the original texts. This is a tool to help better understand the Gospels but does not replace in-depth study. My prayer is that it is useful as you seek to understand better the life and work of our Lord and Savior, Jesus Christ.

We do not have the original manuscripts of the New Testament, but we have an overwhelming amount of evidence that allows us to reconstruct the original text. We have over 5,300 Greek manuscripts (including 10,000 Latin copies and at least 9,300 ancient copies in other languages) of the New Testament. Many of these were copied not long after the original was written. For other important ancient documents, we have far fewer copies, and the copies we have are much farther from the original date than the copies we have for the New Testament.

There are differences in some copies, but scholars can use a logical process to figure out which of the different options are most likely to have been the original. Using the manuscripts we have and textual criticism, we are confident that 99.5% of what we have is an accurate copy of the original documents. None of the material that is in question affects significant doctrine. The translations of the Bible that we read today are based on what we believe was in the original manuscripts.

We do not have a precise timeline for the events in these two books, but the following is a good approximation of when events took place and gives us an outline for the book's organization.

Approximate Timeline of New Testament events

4 B.C.	Jesus' birth
26 A.D.	Jesus begins his ministry
30	Jesus' death, burial, and resurrection, the Holy Spirit comes at Pentecost, and the establishment of the Church
35	First persecution of the Church
36	Saul's conversion
40	First Gentile conversion
43	Founding of church at Antioch; book of Matthew written
48	Paul's first missionary journey
51	Paul's second missionary journey
52	I Thessalonians written
53	II Thessalonians written
54	Paul's third missionary journey

57	I Corinthians and Galatians
58	II Corinthians and Romans written; Paul arrested in Rome
59	Book of Luke written
62	Paul's Roman imprisonment; Ephesians, Philippians, Colossians, Philemon, and James written
63	I Peter, book of Acts, Hebrews, I Timothy, and Titus written
64	Book of Mark written
66	II Timothy and II Peter written
67	Paul's death
70	Destruction of Jerusalem
75	Jude written
85	Book of John written
90	John's three letters written
97	Revelation written

The Life of Jesus

Reorganized Concise Paraphrased Bible

Book IV

By: Obadiah Paulus

ISRAEL IN JESUS' DAY

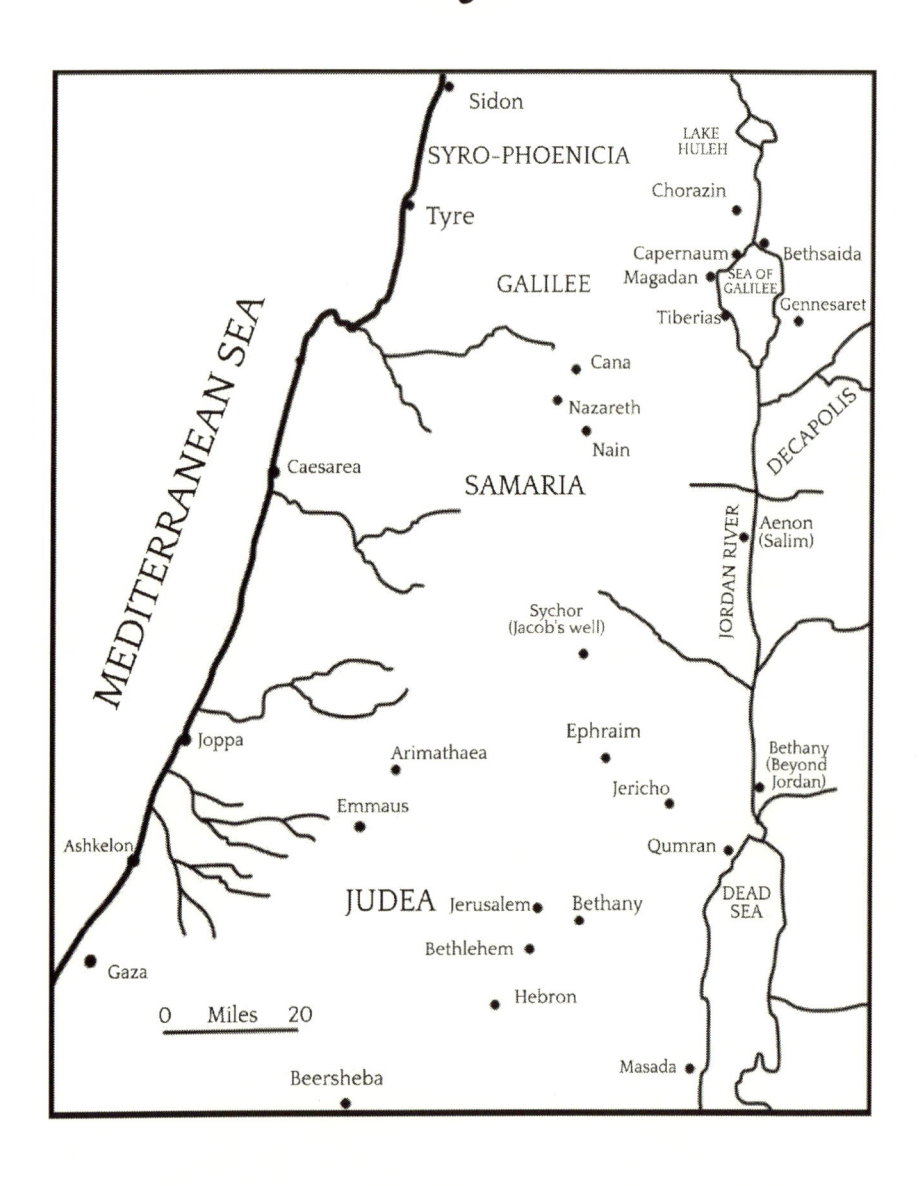

TABLE OF CONTENTS

CHAPTER 1: Introduction to the Life of Jesus	1
CHAPTER 2: Intertestamental Period	3
CHAPTER 3: Preparation for Jesus' Birth	5
CHAPTER 4: The Birth of Jesus	9
CHAPTER 5: Jesus' Early Years	11
CHAPTER 6: The Birth of John the Baptist	14
CHAPTER 7: John's Ministry	17
CHAPTER 8: Baptism and Temptation of Jesus	20
CHAPTER 9: Beginning of Jesus' Ministry	23
CHAPTER 10: Meeting with Nicodemus	26
CHAPTER 11: The Woman at the Well	29
CHAPTER 12: Ministry in Galilee	32
CHAPTER 13: Call of the Four & Various Healings	34
CHAPTER 14: Sabbath Controversies and Withdrawals	40
CHAPTER 15: Appointment of the Twelve	45
CHAPTER 16: The Sermon on the Mount	47
CHAPTER 17: Growing Fame	56
CHAPTER 18: First Public Rejection	61
CHAPTER 19: Secrets About the Kingdom in Parables	64
CHAPTER 20: Continuing Opposition	68
CHAPTER 21: Final Galilean Campaign	72
CHAPTER 22: Death of John the Baptist	75
CHAPTER 23: The Bread of Life	77
CHAPTER 24: The Leaven of the Religious Teachers	82
CHAPTER 25: The Great Confession and the Transfiguration	87
CHAPTER 26: Responsibility to Others	90
CHAPTER 27: The Feast of Tabernacles	95
CHAPTER 28: Further Ministry at the Feast of Tabernacles	99
CHAPTER 29: Private Lessons on Service and Prayer	103
CHAPTER 30: Second Debate with Religious Leaders	108
CHAPTER 31: Sabbath Healings and Further Division	114
CHAPTER 32: Principles of Discipleship	120

CHAPTER 33: Further Parables — 123
CHAPTER 34: Raising Lazarus — 128
CHAPTER 35: Teaching on the Way to Jerusalem — 131
CHAPTER 36: Triumphal Entry and the Fig Tree — 139
CHAPTER 37: Official Challenge to Jesus' Authority — 144
CHAPTER 38: Jesus' Response to Questions — 147
CHAPTER 39: Olivet Discourse — 152
CHAPTER 40: Arrangements for Betrayal — 159
CHAPTER 41: The Last Supper — 161
CHAPTER 42: The Upper Room Continued — 165
CHAPTER 43: Garden of Gethsemane — 171
CHAPTER 44: Jesus' Trial with the Jews — 174
CHAPTER 45: Peter's Denials — 176
CHAPTER 46: Jesus Before Pilate — 178
CHAPTER 47: The Crucifixion — 182
CHAPTER 48: The Resurrection — 187
CHAPTER 49: Resurrection Appearances — 191
CHAPTER 50: Final Instructions — 196
EPILOGUE: What's the Point? — 202

CHAPTER ONE

INTRODUCTION TO THE LIFE OF JESUS
Luke 1:1-4; John 1:1-18

Many people have written accounts about the life and actions of the Messiah. The authors of the Gospels carefully investigated the accounts of the early disciples and other eyewitnesses of how God fulfilled his promises. They used these for their source material and then wrote a careful summary to reassure you of the truth of what others have taught. This is a compilation and a synthesis of those eyewitness accounts.

The Word always existed, even at the beginning of the universe. The Word was with God, and he was God; he was with God in the beginning. He created everything that exists and nothing exists that he didn't create. Life was in him, and this life gives light to everyone. His light shines in the darkness, but the darkness did not understand it, nor could it overpower it.

> **What does "Word" mean?**
>
> The Greek word for word here is *logos*. This word represents the principle of divine reason and creative force of God. In this context, it represents the second person of the Trinity, Jesus Christ.

God sent John the Baptist to tell everyone about Jesus so that they might believe. John was not the light; he was just a witness to the light. Jesus, who is the true light and gives light to everyone, had not come yet.

Although the Word made the world, the world didn't recognize him when he came; even his people in his homeland didn't accept him. But to all who accepted and believed in him, he gave the right to become God's children. They are reborn, and this rebirth is from God and not from any human plan.

So, the Word became human and lived on earth with us in the person of Jesus, and he was full of grace and truth. He came so that we might see his glory, which comes from God the Father. John the Baptist testified about him to the people, shouting, "I was talking about Jesus when I said, 'Someone far greater than me is coming because he existed long before I did.'"

> **Is Jesus really God? Is Jesus really a man?**
>
> The answer to both questions is yes. He never became God; he was God from the moment he was born, and he continued to be God throughout his life, in his death, and after his resurrection. He claimed to be God on multiple occasions (see later inset) and his audience clearly understood his claims (this is why he was killed). Numerous passages state that he is God, including passages in Philippians and Colossians; so, we know his followers understood his nature. He had a miraculous birth and lived a sinless life. He performed miracles, demonstrating his power over nature (which, as God, he created), including raising himself from the dead.
>
> Jesus was also fully man. He was born and suffered all the same things that humans do, including hunger, fatigue, and a natural growth process. This can be difficult to reconcile because he was also fully God, but there is nothing in human nature that precludes also being God. The Chalcedonian Creed of 451 sums up this position when it says, "in the one person, Jesus Christ, there are two natures, a human nature and a divine nature, each in its completeness and integrity, and that these two natures are organically and indissolubly united, yet so that no third nature is formed thereby."

God's unfailing love has blessed us over and over. Moses gave us the Law, but Jesus Christ gave us God's unfailing love and truth. No one has ever seen God; but his only Son, who is God and lives with the Father, has told us about him.

CHAPTER TWO

INTERTESTIMENTAL PERIOD

God had been silent for roughly 400 years between the last prophet and the birth of Jesus. During this time, God was preparing the earth for his arrival. Israel had some brief independence, but nothing like what they had once enjoyed. The people remembered the promises made to their ancestors. They were anxiously awaiting the arrival of the Messiah, the Anointed One, who would fulfill Old Testament prophecies and restore Israel to prominence.

> **What does Messiah mean?**
>
> The term Messiah means "Anointed One." The Messiah was the promised deliverer of Israel who would restore them to world prominence. Throughout the Old Testament, multiple prophecies told of where he would be born, details of his life and ministry, and resurrection. Jesus fulfilled many of these with his first coming and will fulfill the rest when he returns. In Christianity, we refer to the Messiah as the Christ. Thus, the name Jesus Christ means Jesus the Messiah.

The Romans were in charge and they ruled over most of the known world. There was a common currency, peace, and extensive highway system that allowed for travel and the gospel's eventual spread. The Israelites were desperate for liberation and expected the Messiah to be a military ruler to overthrow the Romans and restore their kingdom. While Jesus will one day come as a conquering king, he first came as a suffering servant. The Israelites focused on the prophecies that told of the Messiah doing what they wanted and ignored the prophecies that spoke of his humble service and sacrifice. Therefore, Jesus confused many of his hearers, and they did not understand why he didn't call the people to arms to defeat the Romans.

When Jesus came, the Pharisees and Sadducees were the chief Jewish religious divisions. The Israelites had lost the Promised Land, and the glory of the original temple so, they were determined to keep the Law, the last vestige of God's promises they had left. The Pharisees were so dedicated to following the Law that they set up additional rules around the laws so that they would not even come close to breaking God's commands. While their intentions were good, they ended up loving the rules more than they loved God. Pharisees were typically ordinary people who had formal education in Jewish Law.

The other party was the Sadducees, and they were typically wealthy aristocrats. They wanted to follow God's rules but wanted to adjust them to fit into the culture around them. They changed some of their beliefs to fit in with popular opinion and sacrificed some of their standards to gain popularity with the rulers of the land. They were religious rationalists who denied the existence of miracles and the afterlife.

Jesus' teaching went against both groups' beliefs and they were the groups that Jesus clashed with the most. Jesus taught to love God and others, but the Pharisees and Sadducees were far more worried about following the rules and looking good than loving God and treating the people well. They did everything that they could to maintain public perception and their elevated social standing. Despite their seeming holiness, their hearts were far from God. Jesus' conflict with them was shocking to the people because they held their leaders in high regard.

CHAPTER THREE

PREPARATION FOR JESUS' BIRTH
Matthew 1; Luke 3:23-38; 1:26-56

Jesus was the descendant that God promised to Eve in the garden, to Abraham, and to David. Both Mary, his mother, and Joseph, his adoptive father, were descendants of Abraham and David. Joseph's lineage was through the kings of Israel and Judah, while Mary's ancestors were from David's line, but they did not sit upon the throne.

Some of his ancestors were righteous men of God who were full of faith and love; others were wicked and sinful. We can read many of their stories in the Old Testament, but the most important fact for us is that Jesus was the fulfillment of all of God's promises of a Savior to the Jewish ancestors. He was the solution to our sin and would live a perfect life before becoming the perfect sacrifice for humanity.

Mary was a virgin and had never had sexual relations with any man. But God came to her and she became pregnant with Jesus, who was both fully God and fully human. He needed to be fully God so that he could pay for all of mankind's sin, and he needed to be fully human so that his perfect life and sacrifice could apply to all humanity.

One day, the angel Gabriel came to Mary in the Galilean town of Nazareth. She was engaged to a man named Joseph, a descendant of King David. Gabriel went to her and said, "Greetings, favored one! The Lord is with you!"

Gabriel's words troubled Mary, and she wondered what he meant. But the angel comforted her, "Don't be frightened, Mary, for God is going to bless you! You will become pregnant and have a son, and you are to name him Jesus. He will be very great and will be the Son of God. The Lord will give him the throne of David and he will reign over Israel forever!"

> **Son of God vs. Son of Man**
>
> Son of God and Son of Man are two different titles that the gospel writers used to refer to Jesus. Son of Man focuses on his connection to humanity; Son of God focuses on his connection to divinity. The two are interchangeable in this book.

Mary asked the angel, "How can I get pregnant since I'm still a virgin?"

Gabriel answered, "The Holy Spirit will come upon you, and God's power will overshadow you. Therefore, your baby will be holy and will be the Son of God. Even your relative Elizabeth has become pregnant in her old age, and although she was barren, she is now in her sixth month. Nothing is impossible with God."

Mary replied, "I am the Lord's servant, and I accept his will. May your words come true." Then the angel left.

A few days later, Mary hurried to her relative's hometown in the hill country of Judea and greeted Elizabeth when she arrived. When Elizabeth heard Mary's greeting, her baby leaped in her womb, and the Holy Spirit came upon her. Elizabeth cried out with a loud voice, "God has blessed you above all other women, and your child is blessed too. It's an honor to have the mother of my Lord visit me! As soon as I heard your greeting, my baby jumped for joy. You are blessed because you believed that the Lord would do what he said."

> **What prophecies did Jesus fulfill?**
>
> There are hundreds of Old Testament prophecies that Jesus fulfilled in his birth, ministry, death, and resurrection. Mathematicians have calculated the odds of just some of these coming true about any individual to be infinitesimally small. To have all of them come true identifies Jesus as the Savior of all humanity that God had promised from the beginning.

> Theologians have written entire books on this topic; here is a brief sampling of some of the prophecies that Jesus fulfilled:
>
> - Born of a virgin
> - Born in Bethlehem
> - Descended from King David
> - From the tribe of Judah
> - Would come out of Egypt
> - Sinless life
> - Would be a suffering servant
> - Taught in parables
> - Ministry would begin in Galilee
> - Preceded by a forerunner (John the Baptist)
> - Enter Jerusalem seated on a donkey
> - Betrayed for 30 pieces of silver
> - Crucifixion
> - Resurrection
> - Soldiers would cast lots for his clothes
> - Would not decay in death
> - Mocked and given vinegar to drink at execution

Mary responded and quoted several Old Testament Scriptures, "My soul praises the Lord and my spirit rejoices in God, my Savior! For he noticed his lowly servant girl, and now all generations will call me blessed. For the Lord has done great things for me and his name is holy. He is merciful to all generations, to everyone who fears him. His mighty arm has done tremendous things and he has scattered the proud and arrogant! He has removed rulers from power and lifted the lowly. He has satisfied the hungry with good things and sent the rich away empty-handed. He has helped his servant Israel and has remembered to be merciful. For he promised always to be merciful to Abraham and his descendants."

Mary stayed with Elizabeth and her husband, Zechariah, until Elizabeth's child was born, and then Mary went back home.

Mary returned home to her fiancée, Joseph. She was still a virgin, but she became pregnant by the Holy Spirit. Nazareth was a seaport town that was notorious for prostitution, so there were many rumors about whose child it really was. Jewish engagements were very serious and a couple could only break one with divorce. Because Joseph was a righteous man and ashamed of his pregnant fiancée, he decided to quietly break the engagement so he wouldn't disgrace her publicly.

But an angel of the Lord appeared to him in a dream and said, "Joseph, son of David, do not be afraid to marry her because her baby is from the Holy Spirit. She will have a son, and you are to name him Jesus because he will save his people from their sins." All of this happened to fulfill the Lord's message through the prophet Isaiah: "Look, the virgin will have a child! She will give birth to a son, and he will be called Immanuel, which means God is with us."

When Joseph woke up, he did what the angel of the Lord commanded, and he brought Mary home to be his wife. She remained a virgin until her son was born, and Joseph named him Jesus.

CHAPTER FOUR

THE BIRTH OF JESUS
Luke 2:1-39

About that time, Caesar Augustus decreed that there should be a census of the entire Roman Empire (likely 4 BC). People went to their hometowns to register for this census. Since Joseph was a descendant of King David, he traveled about 70 miles from Nazareth in Galilee to Bethlehem in Judea because it was the city of David. He took Mary with him, and when they arrived, there was nowhere for them to stay, so they slept in a barn with the animals. While they were there, she gave birth to Jesus. She wrapped her newborn snugly and laid him in a feeding trough because there was no room for them in the inn.

That night some shepherds were in the nearby fields, guarding their flocks. Suddenly, an angel of the Lord appeared to them, and the Lord's glory surrounded them. The shepherds were terrified, but the angel reassured them, "Don't be afraid, I bring you good news of great joy for everyone! The Savior has been born tonight in Bethlehem, the city of David! He is the Messiah and Lord! You will know it's him because he will be lying in a manger!"

Suddenly, many other angels joined the angel and they all praised God, saying, "Glory to God in heaven, and peace on earth to everyone that God favors."

After the angels returned to heaven, the shepherds said to each other, "Let's go to Bethlehem and see this wonderful thing the Lord has told us about."

The shepherds ran to the village and found Mary and Joseph watching over the baby lying in the manger. Then the shepherds told everyone what had happened and what the angel had told them. Everyone they talked to was amazed, but Mary treasured these things in her heart and thought about them often. Afterward, the shepherds went back to the fields, praising God for everything they saw and heard.

***

Eight days later, Joseph and Mary circumcised the baby and named him Jesus, just as the angel had told them to do.

After 40 days, his parents took him to Jerusalem to present him to the Lord, in obedience to the Law of Moses. Joseph and Mary were poor, but they obeyed God's Law, bringing a pair of turtledoves or pigeons as a sacrifice.

A righteous and devout man named Simeon lived in Jerusalem and the Holy Spirit was in him. He was eagerly expecting the Messiah to come to rescue Israel, and God revealed to him that he would not die until he had seen the Messiah. When Joseph and Mary came to present the baby Jesus to the Lord, the Holy Spirit led Simeon to the temple. When Simeon saw Jesus, he took the child in his arms and praised God, saying, "Sovereign Lord, now I can die in peace! I have seen the Savior that you have given to all people, just as you promised me. He is God's light to all the nations, and he is the glory of Israel!"

Jesus' parents were amazed at what people were saying about their child. Simeon blessed them and said, "People will reject this child, and he will cause grief for many in Israel, but he will cause great joy for many others. He will reveal the deepest thoughts of men, but a sword will pierce your soul."

A very old prophetess named Anna was also in the temple. She was a widow whose husband had died seven years into their marriage. Anna was now 84 years old and she stayed at the temple day and night, worshiping God with fasting and prayer. She came along just as Simeon was talking with Mary and Joseph, and she began thanking and praising God. She told everyone at the temple who had been waiting for the redemption of Jerusalem about Jesus.

CHAPTER FIVE

JESUS' EARLY YEARS
Matthew 2; Luke 2:40-52

A couple of years later, some wise men from eastern lands arrived in Jerusalem and asked, "Where is the newborn King of the Jews? We saw his star in the east, and we have come to worship him."

Their question deeply disturbed Herod, who ruled Judea for the Romans, and the rest of Jerusalem. He called for the leading priests and teachers of religious law and asked them where the Messiah was to be born. "In Bethlehem, according to the prophecies," they replied.

Then Herod secretly called in the wise men to find out exactly when they first saw the star. They told him that they had first seen it a couple of years before their visit. Herod sent them to Bethlehem and said, "Go look for the child; when you find him, come back and tell me so I can worship him, too!"

After talking to King Herod, the wise men went their way and followed the star until it stopped over Bethlehem. When they arrived at the house where Mary, Joseph, and Jesus lived, they bowed down and worshiped the baby. Then they opened their treasure chests and gave him gifts of gold, spices, and incense. But when they left, they went home another way, because God warned them in a dream to not return to Herod.

After the wise men left, an angel of the Lord appeared to Joseph in a dream and told him, "Get up and run to Egypt with the child and his mother. Stay there until I tell you to return because Herod is going to try to kill the child." That night the little family left for Egypt and stayed there until Herod died. This fulfilled the prophecy that God would call his son out of Egypt.

Herod was furious when he learned that the wise men had tricked him, so he sent soldiers to kill all the boys in and around Bethlehem under the age of three. This also fulfilled Old Testament prophecy.

***

When Herod died a few years later, an angel of the Lord appeared to Joseph in a dream and told him to leave Egypt, saying, "Take Mary and Jesus back to Israel because those who were trying to kill Jesus are dead." So, Joseph returned to Israel with Jesus and his mother. But when he learned that Herod's son Archelaus was the new ruler in Judea, he was afraid. An angel came to Joseph in a dream and told him to return home, so they returned to Nazareth, a small town in Galilee where they had first become engaged. This fulfilled the prophecy that the Messiah would be a Nazarene. Jesus grew up healthy and strong; he was full of wisdom beyond his years, and God blessed him.

> **What prophecy said the Messiah would be a Nazarene?**
>
> There is no explicit Old Testament passage stating that the Messiah would be a Nazarene, but this is a prophecy that was likely in another writing that is not in the Bible. A prophet speaks on behalf of God and some prophets did not have their prophecies recorded in Scripture.

***

When Jesus was twelve years old, his family traveled the 65 miles from Nazareth to Jerusalem for the Passover festival, just like they did every year. After the festival was over, his parents headed back to Nazareth, but Jesus stayed in Jerusalem. Joseph and Mary thought he was with some of the other travelers, so they didn't miss him at first. But when they couldn't find him, they went back to Jerusalem to look for their boy. Three days later, they found Jesus sitting with the religious leaders in the temple listening to them and asking questions. Everyone there was amazed at his understanding of religious matters.

His parents were astonished when they found him and Mary asked, "Son, why have you done this to us? Your father and I have been frantically searching for you!"

Jesus answered, "You didn't need to look for me! Didn't you know I would be in my Father's house?" Even at twelve years old, Jesus knew his true nature, but his parents didn't fully understand. Jesus went back to Nazareth with them and he continued to obey his parents. Mary stored all that Jesus said and did in her heart. As he grew up, Jesus became wiser and impressed both God and men. He worked with his father as a carpenter and eventually took over the business once Joseph died.

CHAPTER SIX

THE BIRTH OF JOHN THE BAPTIST
Luke 1:5-25, 57-79

Before Jesus began his ministry, God sent John the Baptist to tell everyone about him so that the people might believe. John was not the promised Savior; he was just a witness who pointed people to Jesus. Just as Jesus had a miraculous birth, John also had an extraordinary beginning.

John's father was a Jewish priest named Zechariah and his mother was also from the priestly line of Aaron (both were related to Mary). Both were righteous and carefully obeyed all of God's commandments. But now they were getting old and they had no children because Elizabeth was barren.

One day, Zechariah had a once-in-a-lifetime opportunity to enter the sanctuary and burn incense to the Lord. While he was in the temple, an angel of the Lord appeared, standing to the right of the incense altar. When Zechariah saw him, he was scared. But the angel said, "Don't be afraid, Zechariah, God has heard your prayer. You and Elizabeth will have a son and you are to name him John. He will bring you great joy and gladness, and many will rejoice with you at his birth because your son will be great in the Lord's eyes. He must never drink alcohol, and the Holy Spirit will fill him before he is even born. Your son will persuade many Israelites to return to the Lord their God and he will precede the Messiah in the spirit and power of Elijah (the Old Testament prophet). He will turn the hearts of fathers back to their children and help the disobedient accept godly wisdom; he will prepare the people for the coming of the Lord."

Zechariah recognized all the prophecies the angel referenced, but something troubled him, so he asked, "My wife and I are both old, so how do I know this will happen?"

The angel replied, "I am Gabriel, I stand in God's presence, and he has sent me to bring you this good news! But since you didn't believe my message, you won't be able to speak until the child is born. This is a sign so that you will know that all of this will happen at the proper time."

The people outside had been praying and wondered why Zechariah took so long to come out. When he finally did, he kept gesturing, but he couldn't speak. Then they realized that he must have seen a vision.

Zechariah went home to his wife Elizabeth after finishing his service at the temple. Soon afterward, she became pregnant; then she went into seclusion for five months, saying, "The Lord has dealt with me kindly and taken away my disgrace by giving me this child." It was during this time that her relative, Mary came to visit her.

Elizabeth gave birth to a boy. Her neighbors and relatives shared her joy when they heard about how God had been merciful and kind to her.

On the eighth day after their son had been born, friends and relatives came together to circumcise the child, and they wanted to name him after his father, Zechariah. But Elizabeth protested, "No! His name is John!"

This shocked the crowd and they argued, "But no one in your family is named John." So, they made gestures to Zechariah to ask what he wanted to name the baby. He asked for a writing tablet, and to everyone's surprise, he wrote, "His name is John." Instantly, he could speak again, and he began praising God.

The whole neighborhood was in awe and news of these events spread quickly throughout the area. Everyone who heard about it asked how he would turn out because the Lord's hand was with him.

Then the Holy Spirit came upon his father, Zechariah, and he prophesied, quoting numerous Scriptures: "Praise the Lord, the God of Israel, because he has visited and redeemed us. He has sent us a mighty Savior from the royal line of his servant David, just as he promised through his holy prophets years ago. He will save us from our enemies and from all who hate us. God has been merciful to our ancestors by remembering his holy covenant with them, the oath he swore to our ancestor Abraham. God will rescue us from our enemies so that we can serve him without fear, in holiness and righteousness forever.

"My son, you will be called the Prophet of God, because you will prepare the way for the Lord. You will tell his people about salvation through the forgiveness of their sins. Because of God's tender mercy, the rising sun from heaven is about to break upon us. It will shine on those who sit in darkness and the shadow of death, and guide us to the path of peace."

CHAPTER SEVEN

JOHN'S MINISTRY
Matthew 3:1-11; Mark 1:1-8; Luke 3:1-16; John 1:19-28

John grew up and became strong in spirit, and he lived out in the desert until beginning his public ministry to Israel.

About a year before Jesus began his ministry, the word of God came to John, Zechariah's son, in the wilderness. John started by preaching in the Judean countryside on both sides of the Jordan River. The prophets spoke of John when they said, "I will send my messenger before you, and he will prepare your way. He is a voice shouting in the wilderness: 'Prepare the way for the Lord; make a straight road for him! Fill in the valleys and level the mountains and hills! Straighten the curves and smooth out the rough places, and all people will see God's salvation.'"

This messenger was John the Baptist. He wore clothes made of camel hair with a leather belt and ate locusts and wild honey. People from Jerusalem and all over the Jordan Valley went out to the wilderness to hear him preach. He said, "Repent! Turn away from your sinful thoughts and actions and turn to God, because the kingdom of heaven (or kingdom of God) is near." He told the people to show their repentance and receive forgiveness through baptism. After they confessed their sins, he baptized them in the Jordan River.

> **Kingdom of heaven or kingdom of God?**
>
> Matthew's account of Jesus' life speaks of the kingdom of heaven, while Luke's Gospel uses the kingdom of God. The two phrases are basically synonyms, although the kingdom of heaven refers to people on earth, while the kingdom of God includes all of creation. The two writers used different words because of their different audiences. This kingdom of heaven is one where God will rule over all the earth and judge the nations. Although he has not fulfilled all the prophecies in

> Scripture, Jesus' arrival ushered in the kingdom. He will fulfill the rest of these when he returns to earth. The two terms are interchangeable in this text.

But when John saw some of the Pharisees and Sadducees coming out, he denounced them and exclaimed, "You brood of vipers! Who warned you to flee God's coming judgment? Prove you have repented by the way you live your lives. Don't think you're safe just because you are descendants of Abraham; God can change these stones into children of Abraham if he wants. The axe of God's judgment is ready to cut you off because he will chop down every tree that doesn't produce good fruit and throw it into the fire."

The crowd asked, "What should we do?"

John replied, "If you have two coats, give one to the poor; if you have food, share it with the hungry."

Some tax collectors also came for baptism and asked, "Teacher, what should we do?"

He answered, "Make sure you don't collect more taxes than the Roman government requires."

A group of soldiers asked, "What about us?"

John said, "Don't extort money and don't accuse people falsely; you should be content with your pay."

Everyone was expecting the Messiah, and they wanted to know if it was John. He answered them by saying, "I baptize people with water for repentance, but someone is coming after me who is much greater than I am; in fact, I'm not even worthy to untie his sandals. He will baptize you with the Holy Spirit and with fire. He is ready to separate the good from the bad; he will keep the good and burn up the bad with never-ending fire." John used many such warnings as he exhorted the people and announced the Good News to them.

Eventually, John's popularity became so great that even the Jewish leaders had heard of his ministry and sent priests and temple assistants from Jerusalem to Bethany to ask John if he claimed to be the Messiah. He denied it and said, "I am not the Messiah."

"Well then, who are you?" they asked. "Are you Elijah?"

"No," he replied.

"Are you the Prophet that Moses promised would come?"

"No."

"Then tell us who you are, so we can answer the ones who sent us."

John replied in the words of Isaiah: "I am a voice shouting in the wilderness, 'Prepare a straight path for the Lord!'"

Some of the Pharisees said, "If you aren't the Messiah, Elijah, or the Prophet, what right do you have to baptize?"

John replied, "I baptize with water, but someone you don't know is here who will soon begin his ministry. I'm not even worthy of being his servant."

CHAPTER EIGHT

BAPTISM AND TEMPTATION OF JESUS
Matthew 3:13-4:11; Mark 1:9-13; Luke 3:21-23; 4:1-13; John 1:29-34

The next day John saw Jesus coming and God opened John's eyes to reveal who Jesus was. John said, "Look, the Lamb of God who takes away the world's sin. I was talking about him when I told you that someone much greater than I am was coming because he existed long before me. Even though he is my cousin, I did not recognize him as the Messiah, but I came, baptizing, to reveal him to Israel."

Jesus came from Nazareth, in Galilee, to have John baptize him with the rest of the crowds because he wanted to identify with the people he came to save and to set an example for all. But John protested, "You should baptize me, not the other way around."

But Jesus said, "Let it be for now because it is the right thing to do." So, John baptized him.

As Jesus came up out of the water, the heavens opened, the Holy Spirit descended, and settled on him like a dove. Then a voice from heaven said, "You are my Son, I love you, and I am very pleased with you."

John said, "When God sent me to baptize, he told me that the man I saw the Holy Spirit descend and rest upon, is the Son of God. Well, I saw the Holy Spirit descend like a dove and rest upon Jesus; he is the one you seek. He will baptize you with the Holy Spirit because he is the Son of God."

***

What is the Trinity?

The Trinity is an essential doctrine to the Christian faith; however, it is tough to understand. A careful examination of Scripture shows us how we derive the doctrine of the Trinity. The Bible clearly shows that God the Father, Jesus the Son, and the Holy Spirit are all divine and each possesses the full essence of God. However, the Bible also clearly shows us that there is an indivisible unity of God and that he is one in nature (Christians do not believe in three gods). We also see that all three exist simultaneously in Jesus' baptism. With these things in mind, we can conclude that God is an undivided being who exists simultaneously as three persons, and all three are fully God.

The word trinity is not in the Bible, but both the Old and New Testaments imply the doctrine. Some people agree that the Father, Son, and Holy Spirit are equally divine, but they argue that each is a different manifestation of God at different times. However, this passage shows that all three exist simultaneously.

Others agree that the Father, Son, and Holy Spirit are all divine, and all three exist simultaneously, but they argue that God the Father is greater than Jesus, who, in turn, is greater than the Holy Spirit. However, while there may be a subordination of position, there is no subordination of nature. Another way of looking at this is a boss and an employee. The boss may have a greater position than the employee, but the boss is not fundamentally better than the employee. In the same way, God the Father has a superior role to Jesus, but they are equally divine. Each member is fully divine and cannot be subordinate to any being.

Some people have problems with the doctrine of the Trinity and argue that a being cannot be three and one simultaneously. Part of the reason we have this problem is that we do not have the words to express God adequately. The Trinity is one of the great mysteries of the Christian faith and we must remember that God created the universe and our logic. God completely transcends natural laws. Our finite minds cannot grasp what is beyond these laws, and we must recognize that we will never fully comprehend God. Because if we could fully comprehend him, he would cease to be God or we would

> become God. Even though it is difficult to understand this concept, the Bible teaches us that God is an undivided being who exists simultaneously as three persons, and all three are fully God.

After the baptism, Jesus left the Jordan River. The Holy Spirit led him out into the wilderness between Jericho and Jerusalem so that the Devil could tempt him. After eating nothing for 40 days and nights, Jesus was very hungry. The Devil had been waiting for an opportune time to tempt Jesus, so he said, "If you are the Son of God, change these stones into loaves of bread."

People often have their least resolve when they are tired and hungry, and Satan wanted Jesus to take a shortcut and use his power to circumvent the natural order, to make life easier. But Jesus said, "Scripture says, 'People don't live on bread alone; they must feed on every word of God.'"

Then the Devil took Jesus to Jerusalem, to the highest point of the temple, a peak about 250 feet above the floor of the Kidron Valley and said, "If you are the Son of God, jump off! Scripture says, 'He will command his angels to protect and guard you. They will lift you up with their hands to keep you from striking your foot on a stone.'"

Jesus replied, "Scripture also says, 'Do not test the Lord your God.'"

Next, the Devil took him to the peak of a very high mountain and showed him all the world's nations and their glory. The Devil told him, "I will give it all to you if you will bow down and worship me. You can have all the glory of these kingdoms and authority over them because I can give them to whomever I want."

Taking this path would remove the coming pain and suffering of the cross, but Jesus shot back, "Get out of here, Satan! Scripture says, 'You must worship the Lord your God and serve him only.'"

When the Devil gave up on tempting Jesus, he left until the next opportunity came up. Then the angels came and cared for Jesus.

CHAPTER NINE

BEGINNING OF JESUS' MINISTRY
John 1:35-2:25

After his temptation, Jesus returned to the Jordan River, where John was baptizing. John was standing with two of his disciples when he saw Jesus walking by. John looked at him and declared, "Look, the Lamb of God!" John's two disciples left and followed Jesus.

Jesus saw them following him and he asked, "What do you want?"

They replied, "Teacher, where are you staying?"

"Come and see," he said. It was about four in the afternoon when they went with him, and they stayed with him for the rest of the day.

Andrew was one of the men who followed Jesus that day. The first thing Andrew did afterward was to find his brother Simon and tell him they had found the Messiah.

Andrew brought Simon to meet Jesus, and he looked intently at Simon and said, "You are Simon, the son of John, but I will call you Peter."

The next day Jesus headed for Galilee. On the way, he found a man named Philip and called, "Come, be my disciple."

Philip, who was from Andrew and Peter's hometown, went to find Bartholomew (also known as Nathaniel) and told him, "We have found the one Moses and the prophets wrote about! He is Jesus of Nazareth, Joseph's son."

Nazareth had a reputation as being a backwoods town with little going on. Bartholomew sneered, "Can anything good come from Nazareth!?"

"Just come and see," Philip replied.

As they approached, Jesus said, "Here comes an honest man, a true son of Israel."

"How do you know me?" Bartholomew asked.

Jesus answered, "I saw you under the fig tree before Philip got you."

Bartholomew exclaimed, "Teacher, you are the Son of God, the King of Israel!"

Jesus asked him, "Do you believe all this because I told you I saw you under the fig tree? You will see greater things than this. I tell you the truth, you will see heaven open and the angels of God ascending and descending on the Son of Man."

***

The next day Jesus, his mother, and his disciples were at a wedding celebration in the village of Cana. During the party, the hosts made a huge social blunder by not having enough wine for the entire celebration. Mary told Jesus, "They have no more wine, do something to help."

Jesus answered, "Mother, that concerns you, not me. It's not my time."

But his mother told the servants, "Do whatever he tells you."

Six 20- to 30-gallon, ceremonial stone water pots were nearby. Jesus told the servants to fill the jars to the brim with water; after they obeyed, he told them to take a cup full to the master of ceremonies.

When the master of ceremonies drank from the cup (which was now full of wine), he called the groom over. Not knowing where the wine was from, he said to the groom, "Usually a host serves the best wine first and then serves the cheaper wine once everyone has been drinking. But you have kept the best wine until now!"

This was Jesus' first miracle and revelation of his glory. His disciples saw this miracle and believed in him. After the wedding, he went to Capernaum for a few days with his mother, brothers, and disciples.

***

Around the time of Passover, Jesus went up to Jerusalem. At the temple, he saw merchants selling animals for the sacrifices and money changers behind their counters. Furious, he drove out the animals, overturned the tables, and scattered the moneychangers' coins everywhere. He made a whip from some ropes and chased the merchants out, yelling, "Get this stuff out of here! How dare you turn my Father's house into a marketplace!"

> ### Cleansing the temple
>
> People who came to worship at the temple could only donate money in temple currency and the moneychangers would charge hefty fees to purchase it. Inspectors had to approve animal sacrifices, and they were very picky about outside animals, but there were always pre-approved animals available for a ridiculously high price. These men had figured out how to gouge the worshippers to make a tremendous profit for themselves. Jesus didn't mind people making a reasonable living, but he was furious at how they were making a mockery of Passover and the sacrificial system.

Later his disciples remembered that Scripture said, "Passion for God's house will consume me."

The Jewish leaders were really upset and demanded, "Show us a sign to prove you have the authority to do these things."

Jesus answered, "Destroy this temple, and I will raise it up in three days."

The Jews said, "It took 46 years to build this temple, and you will raise it up in three days?" But what Jesus meant was the temple of his body. After he rose from the dead, his disciples remembered what he'd said, and they knew both Jesus and the Scriptures were true. Many people were convinced that he was the Messiah because of his miraculous signs at the Passover. But Jesus didn't trust them because he knew human nature and their hearts.

CHAPTER TEN

MEETING WITH NICODEMUS
Matthew 4:12; Mark 1:14; Luke 4:14; John 3:1-4:4

One night, a Pharisee named Nicodemus came to speak with Jesus and he said, "Teacher, we know you are from God because you could not do these miracles or have this kind of wisdom if God weren't with you."

Jesus replied, "I tell you the truth, no one can see the kingdom of God unless he is born again." Here Jesus was talking about regeneration, not reincarnation.

Nicodemus thought that Jesus meant a physical rebirth and he exclaimed, "What do you mean? How can a grown man go back into his mother's womb and be born again?"

Jesus replied, "The truth is, no one can enter the kingdom of God without being born in the flesh and the Spirit. Flesh can only give birth to flesh, but the Holy Spirit gives birth to spirit. You shouldn't be surprised when I say you must be born again. Just as you can hear the wind but cannot tell where it comes from or where it is going, so it is with people who are born of the Spirit."

"What do you mean?" Nicodemus asked.

"You're a respected Jewish teacher," Jesus replied, "and you don't understand these things? We talk about what we know and have seen, but you refuse to believe. If you don't even believe me when I tell you about earthly things, how can you possibly believe me if I tell you about heavenly things? I am the only one who has been to heaven and I have come to earth to tell you about my Father. Just as Moses lifted up the bronze serpent in the wilderness, so the Son of Man must be lifted up. Then, everyone who believes in me will have eternal life.

"For God so loved the world that he gave his only Son so that whoever believes in him will not perish, but have eternal life. God did not send his Son into the world to condemn it, but to save it. Those who trust him won't face judgment, but those who don't trust him will face judgment because they reject the light, the only Son of God, and love the darkness. They hate the light because they want to practice their evil deeds in the darkness and they are afraid that the light will expose their sins. But those who do what is right gladly come to the light, so everyone can see that their deeds have been done through God."

***

After this exchange, Jesus and his disciples left Jerusalem for the Judean countryside and spent some time baptizing people there.

Meanwhile, John the Baptist was baptizing at Aenon, near Salim, because there was plenty of water there and people kept coming to him. John's disciples grumbled to him, "Teacher, the man you called the Messiah is also baptizing people, and everybody is going to him instead of us."

John replied, "A man can only receive what God gives him. I told you that I am not the Messiah; I'm just here to prepare the way for him. Remember that the bride belongs to the groom. The best man waits and listens for him, and rejoices with him; I rejoice at Jesus' success. He must become greater, and I must become less.

"He has come from heaven and is greater than anyone else. I am from the earth, and I only understand earthly things, but he understands heavenly things. He tells people about what he has seen and heard. Few people believe him, but those who believe him discover that God is true. God sent him and he speaks the word of God because he gives the Holy Spirit without limit. The Father loves the Son and has given him authority over everything. Whoever believes in God's Son will have eternal life, but God will pour out his wrath on those who reject him."

Not long after this, Herod Antipas (not the same Herod who tried to kill the infant Christ) arrested John because he was afraid of his message. Word spread about Jesus, and soon, the Pharisees heard that Jesus' disciples were baptizing and making more disciples than John. When Jesus realized that the Pharisees knew about him and that Herod had arrested John, he left Judea and headed back to Galilee. He took the most direct route through Samaria, propelled by the Holy Spirit's power.

Why were there so many Herods?

Herod was a family name of a group of rulers during the First Century. They all descended from Herod the Great, the one who tried to kill the infant Jesus.

CHAPTER ELEVEN

THE WOMAN AT THE WELL
John 4:5-45

Eventually, Jesus came to the Samaritan village of Sychar near the plot of land that Jacob had given his son Joseph. Jesus was tired from his journey, and he sat down by Jacob's well at about noon while his disciples went into town to buy some food.

Jesus had only been sitting for a little while when a Samaritan woman came out to draw water. Most women came to draw water early in the morning, but this woman came at noon so that she wouldn't have to talk to her neighbors. Jesus was thirsty, so he asked her for a drink. The woman was shocked because most Jews refuse to speak with Samaritans because of their intense hatred for them, so she said, "If you're a Jew and I'm a Samaritan, why are you asking me for a drink?"

Jews and Samaritans

The Jews and Samaritans were both groups descended from Jacob but had very different histories after the division of the Israelite kingdom. The division between them was religious, ethnic, and political. After the Israelite kingdom divided, the Samaritans had made some religious compromises and intermarried with some nations that the Jews found deplorable. The Jews viewed them as half-breeds and wanted nothing to do with them; many Jews wanted the destruction of the Samaritans. The hate flowed both ways and both groups looked down on the other.

The fact that she was not only a Samaritan but also a woman made it unlikely that a Jew, let alone a Jewish teacher, would talk to her. But Jesus loved her and saw her need, not her race. It is also interesting to note that Jesus claimed to be the Messiah very clearly. He was willing to claim to be the Messiah in Samaria, where they did not have as many distorted notions of the Messiah.

Jesus answered, "If you knew the gift that God has for you and who I am, you would have asked me for a drink; and I would have given you living water."

The woman protested, "You don't have anything to get the water with and it's a deep well. Where would you get this living water? Are you greater than our ancestor Jacob, who gave us this well?"

Jesus replied, "Everyone who drinks this water will be thirsty again, but whoever drinks the water I give will never thirst again. The water I give will become a spring of water that gives eternal life."

The woman thought that Jesus was talking about physical water and did not understand that he spoke of a spiritual water, so she said, "I want some of that. It would be great never to get thirsty and not have to come out here to get water."

Jesus said, "Go get your husband and come back."

She answered sheepishly, "I don't have a husband."

Jesus replied, "It's true that you don't have a husband. In fact, you have had five husbands, and you're not even married to the man you live with now."

The woman was shocked. But she saw an opportunity to ask a religious teacher a question because in her life she never had access to a teacher. So, she said, "Sir, I can see you're a prophet, so maybe you can answer this question. Our fathers worshipped here on Mount Gerizim, but the Jews say we should worship in Jerusalem. Where should we worship?"

Jesus answered, "Believe me, a time is coming when it won't matter where you worship God. You Samaritans worship what you don't know; we worship what we know, for salvation comes from the Jews. But from now on, true worshippers will worship God in spirit and truth. That's the kind of worshipper God is looking for; God is spirit and we must worship him in spirit and truth."

The woman said, "I know the Messiah is coming and he will explain everything to us."

Then Jesus declared, "I am the Messiah!"

When his disciples returned, they were surprised to find him talking to a woman, but no one asked why he had been talking to her or about their conversation. The woman left her water jar by the well and went to tell the village, "Come see a man who told me everything I ever did. Could this be the Messiah?" So, the people came out to see Jesus.

Meanwhile, his disciples were urging him to eat. But Jesus said, "I have food to eat that you don't know about."

The disciples asked each other, "Who brought him food?"

Then Jesus explained, "My food is to do God's will and finish the work he sent me to do. Do you think the harvest will only begin when summer ends four months from now? Open your eyes and look at the fields of people coming here; they are ripe for harvest now. The reaper is already earning his wages and his harvest is people who have eternal life. The saying, 'One sows and another reaps' is true. I am sending you out to reap what you have not sowed; others have already done the work and you will gather in their harvest. But the sower and the reaper will share the same joy."

Many of the Samaritans trusted Jesus because of what the woman said, but many more believed he was the Savior after hearing him speak. They came out to him and asked him to stay with them for two days. After that, he left for Galilee, although he knew they would eventually reject him.

CHAPTER TWELVE

MINISTRY IN GALILEE
Matthew 4:13-17; Mark 1:14-15; Luke 4:14-31; John 4:46-54

In Galilee, Jesus received a great welcome because of what he had done at the Passover feast in Jerusalem.

He began to preach, "At last, the time has come. The kingdom of God is near! Turn from your sins and believe the Good News." They all praised him as he taught in their synagogues, and soon everyone throughout the surrounding countryside knew about him.

Around this time, Jesus visited Cana again, where he had turned the water into wine. While he was there, a government official from Capernaum came to see him. When the official found Jesus, he begged him to come heal his son who, was very sick and about to die.

"Must I keep doing miracles and wonders before you people trust me?" Jesus exclaimed.

The official begged, "Please come now before my boy dies."

Then Jesus told him, "Go back home, your son will live." Hoping and believing in Jesus, the government man headed home.

While he was on his way, some of his servants ran up and told him that his son was better. He asked them what time he got better, and they said, "His fever suddenly left around one in the afternoon." This was the exact time that Jesus had said, "Your son will live." So, the official and his entire household trusted in Jesus. This was Jesus' second miracle in Galilee.

***

Jesus went to his hometown of Nazareth; and went to the synagogue on the Sabbath. In Jewish synagogues, men typically sat to read Scripture while the people stood to listen. Jesus, instead of sitting to read, stood up to read from the scroll of Isaiah and found where it says, "The Spirit of the Lord is on me because he has appointed me to preach good news to the poor. He has sent me to proclaim that prisoners will be freed, that the blind will see, that the oppressed will be released, and proclaim that the Lord's favor has come." When he finished reading, he rolled up the scroll, gave it back to the attendant, and sat down.

Everyone was confused because he had stood to read and had stopped reading in the middle of a passage. The rest of the passage went on to talk about how God was going to restore the kingdom of Israel and pass judgment on his enemies. They intently stared at him, waiting for him to continue, and he said, "This Scripture is fulfilled before your eyes."

People spoke well of him and his gracious words amazed them. Puzzled, they asked, "Isn't this Joseph's son? How did he get this kind of understanding and authority to teach?"

Then Jesus said, "Surely you will quote this proverb to me: 'Physician, heal yourself. We want to see you do what we heard you did in Capernaum.' I tell you the truth, no prophet is accepted in his hometown.

"There were many needy widows in Israel during Elijah's time when it didn't rain for three-and-a-half years. Yet God didn't send Elijah to any of them but to the widow Zarephath in a foreign land. Or think of the prophet Elisha who healed Naaman, a foreigner, rather than the lepers in Israel."

All the people in the synagogue were furious when they heard this. They understood that he was claiming to be the Messiah, but they wanted a conquering king and were disappointed that he did not meet their expectations. They thought he was blaspheming against God, so they jumped up, drove him out of town, and took him to a cliff to throw him off it. It wasn't Jesus' time to die, so as they neared the cliff, he walked through the crowd and went on his way.

Instead of staying in Nazareth, Jesus went to Capernaum, by the Sea of Galilee. This fulfilled Isaiah's prophecy that a light would shine on those living in the shadow of death in Galilee.

CHAPTER THIRTEEN

CALL OF THE FOUR AND VARIOUS HEALINGS
Matthew 4:18-25; 8:2-4; 9:1-17; Mark 1:16-2:22; Luke 4:31-5:39

One morning, as Jesus was preaching while he walked along the shore of Galilee, people crowded around him to listen to his teaching on the word of God. He saw two empty boats near the water's edge where Peter and Andrew were washing their nets after fishing all night. Jesus got into one of the boats and asked Peter to push it out into the water. Then he sat down in the boat so that the crowds could hear him and he taught the people.

When he had finished speaking, he told Peter, "Go out into deep water, let down your nets, and you will catch many fish."

The middle of the day was not the best time to catch fish, so Peter protested, "Master, we worked hard all night and didn't catch anything, but if you say so, I'll try again." They rowed out and threw their nets into the water. When they tried to pull the nets back in, they were so full of fish that they began to tear. They called their partners in the other boat to come help them, and they filled both boats with so many fish that the boats began to sink.

When Peter realized Jesus' power, he fell to his knees and begged, "Lord, please leave me because I'm a sinful man!"

Jesus replied, "Don't be afraid, from now on you will catch men." So, the fishermen pulled their boats onto shore and left everything to follow Jesus. The fish they caught would have been extremely profitable and would have provided a comfortable living, but Jesus' words were far more compelling.

Andrew and Peter's partners, James and John, had been sitting in a boat with their father, Zebedee, mending their nets. Jesus called them to follow him too, and they immediately left the boat and their father to follow him.

***

Jesus and his companions stayed in the town of Capernaum, and every Sabbath he went to the synagogue to teach the people. People were amazed because he taught with so much authority and conviction, unlike their teachers of the religious law.

Once, when he was in the synagogue, a man with an evil spirit cried out, "Leave us alone! What do you want with us, Jesus of Nazareth? Have you come to destroy us? I know who you are—the Holy One of God!"

"Be quiet, and come out of him!" Jesus commanded. The demon that possessed the man screamed and threw the man into a convulsion, but came out without injuring him further.

Astonished, all the people could talk about was, "What kind of teaching is this? He has such authority that even the evil spirits obey his commands." News about Jesus spread quickly throughout the surrounding area.

After Jesus and his disciples left the synagogue that day, they went to Peter and Andrew's house, where Peter's mother-in-law was sick with a high fever. "Please heal her," they begged. Jesus went to her bedside, took her by the hand, rebuked the fever, then helped her sit up. The fever left immediately, and she felt well enough to get up and prepare a meal for them.

That evening at sunset, people brought all sorts of sick and demon-possessed people to Jesus. A huge crowd gathered outside to see what would happen. Jesus went to work and healed many sick people and cast out their demons. As they came out, the demons shouted, "You are the Son of God!" because they knew he was the Messiah. But Jesus rebuked those demons and told them to be quiet. All this fulfilled Isaiah's prophecy: "He took our sicknesses and removed our diseases."

> **Demon possession?**
>
> Demon possession is when an evil spiritual being (demon) comes into a person and controls their mind and physical body. The Bible does not tell us how a person can become demon-possessed, but it is only when people open themselves up to Satan's control through their choices and lifestyle. People who trust Jesus cannot be demon-possessed because demons cannot co-exist with the Holy Spirit in a person's soul. However, believers can still be influenced by demons. There are many cases of demon possession in the Bible, and it seems unlikely that it is as common in modern times. Demon possession is different than sickness or mental illness, as shown in this passage.
>
> It is also interesting to note that Jesus told the demons not to identify him as the Son of God. He did this because it was not the right time for this proclamation. Jesus still had much to do before his death and this identification would have accelerated matters too quickly.

***

The next morning before dawn, Jesus went out to the wilderness to pray alone. He knew that he needed to stay in constant contact with his Father despite his busy schedule. The people looked all over for him, and when they found him, they begged him to stay.

But Jesus said, "I must preach the good news of the kingdom of God in other places too because that is why I came." So, he traveled throughout Galilee, teaching in the synagogues and preaching everywhere he could. He also healed people with every kind of sickness and disease and cast out many demons.

News about him spread far beyond Galilee so that the sick came from more than 100 miles away for healing. Jesus healed them all: epileptics, paralytics, and the demon-possessed. Large crowds followed him wherever he went.

In one of the towns, Jesus met a man with an advanced case of leprosy. The man came to Jesus and fell face down on the ground, worshipping him. "Lord," he begged, "if you want, you can heal me."

Moved with pity, Jesus reached out and touched the man. Leprosy was an unclean disease in those days, and lepers were outcasts from the community. This was probably the first time anyone had touched him in years. "I am willing," he said. "Be clean!" Instantly the leprosy was gone. Jesus told him, "Go to the priest and let him examine you, but don't talk to anyone along the way. Take the offering that the Law requires for those healed of leprosy, so everyone will have proof of your healing."

But as the man went on his way, he told everyone what had happened. Therefore, so many people crowded around Jesus that he could no longer publicly enter a city. He had to stay out in the secluded places, and people came to hear him preach and for healing. But Jesus often withdrew to the wilderness to pray.

***

Several days later, Jesus took a boat back to Capernaum, and the news of his arrival there spread quickly through the town. Crowds of people came to the house where he was staying and soon, there was no room left, not even outside the door. As usual, there were some Pharisees and teachers of the religious law in the crowd. God's healing power was with Jesus and he preached the word to all of them.

Four men arrived carrying a paralyzed man on a sleeping mat; they tried to push through the crowd to Jesus, but they couldn't reach him. Frustrated, they went up onto the flat roof, removed some tiles, and lowered the sick man down into the middle of the crowd. Jesus saw their faith and said to the paralyzed man, "Take heart, my son, your sins are forgiven."

The Pharisees and teachers of the religious law became indignant and said to themselves, "This is blasphemy! Who does he think he is? Only God can forgive sins!"

Jesus knew what they were thinking, so he asked, "Why do you think this is blasphemy? Is it easier for me to say, 'Your sins are forgiven' or 'Get up and walk?' But I will prove to you that the Son of Man has the authority of God to forgive sins." Then he turned to the paralyzed man and said, "Stand up, take your mat, and go home."

The man jumped up, took his mat, and pushed his way through the stunned audience. Fear and amazement swept through the crowd, and they all praised God, exclaiming, "We've never seen anything like this!"

***

Once again, Jesus went out beside a lake and taught the crowds that followed him. On his way to the lake, he saw Levi, who Jesus renamed Matthew, sitting at his tax collector's booth. Tax collectors were notorious for extortion and people hated them. Levi was also a Jew and that was even worse because the people saw him as a traitor. Jesus said, "Come follow me." Levi got up, left everything behind, and followed him.

That night, the newly renamed Matthew invited Jesus and the other disciples to have dinner with him, his fellow tax collectors, and others of questionable morality. When the Pharisees saw him eating with such sinners (these people were always with Jesus), they complained to his disciples, "Why does your teacher eat with such scum?"

Jesus overheard them and replied, "Healthy people don't need a doctor, sick people do. Learn what this means, 'I desire mercy, not sacrifice.' I have not come to call the righteous but sinners."

Fasting was a common practice of religious men at the time and it was a way of drawing closer to the Lord. John's disciples and the Pharisees were fasting and they complained that Jesus' disciples were feasting rather than fasting. They came to Jesus and asked, "Why do John's disciples and the Pharisees fast, but your disciples don't?"

Jesus answered, "Should the wedding guests mourn while celebrating with the groom? Of course not, no one fasts when they are with the groom. Someday I will be taken from them and then they will fast."

Then he gave them this illustration, "No one sews an unshrunk patch on an old piece of clothing. If they do, the patch shrinks and pulls away from the clothes, leaving an even bigger hole than before. Also, no one puts new wine into old wineskins. If they do, the wineskin will burst; then they will lose the wine and ruin the wineskin. One must put new wine into new wineskins and then both the wine and the wineskins are safe. No one who drinks the old wine wants to drink the new wine because they say the old is better."

> **What about wineskins?**
>
> Jesus uses the analogy of wineskins to contrast his teaching and Pharisees' teaching. In modern times, we can look at this as differences in worship styles. The gospel is always the same, but its presentation changes. New generations will express their faith differently and that's valid. We don't need to practice the same as others, because we may be happy with our expression of faith. Forcing people to conform will only cause division. Therefore, new churches that express faith differently will reach more people (e.g. traditional versus modern worship).

CHAPTER FOURTEEN

SABBATH CONTROVERSIES AND WITHDRAWALS
Matthew 12:1-21; Mark 2:23-3:12; Luke 6:1-11; John 5

One Sabbath (the Jewish day of worship), Jesus went up to Jerusalem for one of the Jewish feasts. Inside the city, near the Sheep Gate, was the Pool of Bethesda. It had five covered porches where crowds of sick, blind, and paralyzed people lay because when the waters stirred, they could heal people. One man Jesus saw lying there had been there for 38 years! Jesus asked, "Do you want to get well?"

The man gave an excuse instead of answering Jesus' question, "But I have no one to help me into the pool when the waters are stirred. Whenever I try to get there, someone always gets there ahead of me," the man complained. It soon became clear he was making a living on alms that people gave him.

So, Jesus told him, "Stand up, pick up your mat, and walk." Instantly, the man was healed, picked up his mat, and walked.

Since it was the Sabbath, some Jewish leaders objected and said to the man, "You can't do that, it's the Sabbath and it's illegal to carry that sleeping mat."

The man replied, "But the man who healed me told me to pick it up and walk."

The Pharisees demanded, "Who told you to pick it up and walk?"

The man didn't know it was Jesus because he had disappeared into the crowd.

Later, Jesus found the man in the temple and said to him, "Now that you're healed, stop sinning, or something worse might happen to you." Upset that Jesus had healed him and taken away his means for getting money without working, the man went to the Jewish leaders and told them that it was Jesus who had healed him.

The Pharisees harassed Jesus for breaking the Law by healing the man on the Sabbath. But Jesus replied, "My Father never stops working, so why should I?" Therefore, the Jews tried to kill him because he was not only breaking the Sabbath, but he was calling God his Father, equating himself with God.

Jesus knew their thoughts, so he said, "I tell you the truth, I can do nothing by myself because I can only do what I see my Father doing. Whatever the Father does, I do as well because the Father loves me and tells me everything that he is doing. You will see me do even greater things than this healing; just as the Father can raise people from the dead, you will see me raise whomever I wish. Furthermore, the Father has entrusted me to judge the world so that everyone will honor me, just as they honor the Father. In fact, whoever does not honor me, does not honor the Father.

"Whoever listens to my words and believes in God who sent me will have eternal life and won't be condemned. A time is coming and has arrived when the dead will hear the Son of God's voice and live. Just as the Father has the power to give life, so he has granted the Son to have the power to give life; he has given me the authority to judge humanity because I am the Son of Man.

"Don't be amazed; a time is coming when all the dead will hear his voice and rise. Those who have done good will rise to eternal life, and those who have done evil will rise to judgment. But I cannot do anything by myself; I only judge as my Father tells me. Therefore, my judgment is just because it is not mine; it is God's will.

"If I testify about myself, you will say my testimony is not valid. Someone else testifies about me, and his testimony is valid. You asked John and he told you the truth. Human testimony is not always right, but his was. You hold him in high regard and I mention him for your salvation.

"John gave you light and you enjoyed it, but I have a greater witness than John: my teaching and my miracles. My Father has assigned these to me and they testify that he has sent me. The Father has also testified about me, but you have never heard his voice or seen him. His word is not in your hearts because you have not believed me. You study the Scriptures because you think that will give you eternal life. These Scriptures point to me, yet you still refuse to believe.

"I don't receive glory from you because I know you don't have God's love in your hearts. I have come in my Father's name, yet you refuse to accept me; but if someone comes in his own name, you will accept him. How can you believe if you accept praise from each other but don't try to get praise from God?

"But I'm not the one who will accuse you before the Father. Moses will accuse you because you have set your hopes on him. If you trusted Moses, you would trust me because he wrote about me. But since you don't believe what he wrote, why would you believe what I say?"

***

On another Sabbath, Jesus was walking through some grain fields with his disciples. They were hungry, so they broke off the heads of wheat, rubbed off the husks in their hands, and ate the grains. When the Pharisees saw this, they protested, "Don't you know that you're breaking the Law by working on the Sabbath?"

Jesus answered, "Haven't you read what King David did when he and his companions were hungry? He went into God's house with his companions, and they ate the sacred bread that was only for the priests. Or haven't you read in the Law of Moses that the priests work in the temple on the Sabbath? I tell you that one greater than the temple is here. You would not condemn the innocent if you knew the meaning of this Scripture: 'I desire mercy, not sacrifice.' The Sabbath is for the benefit of people, not people for the benefit of the Sabbath. And I, the Son of Man, am the master of even the Sabbath."

***

On another Sabbath, he went into the synagogue and noticed a man with a deformed hand. The Pharisees and teachers of the religious law were looking for a reason to accuse Jesus of some sort of crime, so they watched to see if he would heal the man. They asked Jesus, "Is it legal to heal on the Sabbath?"

But Jesus knew their thoughts and said to the man, "Get up and stand where everyone can see you." So, the man got up. Then Jesus said to his critics, "Which is legal to do on the Sabbath, good or evil, to save life or destroy it? If one of you had a sheep and it fell into a pit on the Sabbath, wouldn't you do work and pull it out? Of course you would, and this man is much more valuable than a sheep. Therefore, it's lawful to do good on the Sabbath."

Jesus looked around at them, distressed by their stubborn hearts. "Stretch out your hand," he told the man. The man stretched out his hand and it was whole again. But the Pharisees were furious and they began to talk with Herod's supporters to figure out how they could kill Jesus.

But Jesus knew their plans, so he and his disciples went out by the lake. The news of his miracles had spread, and people came from as far as 50 miles away to see for themselves.

Jesus told his disciples to have a small boat ready for him in case the crowd grew too large. He had healed many people that day, so many more sick people crowded around, trying to touch him. Whenever those possessed by evil spirits saw him, they would fall down in front of him and scream, "You are the Son of God!" But Jesus ordered them not to say who he was. He healed all the sick people but warned them to keep his identity a secret. This fulfilled Isaiah's prophecy, "Look at my Servant, whom I have chosen. I love him, and he pleases me. I will put my Spirit upon him, and he will proclaim justice to the nations. He will not fight or cry out; he won't raise his voice in public. He won't crush the weak or put out hope until he leads justice to victory. His name will be the hope of the entire world."

Jesus and the Sabbath

The Sabbath was the Jewish day of religious observance from Friday to Saturday evening. Jesus was trying to teach the Jews that God made the Sabbath to benefit them, not the other way around. God wanted people to observe the Sabbath so that they would spend time with him and rest, not so that they could have more rules to follow. As a part of their zeal to keep the Law, rabbis created many rules about forbidden activities on the Sabbath. These included travel, preparation of food, and the types of tasks a person could do.

Some of the regulations on work became ridiculous. For example, people could not look in a mirror because they might see a gray hair and want to pluck it. People also could not move furniture unless it was a ladder, and then they could only move it four paces. While these additions came from a good place, the emphasis became more about the rules than about the Sabbath.

One of the Sabbath prohibitions was healing unless the victim was in danger of dying the next day. This man was in no danger of dying. Since Jesus created the Sabbath, his interpretation of permitted activities had far more authority than the religious leaders.

CHAPTER FIFTEEN

APPOINTMENT OF THE TWELVE
Mark 3:13-19; Luke 6:12-19

One evening Jesus went to a mountain to pray, and he spent the entire night in prayer. In the morning, he called his many followers to him and chose twelve of them to be apostles that would spread his message. He sent them out to preach and he gave them the authority to cast out demons. These are the Twelve he chose: Simon (whom he named Peter), James and John (the sons of Zebedee, now nicknamed the "Sons of Thunder"), Andrew (Simon/Peter's brother), Philip, Bartholomew, Matthew, Thomas, James (son of Alphaeus), Thaddaeus, Simon (the Zealot), and Judas Iscariot (who later betrayed him).

Disciple	Interesting Notes
Simon (Peter)	Andrew's brother. He was originally a fisherman and became the leader of the early church. The Gospel of Mark records the life of Jesus from his perspective.
James (son of Zebedee)	John's brother. Originally, a fisherman. Commonly, believed to be the first disciple martyred.
John	This was not John the Baptist but James' brother. Possibly, the youngest of the disciples, and the only one to die of old age. The Gospel of John records the life of Jesus from his perspective.
Andrew	Peter's brother.
Philip	
Bartholomew	Also known as Nathaniel.

Levi (Matthew)	Had been a tax collector and likely hated by the Jews.
Thomas	Demanded proof that Jesus had really risen.
James (son of Alphaeus)	Possibly Matthew's brother.
Thaddaeus	Sometimes referred to as Judas, but distinct from Judas Iscariot.
Simon (the Zealot)	Zealots hated Roman rule and often carried blades that they used to kill Romans when given the opportunity. He probably had a tough time with Matthew.
Judas Iscariot	Treasurer for the group; he betrayed Jesus for 30 pieces of silver.

When they came down the slopes of the mountain, the disciples stood with Jesus on a large, level area. Many of his followers and the crowds from all over stood around him because they had come to hear him speak and for healing; Jesus cast out many evil spirits that day. Everyone tried to touch him because power was coming from him and healing them all.

CHAPTER SIXTEEN

THE SERMON ON THE MOUNT
Matthew 5-7; Luke 6:20-49

> **The Sermon on the Mount**
>
> This is a compilation of many of Jesus' teachings and is the longest uninterrupted discourse that he gives in Scripture. In this teaching, Jesus takes many traditional interpretations and turns them on their ear. Most Jewish instruction dealt with actions, but Jesus expanded it to include attitude and heart condition. He also taught that our actions should reflect what is happening inside us and not a way to gain recognition from others. He addressed the legalistic misinterpretation of the Law and resetting their understanding of what God told his people all along.

One day, as the crowds were gathering, Jesus went up the mountainside with his disciples and sat down to teach them. A crowd followed and he turned to his disciples and said,

"Blessed are the poor in spirit because the kingdom of heaven is theirs.

"Blessed are the hungry because God will satisfy them.

"Blessed are those who weep because they will laugh.

"Blessed are those who mourn because God will comfort them.

"Blessed are the gentle and lowly because they will inherit the earth.

"Blessed are those who hunger and thirst for righteousness because God will fill them.

"Blessed are the merciful because God will show them mercy.

"Blessed are the pure in heart because they will see God.

"Blessed are those who make peace because they will be children of God.

"Blessed are those who are persecuted for living for God because the kingdom of heaven is theirs.

"Blessed are you when people hate, mock, persecute, reject, and lie about you because you are identified with me, the Son of Man. Rejoice when that happens because a great reward waits for you in heaven. Remember, that's how your ancestors treated the prophets.

"But woe to the rich because they already have their comfort.

"Woe to those who are well-fed because they will go hungry.

"Woe to those who laugh now because they will mourn and weep.

"Woe to you when everyone praises you because that's how your fathers treated the false prophets.

"You are the salt of the earth, but what good is it if the salt loses its flavor? It cannot become salty again; it's worthless and is thrown out and trampled.

"You are the light of the world; a city on a hill cannot be hidden. People don't light a lamp and then put it under a basket; instead, they put it on a stand so everyone can see it. In the same way, let your good deeds shine for all to see, so that they will praise your Father in heaven.

"I have not come to abolish the Law or the Prophets; in fact, I have come to fulfill them. I tell you the truth, until heaven and earth disappear, not one letter or pen stroke will pass away until it accomplishes its purpose. Anyone who breaks the least of these commands and teaches others to do the same will be least in the kingdom of heaven, but whoever obeys God's Laws and teaches others to do the same will be great in the kingdom.

"I warn you that unless you are more obedient than the Pharisees and the teachers of the Law, you won't make it into the kingdom of heaven.

> **Jesus and the Law**
>
> Jesus was not invalidating the Old Testament; he was giving a proper interpretation of it. The Pharisees had developed a hierarchy of the commandments and Jesus shows them that all of it matters. In this next section, he pairs what was considered an important command with a lesser one. He uses these to reveal the heart behind the Law.

"You have heard it said, 'Do not murder' and that 'murderers will be subject to judgment.' But I tell you that if you are angry with someone without cause, you will be subject to judgment. If anyone calls someone else worthless, they will bring him before the court, and whoever calls someone else a fool is in danger of hell.

> **Calling someone a fool**
>
> The Hebrew word for fool went beyond intellect and implied a moral and religious judgment. Jesus warns his audience about calling others fools in the context of unrighteous anger. In other places, Jesus called the Pharisees fools, but as God in the flesh, he knew their hearts and had justifiable outrage.
>
> It's also important for us to see what Jesus did with his anger. The Gospels tell us that when he was angry, he healed a man and cleansed the temple. Our anger should motivate us to good deeds, not sin.

"Therefore, if you are presenting an offering to God in the temple and remember that someone has something against you, leave your offering and go make things right. Then come back and offer your gift.

"Settle things quickly with your opponent at law on the way to court, or else he may hand you over to the judge, and they will throw you in prison. Then you won't get out until you have paid the last penny.

"You have heard it said, 'Do not commit adultery.' But I say that if you even lust after a woman, you have already committed adultery in your heart. If your right eye causes you to sin, gouge it out and throw it away because it is better to lose one part of the body than to go to hell. If your right hand causes you to sin, cut it off and throw it away, because it is better to lose one part of your body than to go to hell.

"You have heard it said, 'Anyone can divorce his wife by giving her a certificate of divorce.' But I tell you that anyone who divorces his wife, unless she has been unfaithful, causes her to commit adultery; anyone who marries a divorced woman commits adultery.

"You have also heard it said, 'Don't break your vows, but keep the oaths you have made to the Lord.' But I tell you not to swear at all. Don't swear by heaven, because it is God's throne; don't swear by the earth, because it is God's footstool; don't swear by Jerusalem, because it is the city of the Great King; and don't swear by your head, because you can't even make one hair white or black. Let your 'Yes,' be 'Yes,' and your 'No,' be 'No.' Anything beyond that is wrong.

"You have heard it said, 'An eye for an eye, and a tooth for a tooth.' But I tell you not to resist an evil person. If someone slaps your right cheek, turn the other cheek as well. If someone wants to sue you and take your shirt, give him your coat as well. If a soldier demands that you carry his gear for a mile, carry it for two. If someone wants something from you, give it to him, and don't try to turn away those who want to borrow things from you.

"You have heard it said, 'Love your neighbor and hate your enemy.' But I say love your enemies, do good to those who hate you, bless those who curse you, and pray for those who persecute you. Doing these things will prove that you are children of your Father in heaven. Remember that he is kind to the unthankful and the wicked. Be merciful just as he is merciful because he gives sunlight to both the evil and the good, and he sends rain on the just and the unjust too.

"What good is it if you only love those who love you? Even sinners do that. What good is it if you are only kind to your friends and only do good to those who do good to you? Sinners do that too. Furthermore, everyone lends to others when they expect to get their money back. Do good to your enemies and lend to them without expecting to get anything back. You are to be perfect, just like your heavenly Father is perfect.

"Be careful that you're not just doing good deeds to impress others because you will lose your reward in heaven. When you give to charity, don't shout about it like the hypocrites do, they already have their reward. When you give, don't let your left hand know what your right hand is doing; your giving should be in secret so that your heavenly Father will reward you.

"When you pray, don't be like the hypocrites, who like to pray in public so everyone will see them. Instead, go into your room and pray behind closed doors so that your heavenly Father will reward you.

"Also, don't go on and on with meaningless repetition like some people in other religions. They think their god will listen because of their many words, but remember that your Father knows what you need, even before you ask.

"This is how you should pray: Father in heaven, I honor your name. May your kingdom come and your will be done on earth like it is in heaven. Give us our bread for today, and forgive our sins, just like we've forgiven those who have sinned against us. Lead us away from temptation, and deliver us from the evil one. For the kingdom, power, and glory are yours forever. Amen.

"If you forgive people who sin against you, your heavenly Father will also forgive you; but if you refuse to forgive others, then God won't forgive you either.

"When you fast, don't make it obvious by looking gloomy and sad. If you do that, you already have your reward from men. When you fast, comb your hair and wash your face so that it won't be obvious that you're fasting. Then your heavenly Father will reward you.

"Don't store up treasures on earth where they will eventually wear out or be stolen. Store up treasures in heaven, where they will never wear out, and they cannot be stolen. Your heart and thoughts will be wherever your treasure is.

"Your eye is the lamp of your body; if your eyes are good, then your whole body will be full of light. But if your eyes are bad, then your body will be full of darkness, and if you think your darkness is light, how deep that darkness is.

> **What did Jesus mean by good and bad eyes?**
>
> This teaching is in the context of material possessions and we cannot interpret it without considering what is before and after. The eye reveals what we focus on, whether God or money. If our eyes focus on him, then we will be full of light, but on possessions, we will be full of darkness.

"No one can serve two masters. You will hate one and love the other, or devote yourself to one and despise the other. In the same way, you cannot serve both God and money.

"Therefore, don't worry about everyday life and whether you have enough food, drink, or clothes. Isn't life more than these things? Look at the birds; they don't worry about planting, harvesting, or storing up food because their heavenly Father feeds them. You are worth so much more than they are; so, don't worry, because all your worrying won't add a single second to your life.

"Why worry about clothes? See how the lilies of the field grow without hard work, yet not even Solomon dressed as beautifully as they are. If God clothes the grass of the field that will be dead tomorrow, don't you think he will clothe you? Where's your faith?

"So, don't worry about having enough food, drink, and clothing. The world runs after all these things, and your heavenly Father knows that you need them. Make your primary concern the kingdom of heaven and he will take care of everything else. Don't worry about tomorrow, because tomorrow will have worries of its own; every day has enough trouble.

"Don't judge, or others will judge you by the same standard. Stop criticizing, or it will all come back on you because others will treat you just like you treat them. Others will use your standard for judgment to judge you.

> **Judgment**
>
> Jesus is saying that the standard we use to judge others applies to us as well. Since God will judge us by his standard, it is all right to tell other believers that they are sinning. However, we must also make sure that we are diligently getting rid of sin in our lives. In other places in the Bible, God instructs us to judge our fellow believers to keep them from sinning. We cannot live our lives without making judgments, so Jesus is telling people to make righteous judgments.
>
> However, our job is not to be the morality police for those who do not claim to be Christians. If people do not claim to follow Christ, we should not stand in a place of judgment; God will do that.

"If you forgive others, they will forgive you too; if you give, you will receive. People will give back to you in the same measure that you give. They will pour into your lap as much as they can.

"What good is it for one blind man to lead another blind man? The first will end up leading the other one into a pit. A student is not greater than his teacher but will become like his teacher.

"Don't worry about the speck of sawdust in your friend's eye when you have a log in your eye. How can you even think of saying, 'Let me help you with that speck,' when you can't even get close enough because of the log in your eye? You hypocrite, first take the log from your eye, and then you will be able to deal with the speck in your brother's eye.

"Don't give dogs what is sacred, and don't give pearls to pigs. If you do, they will trample the pearls and then turn and attack you.

"Keep asking, and you will receive; keep looking, and you will find; keep knocking, and the door will be open. Everyone who asks, receives, everyone who seeks, finds, and everyone who knocks has the door open.

"If a child asks for a loaf of bread, parents won't give him a stone instead, and if he asks for a fish, they won't give him a snake. If you, who are evil, know how to give your children good gifts, how much more will God give good gifts to those who ask him?

"Treat others like you want to be treated; this is a summary of everything the Law and the Prophets teach.

"You must enter God's kingdom through the narrow gate. The highway to hell is broad, and the gate is wide, and many will choose that way; but the road to life is narrow and few people find it.

"Beware of false prophets who come in sheep's clothing, but are really wolves that will tear you apart. You can identify them by how they act, just like you can identify a tree by its fruit. A good tree cannot produce bad fruit and a bad tree cannot produce good fruit. Similarly, a good person does good deeds from a good heart, but an evil person does evil from an evil heart; remember that your heart determines what you are. They will chop down and burn every tree that doesn't produce good fruit.

"Not everyone who sounds religious is godly. They may refer to me as Lord, but they won't enter the kingdom of heaven because they don't obey my Father's commands. On judgment day, they will come to me and say, 'Lord, we prophesied, cast out demons, and performed many miracles in your name.' But I will say, 'I never knew you. Go away, you evildoers.'

"So, why do you call me Lord when you won't obey me? Whoever listens to my teaching and obeys is like a wise person who builds his house with a strong foundation on solid rock. When the rain comes and the floodwaters rise, it stands firm because of its foundation. But whoever hears my words and doesn't obey them is like a foolish man who builds his house on the sand. When the rain comes and the floodwaters rise, it will fall with a mighty crash because it has no foundation."

The crowds were amazed at Jesus' teaching because he taught with authority, and not like their other religious teachers. Rather than just quoting what other teachers said about God's word, he spoke with authority. So, a great crowd followed him down the mountain, and Jesus went back to Capernaum.

Is this an unattainable goal?

Yes. Jesus even goes so far as to command that we be perfect. Teachings like this show us that we need God's grace and Jesus' death on the cross to justify ourselves before God because we cannot possibly obey all his commands all the time. Just because perfect obedience is unattainable doesn't mean we stop working towards it; following God's teaching draws us closer to him and is evidence of our faith. Jesus meant every word of this teaching and this is what we strive to attain.

CHAPTER SEVENTEEN

GROWING FAME
Matthew 8:5-13; 11:2-30; Luke 7

A Roman officer had a very valuable servant who was sick and dying, so he sent some respected leaders to ask Jesus to come heal his servant. They begged Jesus to come help the man, saying, "If anyone deserves your help, it's him; because he loves the Jews and he even built a synagogue for us."

So, Jesus went with these leaders, but before they got to the house, the officer sent some friends to say, "Lord, don't trouble yourself by coming to my home, because I'm not worthy of such an honor. In fact, I'm not even worthy to meet you face-to-face; you can heal my servant by just saying the word. I know because I am under authority and have soldiers under me, and when I tell them to come, they come, and if I tell my servants to do something, they do it."

This amazed Jesus; he turned to the crowd and said, "I tell you the truth, I haven't seen such faith in all of Israel. Many will come from the east and west to eat with Abraham, Isaac, and Jacob in the kingdom of heaven, but many Jews will be cast into the outer darkness where there will be weeping and gnashing of teeth."

Then Jesus turned to the officer's friends, "Go home, what you've believed has happened." When the officer's friends got home, they found the slave completely healed.

***

Soon afterward, with a huge crowd following him, Jesus went to Nain along with his disciples. As he approached the village, a funeral procession for the only son of a widow was passing by. Jesus had compassion for the woman, and he told her not to cry, went over to the coffin, and touched it. The men carrying the coffin stopped and Jesus said, "Young man, get up." The dead boy sat up and began talking to those around him, so Jesus gave him back to his mother.

Fear and awe swept across the crowd, and they all praised God, saying, "A mighty prophet has arisen and we have seen God's hand at work." It wasn't long before news of Jesus' deeds spread all over Judea.

***

Herod Antipas had thrown John the Baptist into prison because John had publicly criticized Herod for marrying his brother's wife, Herodias. John heard about Jesus' deeds while he was in prison, so he sent some of his disciples to ask him if he was the Messiah. John had identified Jesus as the Messiah, but his arrest made him doubt. John's disciples found Jesus and asked, "John the Baptist wanted us to ask you if you are the Messiah we've been expecting, or should we look for someone else?"

At that time, Jesus cured many people of their diseases, cast out evil spirits, and restored sight to the blind. Jesus said to John's disciples, "Go back and tell John what you have seen and heard, the blind see, the lame walk, lepers are cured, the deaf hear, the dead are raised, and the poor have the good news preached to them. Blessed are those who aren't offended by me." This was a reference to prophecy and told John's followers that Jesus was the Messiah.

As John's disciples were leaving, Jesus talked to the crowd about John, "Did you go out to the desert to see a reed blown around in the wind? Or were you expecting to find a well-dressed man in fancy clothes? People who wear beautiful clothes live in palaces, not in the wilderness. Did you go out to see a prophet? John was more than just a prophet; John is the one Isaiah was talking about when he wrote, 'Look I'm sending my messenger before you to prepare a way before you.'" Even though John did not fully understand his role, Jesus gave clarity and claimed to be the promised Messiah.

Jesus continued, "I tell you the truth, out of everyone who has ever lived, no one is greater than John the Baptist, but even the most insignificant person in the kingdom of heaven is greater than he is. From the time of John's preaching until now, the kingdom of heaven has forcefully advanced, and violent men attack it. Before John came, all the prophets looked forward to now, and if you are willing to accept it, he is the Elijah that the prophets said would come. Anyone willing to hear should listen to me and understand."

When the people heard this, they all agreed that God's plan was right because John had baptized them. But the Pharisees and experts in the law rejected God's purpose for them because they refused John's baptism.

> **Who was John the Baptist?**
>
> John was the prophet who prepared the people for Jesus' arrival. He was not a reincarnated Elijah, but he served the same function that Elijah did. Elijah was an Old Testament prophet who came to bring reconciliation. The prophet Malachi prophesied that God would send Elijah as a forerunner to the Messiah. John was positionally greater than everyone else because God chose him to do a special task, but he was not better than others.

Then Jesus asked, "How can I describe this generation? They are like a group of children in the marketplace that call out to each other: 'We played happy songs for you and you didn't dance, so we sang sad songs and you didn't cry.' For John the Baptist didn't eat bread or drink wine and you called him demon-possessed. Then the Son of Man eats bread and drinks wine, and you call me a glutton, drunkard, and friend of sinners.' But wisdom is shown to be right by the lives of those who listen to it."

Jesus began to denounce the cities where he had done most of his miracles because they had not repented, despite what they had witnessed. "Woe to you, Chorazin and Bethsaida, because if I had done the miracles I did for you in wicked Tyre and Sidon, they would have repented a long time ago. Capernaum, God won't exalt you to heaven; you will end up with the dead. For if Sodom had seen the miracles you have, it would still be here today. It will be much more tolerable for these wicked cities on the Day of Judgment than for those who pretend to be righteous."

> **Who are these cities?**
>
> Sodom was an infamously wicked city that God burned with fire during the time of Abraham. Tyre and Sidon were two cities in the Syro-Phonecian region of the land (just north of Israel) that were famous for their wickedness from the time of the Old Testament prophets through the First Century. Jesus compares the Jewish towns of Chorazin and Bethsaida with these three sinful cities because they had not repented after seeing Jesus' miracles and hearing his teaching.

Jesus prayed, "Father, Lord of heaven and the earth, I praise you because you have hidden these things from the wise and educated, and revealed them to little children. It has pleased you to do it this way.

"My Father has given all things to me. No one knows who I really am except the Father, and no one knows the Father except me and those that I reveal it to."

Then Jesus said to the crowd, "If you are tired and burdened, come to me, and I will give you rest. Take my load and learn from me because I am gentle and humble. You will find rest for your souls because my load is easy and my burden is light."

***

Jesus was a popular dinner guest in the early days of his ministry. One of the Pharisees invited Jesus over for dinner; he went and sat down to eat. A sexually immoral woman heard that Jesus was there, so she brought a beautiful jar of expensive perfume. She knelt behind him, started crying, and then began to wet his feet with her tears. Then she wiped up her tears with her hair, kissed his feet, and poured perfume on them. Letting her hair down was a sign of intimacy; the fact that she did this publicly was a sign of worship.

When the Pharisee hosting the meal saw this, he said to himself, "This proves that Jesus is not a prophet, because he would know that this woman who is touching him is a horrible sinner and has slept with many men."

Jesus knew what he was thinking, so he said, "Simon, I have something to say to you."

Simon replied, "Tell me, teacher."

Jesus said, "Two men owed a moneylender money; one owed him 500 days wages, and the other, 50. Neither one of them could pay back the money, so the moneylender forgave both of their debts. Who do you think loved the moneylender more after that?"

Simon answered, "I guess the one who had the larger debt."

Jesus replied, "That's right."

Then he turned to the woman and spoke to Simon, "Do you see this woman? When I came into your house, you didn't offer me water to wash off my feet, but she washed my feet with her tears and hair. You didn't give me a kiss of greeting, but she has not stopped kissing my feet. You didn't give me oil for my head, but she has poured perfume on my feet. Therefore, her many sins have been forgiven, because she loved much; but a person who has only been forgiven a little only loves a little."

Then Jesus said to the woman, "Your sins are forgiven because of your faith; go in peace."

The men at the table said to each other, "Who does he think he is, telling people their sins are forgiven? Only God can forgive sins."

CHAPTER EIGHTEEN

FIRST PUBLIC REJECTION
Matthew 12:22-50; Mark 3:20-35; Luke 8:1-3, 19-21

Not long afterward, Jesus began a tour of the nearby cities and villages to announce the good news about the kingdom of God. He took his twelve disciples with him and some women that he had cured of evil spirits and disease. In the group were Mary Magdalene, from whom he had cast out seven demons; Joanna, the wife of Herod's household manager, Chuza; Susanna; and many others. These women contributed from their resources to help support Jesus and his disciples.

When Jesus returned to the house where he was staying, the crowds began to gather again, begging for teaching and healing. Before long, he and his disciples didn't even have time to eat. When his family heard about this, they tried to bring him home, saying, "He's out of his mind." They didn't believe he was the Messiah and thought he was wasting his time.

A blind, mute, demon-possessed man was brought to Jesus, and he healed the man so that he could both speak and see. The crowd marveled, "Could this be the Son of David, the Messiah?"

But when the Pharisees from Jerusalem heard about Jesus' miracles, they said, "He's possessed by Satan, the prince of demons and that's where he gets the power to cast out demons."

Jesus knew their thoughts, so he asked, "How can Satan cast out Satan? If a kingdom is at war with itself, how can it stand? If Satan gives me power, then who gives power to your followers when they cast out demons? But if I am casting out demons by the Spirit of God, then the kingdom of God has arrived.

"Let me illustrate my point. You cannot enter a strong man's house and rob him unless you tie him up first. Anyone who isn't helping me is against me and anyone who isn't working with me is against me.

"I tell you the truth, any sin can be forgiven, even blasphemy; but anyone who blasphemes against the Holy Spirit will never be forgiven. Anyone who blasphemes against the Son of Man can be forgiven, but blasphemy against the Holy Spirit won't be forgiven, in this world or the next." He told them this because they were saying he had an evil spirit.

> **What is blasphemy of the Holy Spirit?**
>
> Jesus doesn't explicitly tell us what this means; there is much conjecture about this teaching. The unpardonable sin is a lifestyle of rejecting Christ or ascribing the Holy Spirit's work to Satan. Anyone worried that they may have committed the "unpardonable sin" probably hasn't and can still come to Christ.

He continued, "Make a tree good, and its fruit will be good or make a tree bad, and its fruit will be bad because a tree is recognized by its fruit. You brood of vipers! How can you say anything good when you are so evil? People speak what is in their hearts; good people bring forth good things, and evil people bring forth evil. I tell you that on Judgment Day, people will have to give an account for every careless word that they have said. Your words reflect your judgment and they will either condemn or acquit you."

***

One day some of the Pharisees and teachers of the religious law said to him, "Teacher, we want to see a miracle to prove that you're from God."

Jesus replied, "Only a wicked and faithless generation would ask to see a miraculous sign. The only sign I will show you is that of the prophet Jonah, and just as he was three days and nights in the belly of a huge fish, so the Son of Man will be in the heart of the earth for three days and nights. The people of Nineveh will condemn this generation on Judgment Day because they repented at Jonah's preaching, but something greater than him is here. The Queen of Sheba will also condemn this generation because she came from far away to hear Solomon's wisdom, and now someone greater than Solomon is here, but you refuse to listen to me.

> **Who are Jonah and the Queen of Sheba?**
>
> Jonah was an Old Testament prophet that God sent to warn the wicked Assyrian city of Nineveh to repent. Initially, he ran from God and ended up in the belly of a fish for three days. Jesus used his story as a sign that he would be in the grave for three days. The Queen of Sheba was an Egyptian and Ethiopian queen who visited King Solomon in Israel to see how God had blessed him.

"When an evil spirit leaves a man, it goes into the desert, looking for rest and does not find it. So, it says, 'I will return to the house I left.' When it arrives, it finds the house unoccupied, swept clean, and put in order. Then the spirit gets seven other spirits that are worse than it is, and they all enter the person and live there. The person is worse off than before; that's how it will be with this evil generation."

As Jesus was speaking to the crowd, his family showed up and wanted to talk to him. They couldn't get to him because of the crowds, so they sent a messenger to let him know that they wanted to see him. But Jesus asked, "Who is my mother, and who are my brothers?" He looked at those sitting around him and said, "These are my mother and my brothers; whoever does God's will is my family."

CHAPTER NINETEEN

SECRETS ABOUT THE KINGDOM IN PARABLES
Matthew 13; Mark 4:1-34; Luke 8:4-18

That same day, Jesus left the house and went down by the lake, where a huge crowd soon gathered. He got into a boat, sat down to teach the crowd, and told many stories like this:

"A farmer went out to plant, and as he scattered his seed, some of it fell on a footpath, and birds came and ate it. Other seed fell on rocky places where there wasn't much soil, and the plants grew quickly until the sun scorched and withered the plants because they didn't have roots. Other seeds fell in the thorns and shot up quickly, but the thorns choked them out, and they didn't produce grain. But some seed fell on fertile soil, and it grew up and produced a crop of 30, 60, or 100 times what was planted. Anyone who is willing to hear should listen and understand."

Later, when Jesus was alone with his twelve disciples, they asked him, "Why do you always speak in parables?"

Jesus answered, "Everything secret will eventually be revealed. God has allowed you to understand the secrets of the kingdom of heaven, but others cannot. Make sure you pay attention to my words because the more open you are to my teaching, the more you will understand it. But those who don't pay attention will never understand. I speak in parables to fulfill Isaiah's prophecy: 'You will hear my words, but you won't understand; you will see what I do, but you won't understand what it means. For these people have hard hearts, they cannot hear with their ears, and they have closed their eyes. Otherwise, they might see with their eyes, hear with their ears, understand with their hearts, and turn to me, and I would heal them.'

> **Why did Jesus not want the people to understand?**
>
> This is a reference to Old Testament prophecies about the Messiah. It's not that Jesus didn't want people to understand, but he was helping his followers understand that he was the Messiah and the fulfillment of prophecy.

"But blessed are your eyes because they see and your ears because they hear. Many prophets and godly men wanted access to what you see and hear, but they didn't open their hearts.

"But if you don't understand this story, how will you understand my other stories? This is the explanation of the sower and the seed: The farmer sows God's word and many different people hear it. The seed that falls on the hard ground represents those who hear the good news about the kingdom and don't understand it because the Devil steals it away and prevents them from believing and being saved. The rocky soil represents those who hear the word of God and receive it with joy. But they don't have deep roots, so they wilt under persecution and don't bear any fruit. The thorny ground represents those who accept the good news, but allow the world's worries and cares to keep them from maturing. The good soil represents honest, good-hearted people who truly accept God's word and produce a huge harvest, 30, 60, or even 100 times more than what was planted.

"No one lights a lamp and then puts it under a bowl or a bed; people light a lamp so that they can see. Everything hidden will be made clear and every secret will be brought to light. Anyone that can hear me should listen. Pay attention to what you hear because God will give to you by the same measure that you use, but God will give more. Those who have much will receive more, and those who do not have will lose the little they possess.

"The kingdom of heaven is also like a man who plants seeds in his field. As time goes by, the seed grows because the earth produces crops on its own. The soil produces the grain, first the stalk, then the head, and then the ripened grain; once the grain is ripe, the farmer harvests it.

"The kingdom of heaven is also like a man who plants seeds in his field. But at night, his enemy came and planted weeds among the wheat. When the wheat started to grow, the weeds did too. His servants came to him and said, 'The field you planted with good seeds is now full of weeds.'

"The farmer exclaimed, 'An enemy has done this!'

"'Shall we pull the weeds?' they asked.

"He replied, 'No, you might hurt the wheat. Let them both grow, and when it's harvest time, I'll tell the harvesters to sort it out and burn the weeds.'

"The kingdom of heaven is also like a mustard seed planted in a field. Although it is one of the smallest seeds, it grows into a huge plant where birds can find shelter.

"The kingdom of heaven is like the yeast a woman uses to make bread. She mixes it into a large amount of flour and it permeates every part of the dough."

Jesus told many other stories and said everything to the people in parables. This fulfilled the prophecy that said, "I will speak to you in parables and explain the mysteries hidden since the world's creation." But when he was alone with his disciples, he would explain his parables to them. At one point, they asked him to explain the parable of the weeds in the field.

He answered, "The Son of Man is the farmer who plants the good seed, the field is the world, and the good seed represents the people of the kingdom. The one who planted the weeds is Satan, the weeds are Satan's followers, the harvest is the end of the world, and the harvesters are the angels.

"At the end of the world, it will be just like the harvest. The Son of Man will send his angels to weed out all the evil people and everything that causes sin. Then they will throw it all into the fiery furnace where there will be weeping and gnashing of teeth. After that, the godly will shine like the sun in their Father's kingdom. Anyone who is willing to hear should listen and understand.

"The kingdom of heaven is like a treasure that a man found hidden in a field. After finding it, he hid it again, and then sold everything he had to buy the field.

"The kingdom of heaven is also like a merchant looking for fine pearls. When he found a precious one, he sold everything he owned and bought it.

"The kingdom of heaven is also like a fishing net. When the net is full, the fishermen pull it onto the shore and sort out the good fish from the bad. This is how it will be at the end of the world; the angels will separate the godly from the wicked and throw them into the fire where there will be weeping and gnashing of teeth. Do you understand these things?"

"Yes," they replied.

Then Jesus said, "Every teacher of the religious law who learns about the kingdom of heaven is like a man who brings out of his storehouse both old and new treasures." When he finished these parables, he moved on from there.

CHAPTER TWENTY

CONTINUING OPPOSITION
Matthew 8:18, 23-34; 9:18-34; 13:54-58; Mark 4:35-6:6; Luke 8:22-56

One evening Jesus noticed a large crowd growing, so he and his disciples got into a boat and went to the other side of the lake, and many other boats followed them. On the way across, Jesus fell asleep, and while he was sleeping, a storm developed. The wind was fierce and the waves threatened to sink the ship.

The disciples became frantic and woke him up, shouting, "Lord, save us; we're going to drown!"

Jesus woke up and said to the storm, "Be still!" The storm stopped, and there was a great calm, then he turned to his disciples and asked, "Why are you so afraid? Where is your faith?"

The disciples were afraid and stunned, and they said to each other, "Who is this man that even the wind and waves obey him?"

Then they arrived in the land of Gadarenes, across the lake from Galilee. As they were climbing out of the boat, two demon-possessed men ran out to meet them. Homeless and naked, these men had lived in a cemetery for a long time. They were so dangerous that everyone stayed away from that area. People had tried to restrain them with chains and shackles, but they broke them off their wrists. No one was strong enough to control them, and they would roam through the tombs and hills all night, screaming and hitting themselves with stones.

When they got to Jesus, they fell to the ground before him, and one of them shrieked, "Why are you bothering me Jesus, Son of God? I beg you not to torture us because you have no right to torture us before God's appointed time."

Jesus asked, "What is your name?"

The spirit replied, "Legion, for there are thousands of us." Then the spirits begged him not to send them to the bottomless pit. A large herd of pigs was nearby and the demons said, "If you drive us out, send us into the herd of pigs."

Jesus gave them permission and the evil spirits went into the pigs. Then the entire herd of 2,000 pigs rushed down the steep bank and drowned in the water.

When the pig herders saw their drowned pigs, they ran to the nearby town and countryside, yelling, and people gathered to see what had happened. The people crowded around Jesus and became frightened when they saw the two formerly demon-possessed men sitting there, fully clothed, and sane. The herders told everyone what had happened and the crowd asked Jesus to leave.

> **Why did Jesus destroy the pigs?**
>
> Some people object to the fact that Jesus allowed the demons to destroy someone else's property, but Jesus did not command the demons to go into the pigs; he allowed them to. Jesus was not responsible for the pigs' destruction; the demons were. Just as God allows us to have free will and commit sin, this does not mean that he is responsible for our actions.

As Jesus was getting back in the boat, the two men begged to go with him. "Go tell your friends what wonderful things God has done for you and how merciful he is," Jesus told them. After that, the two men went through the region of Decapolis, telling the astonishing story of what Jesus had done for them.

***

On the other side of the lake, a large crowd was waiting for Jesus. A local synagogue leader, named Jairus, fell down and begged Jesus to heal his twelve-year-old daughter, his only child. "She is about to die. Please come and touch her; heal her so she can live!"

Jesus and Jairus went to see the girl, and the crowd followed behind. A woman was in the crowd who had been bleeding for twelve years. She had suffered a great deal through the years and had spent everything she had to pay doctors, but her bleeding had only gotten worse. She'd heard about Jesus, and thought to herself, "If I can just touch his clothing, I'll be healed." So, she came up behind him, touched the fringe of his robe, and immediately the bleeding stopped.

Jesus knew that he had healed someone, so he turned around and asked the crowd, "Who touched me?"

His disciples replied, "How can you ask that with such a huge crowd around you?"

But Jesus told them, "No, someone deliberately touched me, and I healed them." So, he kept looking around to see who had done it. When the woman realized that Jesus knew, she fell to her knees and told him what she did. The whole crowd heard about her healing and Jesus said to her, "Daughter, your faith has made you well; go in peace, you are healed."

While he was still speaking to her, messengers came from Jairus' home and said, "The girl is dead, don't bother Jesus anymore."

Jesus ignored them and said to Jairus, "Don't be afraid; just trust me, and she'll be all right." At Jairus' home, he saw the crowd, heard the funeral music, and said, "Stop all this commotion and go away, the girl isn't dead; she's only asleep." But the crowd laughed at him. Jesus finally got the crowd away and entered the house with Peter, James, John, and the girl's parents.

Jesus went in, took the girl by the hand, and said to her in a loud voice, "Get up my child!" Immediately she got up and walked around, and Jesus told them to give her something to eat. Her parents were overwhelmed. Jesus insisted that they not tell anyone about it, but the report of this miracle spread quickly across the entire countryside.

> **Why did Jesus tell some to spread the news and others to not?**
>
> Jesus told the men in Gadarenes to spread the news because it was not in Israel and they did not have the same Messianic expectations. He told the Jews in Israel not to spread the story because it was not the right time.

As Jesus was leaving, two blind men followed him, shouting, "Son of David, have mercy on us!"

The men followed him into the house where he was staying and Jesus asked them, "Do you believe I can make you see?"

"Yes, Lord," they replied.

Then he touched their eyes and said, "It will happen because of your faith." Suddenly they could see; Jesus sternly warned them not to tell anyone, but they told everyone about it anyway.

After they left, some people brought him a demon-possessed man who couldn't speak. Jesus cast out the demon, and instantly the man could talk. The crowds were shocked and said, "Nothing like this has ever happened in Israel!"

The Pharisees said, "He casts out demons because the prince of demons gives him power."

***

Jesus left that region and went back to Nazareth with his disciples. The next Sabbath, he taught in the synagogue, and the audience was perplexed. They asked, "Where did he get all his wisdom and the power to perform such miracles? He's just the carpenter, the son of Mary and brother of James, Joseph, Judas, and Simon. All his sisters live with us; what makes him so great?" They were offended and refused to trust him.

"A prophet is honored everywhere except in his hometown and with his family," Jesus told them. Because of their disbelief, he could only heal a few sick people but couldn't do much more; and he wondered at their lack of faith.

CHAPTER TWENTY-ONE

FINAL GALILEAN CAMPAIGN
Matthew 9:35-11:1; Mark 6:6-13, 30; Luke 9:1-6, 10

Jesus traveled through all the cities and villages of that area, teaching in the synagogues, announcing the good news about the kingdom, and healing every disease and sickness. He felt great compassion for the crowds that followed him, seeing that they were helpless and had no one to show them where to go. He told his disciples, "The harvest is great, but there aren't many workers, ask the Lord of the harvest to send more workers into the fields."

Jesus gave them the power and authority to cast out demons and heal every disease and illness. He sent them out in pairs and told them, "Don't go to the Gentiles or the Samaritans but only to the lost sheep of Israel. Tell them that the kingdom of heaven is near, heal the sick, raise the dead, cure those with leprosy, and cast out demons. Give to others, just as you have freely received.

"Don't take anything with you on the journey; don't carry a traveler's bag, food, money, extra clothes, or even a walking stick. Don't hesitate to accept hospitality because workers deserve their wages. Whenever you enter a town, search for a worthy home, and stay there until you leave for the next town. When you enter a house, give it your blessing, and if it is a worthy home, let it stand; if it is unworthy, take the blessing back. If a village doesn't welcome you or listen to you, shake the dust off your feet as you leave that place as a testimony against them. I tell you the truth, Sodom and Gomorrah will face less judgment than that city.

"I am sending you out like sheep among wolves, so be as shrewd as snakes and as innocent as doves. Be on your guard against men, because they will hand you over to the courts and beat you in their synagogues. You will stand trial before government officials because you are my followers and this will be your opportunity to tell the world about me. But don't worry about what you will say in your defense; the Holy Spirit will give you the words to say and will speak through you.

"Family members will turn against each other and turn each other over to be killed. Everyone will hate you because of your allegiance with me, but those who endure to the end will be saved. When one town persecutes you, run to the next. I tell you the truth, the Son of Man will come before you finish going through all the towns of Israel.

"A student is not above his teacher and a servant is not greater than his master. It is enough for the student to become like his teacher and the servant like his master. If they call the master of the house the prince of demons, they will also slander the members of the house. But don't be afraid when they threaten you. A time is coming when everything will be revealed and all secrets will become public. What I tell you in the dark, talk about in the light; what I whisper in your ear, shout from the housetops.

"Don't be afraid of those who can kill you but cannot kill your soul. Instead, fear God who can destroy your body and soul in hell. They sell sparrows for less than a penny, and none of them fall to the ground without your Father knowing about it; you are worth more than a whole flock of sparrows, so don't be afraid. God even knows how many hairs are on your head.

"If anyone publicly acknowledges me here on earth, I will acknowledge that person before my Father in heaven. But if someone disowns me here on earth, I will disown that person before my Father in heaven.

"Don't think that I came to bring peace on earth because I have come to bring a sword. I have come to turn a man against his father, a daughter against her mother, and a daughter-in-law against her mother-in-law. Your enemies will be members of your own family. If you love anyone more than you love me, you aren't worthy of being my disciple. If you don't take up your cross and follow me, then you are not worthy of being my disciple. Those who try to keep their life will lose it, and those who lose their lives for my sake will find it.

> **Does Jesus want us to hate our families?**
>
> No. But Jesus wants the highest level of commitment to him. He wants us to love him so much that any other allegiance seems like rejection. Family is important, but if it keeps us from following God, then we must reject them.

"Anyone who welcomes you is welcoming me and whoever welcomes me is welcoming the Father who sent me. If you welcome a prophet as a spokesperson for God, you will receive a prophet's reward, and if you welcome a righteous man, you will receive a righteous man's reward. Also, if anyone gives a cup of cold water to someone because he is my disciple, he will receive his reward."

When Jesus had finished giving these instructions to his twelve disciples, they went off teaching and preaching throughout the country, telling people to turn from their sins. They cast out many demons and healed many sick people, anointing them with olive oil. After they finished their work, they came back and told Jesus what they had done and taught.

CHAPTER TWENTY-TWO

DEATH OF JOHN THE BAPTIST
Matthew 14:3-12; Mark 6:17-29

Around this time, Herod Antipas sent soldiers to arrest and imprison John at his wife Herodias' request. She had been married to Herod's brother Philip, but now was married to Herod. John told Herod that his marriage was illegal and that made Herodias mad. She wanted to kill John, but couldn't do anything without her husband's approval. Herod knew John was a good man and was afraid of a riot, so he protected him. Herod even liked to talk to John, although it always disturbed him.

Herodias' chance came on Herod's birthday when he threw a banquet for his government officials, military commanders, and the leading citizens of Galilee. Herodias' daughter, Salome, danced for the men and greatly pleased them, so Herod said to her, "Ask me for anything you want, and I'll give it to you. Whatever you want, even up to half my kingdom."

The girl went out to ask her mother, "What should I ask for?"

Her mother answered, "Ask for John the Baptist's head on a tray!"

So, the girl ran back to Herod and said, "I want the head of John the Baptist on a tray, right now!"

Her request distressed Herod, but he didn't want to break his promise in front of his dinner guests. So, he sent an executioner to bring him John's head. The soldier cut off his head and brought it to the girl on a tray; then she took it to her mother. When John's disciples heard what had happened, they took his body, buried it, and then told Jesus what had happened.

After John's death, Herod kept hearing more about Jesus because everyone was talking about him. These reports troubled Herod because some people said that John the Baptist had come back to life and that was why he could do such miracles. Others said he was the prophet Elijah or another one of the ancient prophets raised from the dead. Herod was very curious because he had killed John, so he kept trying to see Jesus.

CHAPTER TWENTY-THREE

THE BREAD OF LIFE
Matthew 14:13-36; Mark 6:31-56; Luke 9:10-17; John 6

John's death grieved Jesus and when he saw that a huge crowd was gathering, he said, "Let's get away and rest for a while." So many people were gathering around him that Jesus and his disciples didn't even have time to eat, so they took a boat across the Sea of Galilee towards Bethsaida, looking for a remote area to be alone.

But many people saw them leave and ran ahead to meet them as they landed. A vast crowd gathered as Jesus got out of the boat. Despite his grief, he had compassion on them because they were like sheep without a shepherd. So, he welcomed them, healed their sick, and taught them many things about the kingdom of God.

Then Jesus went up into the hills and sat down with his disciples around him. He saw a great crowd of people coming up the hill, looking for him, so he turned to Philip and asked, "Where can we buy bread to feed all these people?" Jesus was testing Philip, although he already knew what he was going to do.

Philip replied, "It would take about eight months' wages to feed them!"

Then the disciples said, "We're far from town and it's getting late. Send the crowds away so they can go find food and lodging because there is nothing out here in this desolate place."

"They don't need to go away, you feed them," Jesus replied.

"Impossible!" they exclaimed.

"Go find out how much food you have."

They came back and reported, "All we have is a young boy with five barley loaves and two fish. But what good is that with so many people?"

Jesus answered, "Bring them here." Then he had the people sit down in large groups, took the bread, and blessed it. He broke the loaves and fish, gave some to each disciple, and had them hand it out to the people. Everyone ate as much as they wanted and the disciples still picked up twelve baskets full of leftovers. About 5,000 men and many women and children (around 20,000 total) ate from the five loaves and two fish.

When the crowd realized what had happened, they exclaimed, "He must be the Prophet we've been expecting." Jesus realized that the people wanted to make him king by force, so he made his disciples get back into the boat and go to Bethsaida while he calmed the crowd and sent them home. Afterward, Jesus went up into the hills to pray. He was alone as night came.

***

Three or four miles out in the middle of the lake, the disciples were in serious trouble, struggling against the wind and waves. Jesus walked out to them around three in the morning. Jesus started to walk past them, but when they saw him walking on the water, they thought he was a ghost. They were all terrified, but he said to them, "Don't be afraid, it's me."

Peter called out to him, "Lord, if it's really you, tell me to walk out to you."

"Come then," Jesus replied.

Peter climbed out of the boat and walked on the water toward Jesus. But when he saw the wind and the waves, he got scared, and started to sink. "Save me, Lord!" he shouted.

Instantly, Jesus reached out and grabbed him. "Where's your faith?" he asked. "Why did you doubt me?" They both climbed back in the boat, the wind stopped, and they were immediately at their destination.

The disciples worshipped Jesus, saying, "You really are the Son of God." They were deeply moved because their hearts had been hard and they had not understood what was happening with the fish and the loaves feeding all those people.

They anchored the boat at Gennesaret and climbed out. People there recognized Jesus at once, and soon the news of his arrival spread through the entire countryside. Everywhere he went, people brought him the sick for healing. The suffering begged him to let them touch the fringe of his robe and everyone who touched it was healed.

The next morning, a crowd gathered across the lake, waiting to see Jesus. They knew that his disciples had left before him and they were hoping to see him again. Several boats from Tiberius had come to see him as well. When they realized that he was not there, they got into boats and went to Capernaum to look for him. Upon finding him they asked him, "Teacher, how did you get here?"

Jesus replied, "You don't want to be with me because of the miracle; you just want to be with me because I fed you. But don't be so worried about perishable food; seek the eternal food that I will give you. That's why God has sent me."

The crowd asked, "What does God want us to do?"

Jesus answered, "God wants you to believe in me as the One he sent."

The crowd replied, "If you want us to believe in you, show us a sign. Our ancestors ate manna in the wilderness, so what will you do?"

"I tell you the truth," Jesus said. "Moses didn't give them bread from heaven; my Father did. Now he has sent the true bread of heaven down and he gives life to the whole world."

The crowd responded, "We want that bread for our lives."

"I am the bread of life," Jesus declared. "Whoever comes to me will never be hungry, and whoever believes in me will never be thirsty. But you haven't trusted even though you have seen me. I will never turn away anyone my Father sends me. I have come down from heaven to do God's will, not mine. His will is that everyone who believes in me will have eternal life, and I will not lose any of them but will raise them up on the last day."

People began to say to each other, "Isn't this Joseph's son, Jesus? We know his parents, so how can he say he came from heaven?"

Jesus answered, "Stop grumbling. No one can come to me unless the Father who sent me calls him, and I will raise him up on the last day. Just like Scripture says, 'They will all be taught by God.' Everyone who listens to and learns from God comes to me. No one has seen the Father except me. I tell you the truth, whoever believes has eternal life. I am the bread of life; your ancestors ate manna in the wilderness and died. But here is the bread from heaven, and anyone who eats it will not die. I am the living bread from heaven; anyone who eats this bread will live forever. This bread is my flesh, and I will give my life for the world."

Arguments broke out about what he meant, and the people asked, "How can he give us his flesh to eat?"

Jesus said to them, "I tell you the truth, unless you eat the Son of Man's flesh and drink his blood, you cannot have eternal life. If you do these things, I will raise you up on the last day. My flesh is real food, and my blood is true drink; whoever eats and drinks them remains in me, and I in him. God gives me life, and I will give life to those who feed on me. Your ancestors ate manna and died, but whoever eats this bread will live forever.

What did Jesus mean by eating his flesh and drinking his blood?

This does not mean we must literally eat his flesh; Jesus was using figurative language, just as when he says that he is the door, he does not mean he is made of wood and has hinges. He meant that the people must partake in his life and death and live their lives for his glory rather than their own.

Jesus said these things in the synagogue, and his disciples began to say, "This is a difficult teaching; who can understand it?"

Jesus knew that his disciples were complaining, so he asked, "Does this offend you? What will you think when you see the Son of Man return to heaven? The Spirit gives life, but the flesh accomplishes nothing. My words are spirit, and they give life, but some of you don't believe." Jesus knew from the beginning who would not believe and who would betray him. From this time, many of his disciples besides the Twelve stopped following him.

Jesus turned to the Twelve and asked, "Do you want to leave too?"

Peter answered, "Where would we go; you're the only one with eternal life. We trust you and know you are the Messiah, the Holy One of God."

Jesus replied, "I chose twelve of you, but one of you is a devil." He was talking about Judas Iscariot, who would later betray him. Even though Jesus knew this about Judas, he kept him close by and loved him as much as his other followers.

After this, Jesus moved around in Galilee, staying away from Judea because the Jews there wanted to kill him.

CHAPTER TWENTY-FOUR

THE LEAVEN OF THE RELIGIOUS TEACHERS
Matthew 15-16:12; Mark 7:1-8:26; John 7:1

Some Pharisees and teachers of the religious law traveled from Jerusalem to confront Jesus. They noticed that some of Jesus' disciples didn't follow the Jewish handwashing ritual before they ate. So, they asked Jesus, "Why don't your disciples follow our customs and eat without first washing their hands?"

Jesus replied, "Isaiah was prophesying about you hypocrites when he said, 'These people honor me with their words, but their hearts are far away. Their worship is a joke, and their teachings are just made-up rules.' You have ignored God's commands and substituted your own traditions.

"You break God's commands to observe your own traditions. For example, Moses said, 'Honor your father and mother' and, 'Anyone who curses his father or mother must be put to death.' But you say that if a man tells his parents, 'I cannot help you because I have dedicated what I could have given you to God.' You allow him to dishonor his needy parents. Thus, you nullify the direct commandment of God to protect your tradition."

> **Clean hands and the Law**
>
> The Jews, especially the Pharisees, did not eat until they had poured water over their cupped hands, as required by their ancient traditions. They also didn't eat anything from the market unless it had been washed. They observed other traditions, such as ceremonial washing of cups, pitchers, and kettles. The washing ceremony was a part of the meticulous rules the Jews made after their captivity under the Babylonians. These were a part of an oral tradition based on an interpretation of Moses' Law until they were recorded in 200 A.D. as

> the Mishnah (Jewish teachings). Even though this wasn't Scripture, the Jews held it in the highest regard.
>
> Another tradition was that irresponsible children could "dedicate" money to the temple so that they would not have to give it to their parents. However, this dedication did not mean that they had to give it to the temple. This practice was an example of the Pharisees following the letter but not the spirit of the Law.

Then Jesus said to the whole crowd, "Listen and understand, you are not defiled by what you eat; you are defiled by what you say and do."

A little later, his disciples came to him and asked, "Do you realize that you offended the Pharisees?"

Jesus replied, "Every plant my heavenly Father did not plant will be pulled up by the roots. Ignore those blind guides because if a blind man leads another blind man, both will fall into a pit."

Then Jesus went into a house to get away from the crowds, and Peter said, "Explain what you meant when you said people aren't defiled by what they eat."

Jesus replied, "Don't you understand either? Nothing from the outside can make you unclean because it doesn't go to your heart; it goes to your stomach, and then out of your body. What comes out of you is what makes you unclean. From men's hearts come evil thoughts, murder, adultery, sexual immorality, theft, lies, greed, wickedness, deceit, lewdness, envy, slander, arrogance, and foolishness. These are the things that make you unclean, but eating with unwashed hands could never make you unclean." By saying this, Jesus declared that all foods are acceptable to eat.

***

Heading north to the region of Tyre and Sidon, Jesus tried to keep his arrival secret, but the news spread quickly. A Gentile woman from that region came to him, pleading, "My Lord, Son of David, have mercy on me! My daughter suffers greatly at the hands of a demon."

Jesus ignored her. "Tell her to leave us alone, she's bothering us," the disciples urged.

The woman was a Syro-Phoenician Gentile, so he said to her, "I was only sent to the lost sheep of Israel."

But the woman knelt before him and said, "Lord, help me!"

Jesus replied, "It's not right to take the children's bread and throw it to the dogs."

"Yes, Lord," she replied, "but even dogs can eat the crumbs that fall from the children's plates."

Moved by her faith, Jesus granted her request. Her daughter was instantly healed; when the woman arrived home, her daughter was lying quietly in bed, and the demon was gone.

> **Why did Jesus call this woman a dog?**
>
> Some have interpreted this statement to mean that women are inferior to men. But this was a statement reflecting race relations of the time. Jesus had first come to Israel and his followers would eventually spread the gospel to all people.

***

Jesus left Tyre and went through Sidon, then returned to the Sea of Galilee and Decapolis. Upon his arrival, he climbed a hill and sat down. The crowd brought Jesus a deaf man who could barely talk and begged him to heal the man. Jesus led him away from the crowd and put his fingers into the man's ears. Then he spit on his fingers and touched the man's tongue. Jesus looked up to heaven, sighed, and said, "Be opened." Instantly the man could hear and speak.

The crowd surged up with lame, blind, disabled, mute, and other sufferers, and he healed them all. When the crowd saw these people healed, they were impressed, and they praised the God of Israel.

Jesus asked the crowd not to tell anyone, but the more he told them not to, the more they spread the news. They kept saying, "He does everything well, he even makes the deaf hear and the mute speak."

***

Around this time, another large crowd gathered and they ran out of food again. Jesus called his disciples to him and said, "I feel sorry for these people because they've been with me for three days and haven't eaten anything. But if I send them home without feeding them, they will faint on the way because some of them have come from far away."

His disciples asked, "Where will we find enough food for them out here in the wilderness?" Even though they had seen Jesus feed 5,000 men, they still didn't understand his power.

"How many loaves of bread do you have?" Jesus asked.

"Seven, and a few small fish," they replied. Jesus asked all the people to sit down on the ground. He took the loaves and fish, thanked God for them, and began distributing food to his disciples, who gave it to the crowd.

Everyone ate until they were full and there were still seven large baskets of leftovers. That day, they fed about 4,000 men plus women and children (around 16,000 total).

After eating, Jesus sent the people home and he took a boat to Magadan with his disciples.

***

The Pharisees heard about Jesus feeding the people and came to argue with him. They were testing him, demanding a miraculous sign to prove that he was from heaven.

Jesus sighed deeply and replied, "You know the saying, 'Red sky at night, sailor's delight; red sky at morning, sailor's take warning.' You know how to interpret the weather, but you cannot interpret the signs of the times. Only a wicked and faithless generation would ask for a miraculous sign, but the only sign I'll give you is the sign of the prophet Jonah." Jesus got back into the boat and crossed the lake again.

The disciples forgot to bring food, and there was only one loaf of bread in the boat. As they crossed the lake, Jesus warned them, "Beware of the yeast of the Pharisees, Sadducees, and Herod."

The disciples decided that he said this because they hadn't brought any food. But Jesus knew their thoughts and said, "Where's your faith? Why are you worried about food? Are your hearts too hard to learn or understand? You have eyes but cannot see and have ears but cannot hear. When I fed the 5,000 with five loaves of bread, how many baskets of leftovers did you pick up?"

"Twelve," they answered.

Jesus continued, "How many did you pick up when I fed the 4,000 with seven loaves?"

"Seven," they replied.

"Don't you understand?" he asked. "How can you even think I was talking about food? Beware of the yeast of the Pharisees, Sadducees, and Herod."

Finally, the disciples understood that he was talking about false teaching and not food.

When they came to Bethsaida, some people led a blind man up and begged Jesus to touch him. Jesus took the blind man by the hand and led him outside the village. He put spit on the man's eyes, laid his hands on him, and asked, "Can you see anything?"

The man looked up and said, "I see people, but they look like trees walking around."

Jesus put his hands over his eyes again and then the man could see everything clearly. Then Jesus sent him home and said, "Don't go into the village."

CHAPTER TWENTY-FIVE

THE GREAT CONFESSION AND THE TRANSFIGURATION
Matthew 16:13-17:13; Mark 8:27-9:13; Luke 9:18-36

On their way to the villages of Caesarea Philippi, Jesus asked, "Who do people say I am?"

The disciples replied, "Some say you are John the Baptist, some say Elijah, and some say you're one of the other ancient prophets risen from the dead."

Then Jesus asked, "But who do you say I am?"

Peter answered, "You are the Messiah, the Son of the living God."

Jesus replied, "God bless you Peter, because my heavenly Father revealed this to you. I will build my church upon the rock of your confession and the gates of hell will not overcome it. I will give you the keys of the kingdom of heaven; whatever you lock up here on earth will be locked up in heaven and whatever you open here on earth will be opened in heaven." Then Jesus warned them not to tell anyone he was the Messiah because it was not yet time.

> **Timing**
>
> Jesus told his disciples not to tell people that he was the Christ because the timing was wrong. At times, he may have wanted to keep the crowds small. Other times he may not have wanted the Jews to get the wrong idea because they thought that the Messiah would be a political leader and military conqueror. Finally, Jesus did tell them to spread the word after his resurrection.

From that point on, Jesus began to tell them that the Son of Man must go to Jerusalem, suffer many terrible things, and be rejected by the leaders, priests, and teachers of the religious law. He told them that he would be killed and that he would resurrect on the third day. Jesus talked openly about these things, but Peter took him aside and told him not to say such things.

Jesus turned and looked at his disciples and then sternly told Peter, "Get behind me, Satan! You are a stumbling block; you're only seeing things from an earthly point of view, and not God's."

> **Why did Jesus call Peter 'Satan'?**
>
> Peter's attempt to get Jesus to avoid the cross was the same as Satan's temptation to take power in an inappropriate manner when Satan tempted him in the wilderness. Jesus was speaking to Satan, who was using Peter's words as a temptation, not Peter. Satan was using Peter as a tool, and we must remember that Satan can tempt in just about any situation. We must deny our interests if they conflict with following Jesus.
>
> It is also interesting to note that only moments after making the great confession, Peter had a great failure. Often our most significant failures will come on the heels of our greatest successes. We always need to make sure to keep our guard up against a growing ego.

Then Jesus called the crowds to him and said, "If any of you wants to follow me, you must deny yourself and take up your cross. Whoever wants to save his life will lose it, and whoever loses his life for me and the gospel will save it. What good is it to gain the whole world and lose your soul? Nothing is as valuable as your soul. If anyone is ashamed of me and my message, then the Son of Man will be ashamed of him when he comes with the angels and his Father's glory to judge people according to their deeds. I tell you the truth, some of you who are standing here will not die before you see the kingdom of God arrives with great power."

***

A week later, Jesus took Peter, James, and John to a mountain to pray. As Jesus was praying, his appearance changed so that his face shone like the sun and his clothes became whiter than any natural process could make them. Just then, Moses and Elijah appeared in glory and began talking to Jesus. They talked about how he was on his way to die in Jerusalem to fulfill God's plan.

Peter, James, and John had fallen asleep while Jesus prayed, but now they were wide awake. As Moses and Elijah were starting to leave, Peter blurted out, "Master, it's good that we're here. Let us put up three shelters, one for you, one for Moses, and one for Elijah."

> **Who are Moses and Elijah?**
>
> Moses and Elijah are two central figures from the Old Testament. Moses represents the Law and Elijah represents the Prophets. Together, the two represent all Old Testament Scripture.

A cloud appeared and covered them, and they were terrified. A voice from the cloud said, "This is my beloved son whom I have chosen and I am pleased with him; listen to him."

The disciples were terrified and they fell face down on the ground. But Jesus came over, touched them, and said, "Get up and don't be afraid." Then when they looked around, Moses and Elijah were gone.

As they went down the mountain, Jesus told his disciples not to tell anyone what they had seen until after he had risen from the dead. So, they kept it to themselves, but they often spoke of what Jesus meant when he talked about rising from the dead.

They began asking him, "Why do the teachers of the religious law say that Elijah must return before the Messiah comes?"

Jesus replied, "Elijah comes to set everything in order. But I tell you, Elijah has already come, and they treated him as they wished. In the same way, I will suffer and be rejected." Then the disciples understood that he was talking about John the Baptist.

CHAPTER TWENTY-SIX

RESPONSIBILITY TO OTHERS
Matthew 17:14-18:35; Mark 9:14-50; Luke 9:37-50

When they got to the foot of the mountain, they found a great crowd surrounding the other disciples, and some of the teachers of the religious law were arguing with them. Jesus walked up and asked, "What's all this arguing about?" The crowd surged around him with joy.

One man knelt before Jesus and said, "Teacher, my son is possessed by an evil spirit that won't let him talk. Whenever it seizes him, it throws him to the ground; he foams at the mouth, grinds his teeth, and goes rigid. It hardly ever leaves him alone and is always hurting him. So, I brought my son for you to heal him; your disciples tried, but they couldn't cast out the demon."

Jesus rebuked them, "You stubborn, faithless people, how long will I have to stay with you and put up with you? Bring the boy to me."

When they brought the boy to Jesus, the evil spirit threw the boy into a violent convulsion, and he fell to the ground, writhing and foaming at the mouth. Jesus asked the boy's father, "How long has this been happening?"

The man replied, "Since he was very small. The demon has often tried to kill him by throwing him into the fire or water. Have mercy on us and do something if you can."

"What do you mean if I can?" Jesus asked. "Everything is possible for those who believe."

Instantly, the father exclaimed, "I do believe, but help me not to doubt."

When Jesus saw the crowd gathering around, he rebuked the evil spirit, and said, "Come out of him you deaf and mute spirit, and never bother him again."

The demon shrieked, threw the boy into another convulsion, and left him. The boy lay motionless and appeared to be dead. But Jesus took him by the hand, helped him to his feet, and healed the boy.

Jesus went back inside and his disciples asked him, "Why couldn't we drive out the demon?"

He replied, "Because you lack faith. If you had faith as small as a mustard seed you could tell a mountain to move and it would. Nothing is impossible with faith. Plus, this kind of demon only comes out through prayer."

Then they left that region and traveled through Galilee. Jesus tried to avoid the crowds to spend more time with his disciples. He said to them, "Pay attention! I will be betrayed and killed, but I will rise again on the third day." What he was saying was incomprehensible, but they were afraid to ask for clarification.

> **How were the disciples so dense?**
>
> It seems like Jesus was very clear that he would die and rise again, but we must remember that they believed that the Messiah was going to be a conquering king. It took a long time to undo their misconceptions about the Messiah and what Jesus was accomplishing.

***

When they got to Capernaum, tax collectors came to Peter and asked, "Does your teacher pay the two-drachma temple tax?"

Peter answered impulsively, "Of course he does." Then Peter went to ask Jesus about it.

Before Peter had a chance to say anything, Jesus asked him, "Do kings tax their own sons or others?"

"Others," Peter answered.

Then Jesus said, "Ah, so the sons are exempt. But we don't want to offend them, so go down to the lake and throw out your fishing line.

Open the mouth of the first fish you catch, and you will find a four-drachma coin. Take it and pay both our taxes."

***

As Jesus and his disciples were settling into the house they would stay in while they were in Capernaum, Jesus asked, "What were you discussing on the way here?" Embarrassed, they didn't answer because they had been arguing about which of them was the greatest disciple. He sat down and gathered his disciples around him. He said, "Anyone who wants to be first must be the last and the servant of all."

He called a child over, took him in his arms, and said, "I tell you the truth, unless you repent and become like little children, you will never make it into the kingdom of heaven. Anyone who welcomes a child like this in my name welcomes me, and anyone who welcomes me welcomes the one who sent me. Whoever is least among you is the greatest."

A little while later, John came to him and said, "Teacher, we saw a man casting out demons in your name. We tried to stop him because he's not in our group."

But Jesus said, "Don't stop him because no one can do a miracle in my name and then say something bad about me. Anyone who is not against you is on your side. I tell you the truth, anyone who gives you a cup of cold water because you are my followers will receive a reward.

"But if anyone causes one of these little ones that believes in me to sin, it would be better for that person to be thrown into the sea with a large millstone tied around his neck. Beware that you don't look down on the little ones, because in heaven, their angels are always in God's presence. Woe to the world because of its stumbling blocks. Such things will happen, but woe to whoever causes the stumbling block.

"If your hand or foot causes you to sin, cut it off because it's better to enter life crippled than to go to hell. If your eye causes you to sin, gouge it out because it is better to enter the kingdom of God with one eye than to have two eyes and be thrown into hell 'where the worm does not die and the fire never goes out.'

> **Did Jesus advocate self-mutilation?**
>
> No. We need to be aware of our weaknesses because Satan is very aware of them. If something causes us to stumble, we need to cut it off, no matter how painful it is, so that we won't fall into greater temptation. For example, if we always end up getting into trouble when we hang out with certain friends, it is better to cut them off than maintain relationships that pull us away from God. If we were to take this literally, we would end up cutting off almost every single body part.

"Everyone will be purified with fire. Salt is good for seasoning, but if it loses its flavor, you can't make it salty again. Be like salt amongst each other and live in peace.

"If your brother sins against you, go and show him his fault privately. If he listens to you, you have won your brother. But if he refuses to listen, take one or two others with you so that everything may be established by the testimony of two or three witnesses. If he still refuses to listen, tell the whole church; if he refuses to listen to the church, shun him like a pagan or a tax collector.

"I tell you the truth, whatever you bind on earth will be bound in heaven, and whatever you loose on earth will be loosed in heaven. If two of you on earth agree about anything and ask my Father in heaven to do it for you, he will do it. For where two or three come together in my name, I am there with them."

Then Peter came to Jesus and asked, "Lord, how many times should I forgive someone who sins against me? Seven times?" The day's common teaching was to forgive someone three times, but Peter thought that doubling that and adding one would sound impressive.

Jesus answered, "Not seven times, but seventy times seven." Jesus did not mean keeping track until the 490th time, but that there should be no limit to forgiveness.

> **Forgiveness and access**
>
> Jesus teaches us that we need to forgive without limit, but that doesn't mean we have to allow the same access. If someone violates our trust, we can forgive and restore the relationship, but we do not need to put ourselves in the same position to be hurt again. For example, a business owner may forgive an employee who is stealing from the company, but it does not mean she still has to employ the offending worker.

Jesus continued, "The kingdom of heaven is like a king who wanted to settle accounts with those who borrowed from him. As the settlement began, a servant who owed him millions of dollars came before the king. The servant was unable to repay his debt, so the king ordered that the servant, his family, and all they owned should be sold to repay the debt.

"The servant fell to his knees before the king and begged him to be patient. The king took pity on him, canceled the debt, and let the servant go.

"But when the servant went out, he found a fellow servant who owed him a few dollars. He grabbed this man and began to choke him, demanding that he pay back what he owed.

"His fellow servant begged him to be patient, but he refused. Instead, he had the man thrown in prison until he could repay his debt. When the other servants saw the situation, they were upset, and they told the king what had happened.

"The king called in the man and said, 'You wicked servant, I canceled all your debt because you begged me to. Shouldn't you have mercy on your fellow servant, just like I had mercy on you?' Then the angry king sent the man to prison to be tortured until he should pay back his debt.

"This is how my heavenly Father will treat you unless you forgive your brother from your heart."

CHAPTER TWENTY-SEVEN

THE FEAST OF TABERNACLES
Matthew 8:19-22; Luke 9:51-62; John 7:2-53

When it was time for the Jewish Feast of Tabernacles, Jesus' brothers urged him to go to Judea for the celebration, saying, "You should go to Judea, so your disciples can see your miracles. You cannot become a public figure if you stay hidden like this. Since you do such wonderful things, you should prove it to the world." They said this because they didn't believe he was the Messiah.

Jesus replied, "Although it's the right time for you, it's not the right time for me. The world cannot hate you, but it hates me because I call it evil. You go ahead to the feast, but it's not my time yet." Jesus stayed in Galilee while his brothers went to Judea.

Once the others had gone, Jesus left for Jerusalem in secret. On the way, he sent messengers ahead to a Samaritan village to prepare for his arrival. But the villagers turned the messengers away because Jesus' men were on their way to Jerusalem. When James and John heard about this, they asked, "Should we call fire down from heaven to burn them up?" But Jesus rebuked them, and they went on to the next village.

As they walked along the road, one of the teachers of religious law said to him, "Teacher, I will follow you wherever you go."

Jesus replied, "Foxes have dens to live in, and birds have nests, but the Son of Man has no place to lay his head."

He said to another man, "Come be my disciple."

The man said, "Let me bury my father first."

Jesus said, "Let the dead bury their own dead, but you go preach the coming of the kingdom of God."

Another person said, "I will follow you, but first let me say goodbye to my family."

But Jesus told him, "Anyone who puts a hand to the plow and then looks back is unworthy to serve in the kingdom of God."

What did Jesus mean?

These are some difficult sayings that Jesus said to people who seemed to want to follow him, but we must remember that he knew their hearts and that they were not ready to commit to follow him. The first man wanted to follow, but Jesus wanted him to know that following him would not be a comfortable life and that it would require sacrifice.

The second man asked to bury his father before he followed Jesus, but, likely, his father was still alive, and the man wanted to wait to follow until a significant life event happened first. Currently, we may substitute a different life event that we are waiting for before committing to follow (graduation, getting a job, having kids, retirement, etc.). Jesus wants our faith now, not when it is convenient for us.

The third man asked to say goodbye to his family, and that seems like a reasonable request. But Jesus answers with a proverb that means that someone beginning a new venture must stay focused and not look back on the past if he wants to be successful.

In all three of these situations, Jesus was questioning their level of commitment. He wanted his followers to know what following him entailed and not change their minds once they realized what they needed to sacrifice.

***

The Jewish leaders tried to find Jesus at the festival; everyone was asking where he was. There was a lot of talk about him, but no one wanted to say anything publicly because they were afraid of the people's divided opinions. Some people said that he was a good man, while others said that he was deceiving the people.

About halfway through the feast, Jesus began teaching in the temple courts. The Jews were impressed and asked, "How does he know so much without having studied?"

Jesus answered, "My teaching is not my own, but it comes from the one who sent me. If anyone does God's will, he will find out if my teaching is from God or not. Those who speak on their own are looking for praise, but those who seek the glory of the one who sent them are full of truth. Moses gave you the Law, but none of you obey it, so why are you trying to kill me?"

The crowd responded, "Are you crazy? Who's trying to kill you?"

Jesus replied, "I did one miracle and you're all astonished. Moses gave you circumcision, although it really came from Abraham. If you can circumcise a child on the Sabbath so you don't break the Law, why do you condemn me for making an entire man well on the Sabbath? Stop judging by appearances and make a legitimate judgment."

Some of the people who lived in Jerusalem said to each other, "Isn't this the man they're trying to kill? Here he is, speaking in public, and nobody's saying anything to him. Have the authorities decided that he is the Messiah? But that's not possible because no one will know where the Messiah comes from, and we know where he's from."

Jesus was still teaching in the temple courts and he cried out, "You know me, and where I'm from, but I represent one you don't know. I know him and I know that he is true because he sent me."

The authorities tried to arrest him, but no one laid a hand on him; it wasn't his time yet. People in the crowd began saying that the Messiah would not do any more miraculous signs than Jesus was.

The Pharisees heard the crowd whispering so they sent the temple guards to arrest him. Jesus said to them, "I am with you for only a little while longer, and then I will go back to the one who sent me. You will look for me, but won't be able to find me because you cannot go where I am going."

The Jews were puzzled and said to each other, "Where is he going that we won't be able to find him? Is he going to leave Israel and teach the Greeks? What does he mean that we won't find him and that we cannot go where he is going?"

***

On the last day of the festival, Jesus stood up and shouted, "If anyone is thirsty, come and drink. Whoever believes in me will have rivers of living water flowing from within, just as the Scriptures say." By rivers of living water, Jesus meant the Holy Spirit, whom he would give to his followers after his glorification.

Some said, "This man is the Prophet who comes before the Messiah." Others maintained he was the Messiah. Still others said, "He can't be the Messiah because he's from Galilee. The Scriptures clearly say that the Messiah will be born of David's royal line, in Bethlehem, the town where King David was born." People were divided about him, some people wanted to arrest him, but no one touched him.

Finally, the temple guards went back to the chief priests and Pharisees, who asked them, "Why didn't you arrest him?"

"We've never heard anyone talk like him," the guards declared.

The Pharisees replied, "Has he deceived you too? Have any of the rulers or Pharisees believed in him? Of course not, this mob is ignorant and they are cursed."

Nicodemus, a Pharisee who had spoken with Jesus earlier, asked, "Is it legal to convict someone without first giving him a hearing?"

They replied, "Are you a Galilean too? Check the Scriptures and see that no prophet has ever come from Galilee." The meeting broke up; everybody went home and Jesus went to the Mount of Olives.

CHAPTER TWENTY-EIGHT

FURTHER MINISTRY AT THE FEAST OF TABERNACLES
John 8

Jesus was back at the temple early the next morning. When a crowd gathered around him, he sat down and started to teach. As he was speaking, the religious leaders brought him a woman caught in adultery. They were looking for an opportunity to accuse him of something, so they made her stand in front of the crowd and said, "Teacher, this woman was caught committing adultery. The Law of Moses commands us to stone such women. What do you think we should do?"

Jesus didn't say a word, but instead bent down and started to write on the ground with his finger. They kept asking him for an answer so he stood up and said, "Whoever is without sin should cast the first stone." Then he knelt and started writing again.

When his accusers heard this, they began to slip away one at a time, starting with the oldest, until Jesus was left standing with the woman in the middle of the crowd. Jesus stood up and asked her, "Where are they? Has no one condemned you?"

"No, Lord," she said.

Jesus said, "Neither do I. Go and sin no more."

> **What did Jesus write?**
>
> We don't know what Jesus was writing, but people have suggested that he was listing the Pharisees' sins or writing the names of the Pharisees who had slept with the woman.

***

Later, Jesus said, "I am the light of the world. Whoever follows me will never walk in darkness but will have the light that leads to life."

The Pharisees replied, "You're testifying about yourself, so it is invalid."

Jesus answered, "Even if I testify on my behalf, my testimony is valid because I know where I came from and where I'm going. You judge by human standards, but I don't judge anyone. But if I do judge, my judgment is just because God is with me. The law says that the testimony of two men is valid; you have me and you have my Father who sent me."

They asked, "Where is your father?"

Jesus answered, "You don't know me or my Father, if you knew me, you would know my Father too." Jesus said these things while teaching near the offering boxes where people made donations, but no one arrested him because it wasn't his time yet.

Then Jesus said again, "I'm going away and you will look for me, but will die in your sin, because you cannot come where I'm going."

This made the Jews ask, "Is he going to commit suicide? Is that why we cannot go where he's going?"

Jesus continued, "You're from below, but I'm from above; you're from this world, but I'm not. If you refuse to believe in me then you will surely die in your sins."

"Who are you?" they demanded.

Jesus replied, "I am who I have always claimed to be. I have a lot to judge you on, because the one who sent me is reliable, and I tell the world what he tells me."

He could see that they still didn't understand that he was talking about God, so he said, "When you have crucified me, you will know that I am who I said I am. You will also know that I do nothing on my own, but I only say what my Father tells me to. He is still with me and has not deserted me because I do what he wants."

***

Many people who heard Jesus speak trusted in him, and he said to them, "You are really my disciples if you obey my teachings; then, you will know the truth and the truth will set you free."

They answered, "We are descendants of Abraham and have never been slaves. What do you mean we will be set free?"

Jesus replied, "I tell you the truth, everyone who sins is a slave to sin. A slave doesn't belong in the family, but a son always belongs. If the Son sets you free, you will always be free. I know that you are descendants of Abraham, but you are ready to kill me because you have no room for my word. I am telling you what I heard in my Father's presence, but you are doing what you heard from your father."

"Our father is Abraham," they answered.

Jesus said, "If you were Abraham's children, then you would do what he did. I told you the truth that I heard from God, but you're trying to kill me. Abraham wouldn't do that, so you're doing the things your true father does."

"We're not illegitimate children; God himself is our true father," they protested.

Jesus told them, "If God were your father, you would love me, because he sent me. Why don't you understand what I'm saying? It's because you cannot. Your father is the Devil, and you want to do his will. He was a murderer from the beginning and there is no truth in him. It is natural for him to lie because he is the father of lies, so you don't believe me when I tell the truth. Can you prove me guilty of sin? If I'm telling the truth, why don't you believe me? If you belonged to God, you would hear what he says, but you cannot hear him because you don't belong to him."

"You're a Samaritan and demon-possessed!" the Jews shouted.

Jesus responded, "I'm not demon-possessed, but I honor my Father and you dishonor me. I'm not trying to glorify myself, but God is, so let him be the judge. I tell you the truth, if anyone obeys my word, he will never die."

The Jews called out, "Now we know you are demon-possessed. Abraham and the prophets died, but you say that whoever obeys you will never die. Are you greater than Abraham and the prophets? Who do you think you are?"

"It doesn't matter if I glorify myself," Jesus replied, "but God, whom you say is your father, glorifies me. Even though you don't know him, I do, and I would be a liar like you if I said I didn't. Abraham looked forward to my day with joy and was glad to see it come."

The Jews said, "You're not even 50 years old, how can you say you've seen Abraham?"

Jesus answered, "I tell you the truth, before Abraham was born, I AM!" Then the Jews picked up stones to kill him because they knew that he was claiming to be God, but Jesus hid himself and left the temple.

Did Jesus claim to be God?

Many times, and in many ways, this is the reason that he was ultimately killed. When Jesus says, "I AM," it is a reference to the name God gave for himself (I AM WHO I AM) when he appeared to Moses in the burning bush. Jesus did things that only God could do, like forgive sins and judge people, even when confronted by his opponents. He also accepted worship from his followers. He took on many of the same names and characteristics that only God did in the Old Testament. As a good Jewish teacher, he would not do any of these without understanding that he was claiming to be God.

CHAPTER TWENTY-NINE

PRIVATE LESSONS ON SERVICE AND PRAYER
Luke 10:1-11:13

Jesus chose 70 disciples, including the original Twelve, and sent them in pairs to all the towns and villages that he was about to visit. Before he sent them, he said, "The harvest is ready, but there aren't many workers, so pray that God sends out more workers into the field. I am sending you out like lambs among wolves. Don't take a bag, money, or an extra pair of sandals.

"Don't greet anyone on the road, but bless a house when you enter it. If the man is worthy, your blessing will stand, but if he is not, it will return to you. Don't move around, but stay in one house and take what they give you because a worker is worthy of his wages.

"Heal the sick and tell them that the kingdom of God is near. But if a town does not welcome you, go into its streets and wipe the dust off your feet as a testimony to their coming judgment, reminding them that the kingdom of God is near. Even wicked Sodom will face less judgment than that town.

"Woe to Chorazin and Bethsaida because if Tyre and Sidon saw the miracles they did, they would have repented long ago. It will be more bearable for Tyre and Sidon in judgment than it will be for you. Capernaum won't be lifted to heaven but will go down to death.

"Whoever listens to you, listens to me; whoever rejects you, rejects me; and whoever rejects me, rejects God."

When the 70 returned from their mission, they were elated and said, "Lord, even the demons obey us in your name."

Jesus replied, "I saw Satan fall from heaven like lightning. I have given you the power to overcome the enemy and trample snakes and scorpions without being hurt. But don't rejoice because the spirits obey you, rejoice because your names are written in heaven."

The Holy Spirit filled Jesus and he said, "O Father, Lord of heaven, I praise you for hiding these things from the wise and educated and revealing them to the childlike. It pleases you to do it that way.

"God has pledged all things to me. No one knows me except the Father, and no one knows the Father except me and those to whom I choose to reveal him."

Then he turned to his disciples and said, "You are privileged to see what you've seen because many prophets and kings wanted to hear and see these things, but they could not."

***

One day an expert in the religious law stood up to test Jesus and asked him, "Teacher, what do I have to do to receive eternal life?"

Jesus replied, "What does the Law of Moses tell you?"

The man answered, "'Love the Lord your God with all your heart, soul, strength, and mind,' and, 'Love your neighbor as yourself.'"

"You're right, do this and you will live," Jesus agreed.

But the man wanted to justify himself, so he asked, "Who is my neighbor?"

"Imagine this," Jesus replied. "Suppose a man was going down from Jerusalem to Jericho and on his way, he was attacked by robbers. They beat him up, stole his clothes, and left him for dead on the roadside.

"A Jewish priest came along the road and saw the man, but the priest crossed to the other side of the road. A little while later, a Levite came by and saw him, but he crossed to the other side of the road too.

"Then a Samaritan came along and took pity on the man. He bandaged his wounds and gave him some medicine. Then the Samaritan put him on his donkey and took him to an inn, where he cared for the man. The next day the Samaritan had to leave, so he gave the innkeeper some money with instructions to care for the injured man. He also said that if it cost more money, he would pay the rest the next time he came through that way.

"Now which of these three would you say was a neighbor to the man attacked by bandits?"

The expert said, "The one who had mercy on him."

Jesus told him, "Go, and do the same."

> ### The scandal of the Good Samaritan
>
> The questioner wanted to narrowly define the scope of whom he was responsible to love. But Jesus showed him that we should love everyone we come across who has need. The priest and the Levite in the parable excused themselves from helping because they would have become ceremonially unclean and unable to fulfill their religious obligations. This story also took place on a 17-mile stretch of road that was a common place for robbers to wait for travelers. But Jesus wanted his audience to view people and their needs as more important than ceremony.
>
> The fact that Jesus made the Samaritan the hero of the story was scandalous because the Jews hated them extremely. In modern terms, we can replace the Samaritan with a member from whatever group we view as the lowest or most challenging. God wants us to love even those it's difficult for us to love.

***

As Jesus and his disciples continued to Jerusalem, they came to a village where a woman named Martha welcomed them into her home. Martha was distracted with the necessary preparations to have company, but her sister Mary sat at Jesus' feet and listened to what he had to say. Martha got frustrated, so she came to Jesus and said, "Lord, it's not fair that my sister is making me do all the work, tell her to come help me."

But Jesus said to her, "My dear Martha, you are worried about so many things, but only one thing is essential. Mary has discovered that one thing and I won't take it away from her."

***

Another day while Jesus was finishing a prayer, one of his disciples asked, "Lord, teach us to pray, just like John taught his disciples."

> **How does prayer work?**
>
> Prayer is the way that we communicate with God, it can be silent or out loud. Through prayer, we praise God, confess our sins, and tell him what we need. God tells us that he answers all our prayers, although sometimes he says no or that we need to wait. One of the primary purposes of prayer is to draw us closer to God. It is like casting a fishing line and catching an island. As we reel the island in, we move closer, not the other way around. When we pray, it draws us closer to him.

Jesus said, "This is how you should pray: 'Father, I praise your name, let your kingdom come soon. Give us what we need each day. Forgive our sins, just as we forgive those who sin against us and keep us far from temptation.'"

He continued, "Suppose you went to a friend's house in the middle of the night to borrow three loaves of bread because you had some company and wanted to feed them. Your friend would say, 'Go away, I'm already in bed and I don't have anything to give you.' Even though he won't give you bread just because you're his friend, he will eventually give you bread if you keep knocking long enough.

"So, keep on asking, and you will receive; keep on seeking, and you will find; keep on knocking, and the door will be opened. Everyone who asks, receives; everyone who seeks, finds; and the door is opened to everyone who knocks.

> **Why doesn't God say 'yes' to every prayer?**
>
> Jesus' teaching seems to indicate that God should say 'yes' to all our prayers. But God is not a sky fairy who exists to grant our wishes like a genie in a bottle. His primary concern is his plan, not what we think we need. Sometimes God says no to our requests because it might end up hurting us in the long term. This is like a parent who doesn't give a child everything he or she wants because it is not in their best interest. Sometimes, he tells us to wait because the timing is not right. Ultimately, we must submit to the fact that our lives are about God's glory and not what we might think is best for us.

"Do you fathers give your children a snake if they ask for a fish or a scorpion if they ask for an egg? If you know how to give good gifts even though you are evil, what better gift will your heavenly Father give to those who ask him than the Holy Spirit?"

CHAPTER THIRTY

SECOND DEBATE WITH RELIGIOUS LEADERS
Luke 11:1-13:9

One day, Jesus cast a demon out of a mute man and the crowd was impressed. Some said, though, that he cast out demons because he was the prince of demons. Others demanded another miracle to prove that he was from God.

Jesus knew their thoughts and said, "Any kingdom at war with itself is doomed, and any divided house will fall. If Satan is fighting against himself, how will his kingdom stand? If I drive out demons by the power of Satan, where do your followers get their power? But if I drive out demons by the power of God, then the kingdom of God has arrived.

"When a fully-armed strong man guards his house, his possessions are safe. If someone stronger comes along, that one overpowers him, takes his armor, and carries off his possessions.

"Whoever isn't helping me opposes me; whoever isn't working with me is working against me.

"Now, when a demon leaves a man, it goes through the desert, looking for a place to rest. When it can't find any, it decides to go back. When it gets back, it finds his former home swept and clean, so it takes seven other worse spirits and they all move in. Then the person is worse off than before."

As Jesus was speaking, a woman cried out, "God bless your mother, her womb, and the breasts that nursed you."

Jesus replied, "Rather, God blesses those who hear God's word and obey it."

As the crowd grew, Jesus said, "This wicked generation asks for a sign, but the only sign it will get is the sign of Jonah. As Jonah was a sign for the Ninevites, so I will be a sign for this generation.

"The Queen of Sheba will judge this generation because she came from far away to hear Solomon's wisdom. The Ninevites will also judge you because they repented when they heard Jonah's message. Now someone greater than Solomon and Jonah is here and you refuse to listen.

"No one lights a lamp and then hides it; instead, he puts it on a stand so everyone can see it. Your eye is the lamp of your body, and when your eyes are good, your whole body is full of light. But if your eyes are bad, then your body is full of darkness. Therefore, if your body is full of light and has no darkness, you will be full of light."

***

When Jesus finished speaking, a Pharisee invited him to eat. Jesus went in and reclined at the table. His host was surprised to see that Jesus sat down to eat without first performing the ceremonial washing ritual.

But Jesus said to him, "You Pharisees carefully clean the outside of the cup and the dish, but inside you are full of greed and wickedness! Foolish people, didn't God make the inside as well as the outside? Give what is inside the dish to the poor, and you will be completely clean.

"Woe to you Pharisees, because you tithe the smallest part of your income, but you neglect God's justice and love. You should tithe, but you shouldn't ignore the more important things.

"Woe to you Pharisees, because you love the seats of honor and respectful greetings in the marketplace.

"Woe to you, because you are like unmarked graves that people walk over without knowing it."

One of the experts in the religious law said, "Teacher, you insult us with what you've just said."

Jesus replied, "Woe to you teachers of the religious law, because you crush people with impossibly heavy loads, but do nothing to help them.

"Woe to you, because you build tombs for the prophets, but your own ancestors killed those prophets. Your actions show that you think your ancestors were right and prove that you would have done the same thing. That's why God said, 'I will send them prophets and apostles, and they will kill some and persecute others.'

"This generation will be responsible for the murder of all God's prophets, from Abel's murder to Zechariah, who they killed between the altar and the sanctuary. You will be responsible for all their blood.

"Woe to you teachers of the religious law, because you hide the key to knowledge from the people. You don't enter God's kingdom yourselves, and you prevent others from entering as well."

This made the Pharisees and teachers of religious law furious. From then on, they grilled him with many hostile questions, trying to trap him in something he might say.

Meanwhile, a crowd of thousands gathered so thickly they were trampling each other. Jesus began to speak to his disciples, saying, "Look out for the yeast of the Pharisees, beware of their hypocrisy. The time is coming when everything will be revealed and all secrets will be made public. Whatever you said in the dark will be heard in the daylight, and what was whispered in your ear will be proclaimed from the rooftops.

"Friends, don't be afraid of those who can kill the body and that's all. Fear him who can destroy the body and throw you into hell.

"Aren't five sparrows sold for a couple pennies? God doesn't forget any of them; so, don't be afraid. You are more valuable than an entire flock of sparrows, so valuable that God knows how many hairs are on your head.

"If someone publicly acknowledges me here on earth, the Son of Man will acknowledge him before God's angels. But if anyone denies me here on earth, I will deny him before God's angels. God can forgive those who speak against me, but God won't forgive anyone who blasphemes against the Holy Spirit.

"When you are brought to trial before synagogues, rulers, and authorities, don't worry about what you will say, because the Holy Spirit will give you words in the moment."

***

Someone in the crowd yelled, "Teacher, tell my brother to divide the inheritance with me."

Jesus retorted, "Who made me a judge to settle such disputes?" Then he continued, "Don't be greedy because life is more than what you own.

"Imagine this. A rich man had a field that produced so much crop that he didn't have room to store it all. So, he decided to tear down his barns and build bigger ones. After making this plan, he decided to take a few years off and enjoy life.

"But God said to him, 'Foolish man, you will die tonight. Now who will get your wealth?' That's what it will be like for people who gain wealth for themselves but aren't rich towards God."

Then he turned to his disciples and said, "Don't worry about food and clothes because life is so much more than that. Look at the ravens; they don't plant, harvest, or store food because God feeds them. You are a lot more valuable to God than a whole flock of birds. All your worrying can't even add a single moment to your life. If it cannot do that, what's the point in worrying over bigger things?

"Look at the lilies and how they grow. They don't work to make their clothing, yet not even Solomon clothed himself with such beauty. If God cares so much for flowers, which will die tomorrow, don't you think he will take care of you? You of little faith, don't worry about what you will eat or drink; God will provide. The world keeps itself busy pursuing such things and God knows that you need them. But make his kingdom your primary concern and he will meet all your needs.

"Don't be afraid, little flock, because God is happy to give you the kingdom.

"Sell your possessions and give to the poor. Store up treasure in heaven where it won't wear out, be stolen, or destroyed. Your heart is wherever you keep your treasure.

"Be ready to serve, like men waiting for their master to come back from a party; then you will be prepared to open the door as soon as he returns. It will be good for the servants if they are ready to serve, even if their master comes in the middle of the night. I tell you the truth, he will seat them, put on an apron, and serve them as they sit and eat.

"Understand that if a homeowner knows when a thief is coming, he won't let the thief in. Always be ready because the Son of Man will come when you least expect him."

Peter asked, "Are you telling this parable to just us, or everyone?"

Jesus replied, "Consider the faithful, wise servant the master puts in charge of feeding his family. It will be good for the servant that the master finds doing his job when he returns; he will be put in charge of all his master's possessions. But what if the servant thinks his master won't return for a long time and starts to get drunk and beat the other servants? Then, when the master of the house comes back unexpectedly, he will tear that servant apart, and throw him out of the house.

"The servant who knows what to do and doesn't do it will receive severe punishment. The one who doesn't know he is doing the wrong thing will receive light punishment. God requires a lot from everyone who receives a lot; the more he gives, the more he requires.

"I've come to bring a fire to the earth, and I wish I were already finished. I have a terrible baptism ahead of me, and I'm anxious until it's finished. Don't think that I've come to bring peace on earth, because I've come to bring division and strife. From now on, a family of five will disagree with each other, three against two or two against three. Entire families will all be at odds with each other."

Then Jesus turned to the crowd and said, "When you see clouds to the west, you know it's going to rain, and when you feel a south wind, you know it's going to be hot. Hypocrites! You know how to interpret the weather, but you can't interpret this present time.

"Judge for yourselves what is right. If you're going to court with your adversary, try to reconcile on the way, or else the judge will hand you over to the officer and the officer will throw you in jail. Then you won't get out until you have paid the last penny."

***

About this time, someone told Jesus that Pilate had killed some Galileans while they were sacrificing in the temple. Jesus answered, "Do you think these Galileans were worse sinners than all other Galileans because they died that way? No, and you will perish as well unless you repent and follow God. What about the 18 men the Tower of Siloam fell on (a disaster during the First Century)? Were they the biggest sinners in Jerusalem? No, and unless you repent, you will die too."

Then Jesus told this parable, "A man planted a fig tree and was disappointed when he didn't find any fruit on it. Finally, he told his gardener to cut the tree down and plant something else because he hadn't found any fruit on it in three years. But the gardener replied, 'Sir, leave it alone for one more year, and I'll give it special attention and plenty of fertilizer. If it bears fruit next year, fine; if not, cut it down.'"

CHAPTER THIRTY-ONE

SABBATH HEALINGS AND FURTHER DIVISION
Luke 13:10-21; John 9:1-10:39

One Sabbath, Jesus was teaching in a synagogue and he saw a woman who hadn't been able to stand up straight for 18 years because she had an evil spirit. Jesus called her over and said, "Woman, you are healed." Then he put his hands on her, and she stood up straight and praised God.

The leader of the synagogue was indignant because Jesus had healed her on the Sabbath. "There are six days for working, come get healed on one of those days, not on the Sabbath."

Jesus answered, "You hypocrites, doesn't each of you untie your animals and lead them out for water on the Sabbath? Therefore, wasn't it necessary for me to free this woman from 18 years of Satan's bondage, even if it was on the Sabbath?" His enemies were humiliated when they heard these words, and the people rejoiced at the wonderful things he was doing.

Then Jesus asked, "To what can I compare the kingdom of God? It's like a tiny mustard seed planted in the garden that grows up into a tree where the birds of the air can rest. The kingdom of God is also like yeast used for baking bread. Even though there is a lot of flour, the yeast permeates every part of it."

***

As Jesus was walking along on another Sabbath, he saw a blind man and his disciples asked him, "Teacher, was it this man, or his parents' sin that caused him to be born blind?"

Jesus answered, "Neither one, but he was born blind so that God's power could be shown in his life. We must do God's work as long as possible, but there is a time coming when we won't be able to work. While I am here, I am the light of the world."

He spit on the ground, made some mud, and put it on the man's eyes. Jesus said to him, "Go wash in the Pool of Siloam." So, the man went and washed, and then he could see.

Why do bad things happen?

Many people have a difficult time understanding why God would allow bad things to happen. Some people use it as a case for why he doesn't exist. If God allows us to have free will, he must let our actions play out. Sometimes, bad things happen because of the choices that we have made, sometimes it is because of the choices that others have made, and sometimes it is because creation is under the weight of sin. We don't always know why God allows bad things to happen or how he could use it for his glory, but he has a far greater perspective than we do, and we cannot possibly understand how he makes everything work together. God can use things that we cannot possibly understand to do amazing things in the future.

The disciples had the mistaken notion that all suffering was the direct result of their own or their parents' sin. All suffering is the result of sin, although not always the sufferer's sin (children born with birth defects did not sin before birth).

Suffering came after the fall of Adam and continues today. God always has a purpose for our pain, although we don't always see or understand it. In this instance, the man was born blind for God's glory. God also uses trials and suffering to build our character, to prepare us to comfort others, to discipline us, to further the gospel, or so that we might share in Jesus' suffering. Sometimes the reason for pain is apparent, but in some cases, we may never know why it happened. Our role is not always to understand but to trust God.

Those who knew him as a blind beggar asked, "Is that the same blind beggar we know?" Some said he was, but others disagreed and said he only looked like him.

But the man insisted, "I am that man."

His friends and neighbors asked, "How were your eyes opened?"

He answered, "Jesus made some mud, put it on my eyes, and told me to wash it off in the Pool of Siloam. I did, and now I can see."

"Where is he?" they asked.

"I don't know," the man replied.

His friends and neighbors took him to the Pharisees and they asked him how he could see. The man answered, "Jesus put mud on my eyes, I washed it off, and now I can see."

"This man cannot be from God because he doesn't keep the Sabbath," some of the Pharisees scoffed. But others asked how a sinner could perform such miracles.

Finally, they asked the blind man, "He opened your eyes, so what do you say about him?"

The man replied, "He's a prophet."

The Jewish leaders still didn't believe him, so they called in his parents and asked, "Is this your son? If he was born blind, how can he see?"

The Jewish leaders had decided to kick people out of the synagogue if they said that Jesus was the Messiah, so the parents answered, "He is our son and was born blind, but we don't know how he can see now or who opened his eyes. He's old enough to speak for himself, so ask him."

They called the man who had been born blind back and said, "Tell the truth because we know this man is a sinner."

He replied, "I don't know if he's a sinner or not. All I know is that I used to be blind, and now I can see."

"But how did he heal you?" they kept asking.

The man answered, "I told you once and you didn't listen, so why do you want to hear it again? Do you want to become his disciples?"

Furious, the Pharisees hurled insults at him. "You're one of his disciples, but we're Moses' disciples. We know God spoke through Moses, but we don't even know where this man came from."

Exasperated, the man answered, "That's odd, he opened my eyes, and you don't know where he's from. We know that God doesn't listen to sinners, but only to those who do his will. Nobody has ever made a blind man see; if he weren't from God, there's no way that could happen."

"You were born a sinner; how dare you lecture us?" Then the Pharisees kicked him out of the synagogue.

When Jesus heard about this, he found the man and asked, "Do you believe in the Son of Man?"

The man replied, "Tell me who he is, so I can believe in him."

"You've seen him, and are talking to him right now," Jesus told him.

"Lord, I believe," he said and he worshipped him.

Then Jesus said, "I have come to judge the world so that the blind might see and those who see might become blind."

Some Pharisees heard him. "Are you saying that we're blind?" they asked.

Jesus replied, "If you were blind, you would be innocent, but you are guilty because you say that you can see.

"The man who sneaks into the sheepfold instead of coming through the gate is a thief. The man who comes through the gate is the shepherd and the watchman lets him in. The shepherd calls the sheep by name as he leads them out. The sheep listen to him and follow him because they know his voice. They won't listen to a stranger because they don't recognize his voice."

> **Why are we sheep?**
>
> The Bible compares us to sheep, which were animals that all the people were familiar with in Jesus' day. They are some of the dumbest animals alive; they constantly need care and attention. This analogy shows that we always need God and that he is constantly watching out for us. We like to think of ourselves as knowing what is best for our lives, but we lack the perspective that God has. We need to stay close to him so that he can provide what we need.

The people didn't understand what Jesus was saying to them, so he said, "I tell you the truth, I am the gate for the sheep. Everyone who came before me was a thief, but whoever enters through me will be saved. The thief comes only to steal, kill, and destroy, but I have come to give life to the fullest.

"I am the good shepherd, and I lay down my life for the sheep. The hired hand doesn't own the sheep, so he runs away when he sees a wolf coming; then the wolf attacks and scatters the flock.

"I know my sheep and my sheep know me, just like the Father knows me and I know the Father, and I lay down my life for the sheep. I have other sheep that aren't from this flock and I must bring them in too. Then there will be one flock and one shepherd.

"The Father loves me because I lay down my life, only to take it up again. No one takes my life from me. I lay it down voluntarily because my Father has given me the power to take it up again."

There was a lot of argument after hearing these words. Some of the Jews said that he was demon-possessed and it was pointless to listen to him. Others argued that a demon-possessed man couldn't open the eyes of the blind.

***

Winter came and it was time for the Feast of Dedication in Jerusalem. Jesus was in the temple, walking through Solomon's

Colonnade when the Jewish leaders surrounded him and asked, "How long will you keep us in suspense? If you're the Messiah, tell us plainly."

Jesus answered, "I told you, but you didn't believe me. My miracles should tell you that, but you don't trust me because you aren't my sheep. My sheep recognize my voice and they follow me. I give them eternal life, and no one can take them away from me because the all-powerful Father has given them to me. The Father and I are one."

The Jews picked up stones to kill him. Jesus said, "I have done many good deeds from the Father, for which of these are you stoning me?"

They replied, "We aren't stoning you for doing a good deed. We are stoning you for blasphemy because you're just a man, but you're making yourself out to be God."

Jesus answered, "Your own Law calls men gods. So, if those people, who received God's word, were called 'gods,' why do you call it blasphemy if the Holy One says, 'I am the Son of God?' You should only believe me because I do what my Father says. Even if you don't trust me, trust in the works I have done. Then you will realize that the Father is in me, and I am in the Father."

Was this a denial of deity?

Some critics have used this as a denial of deity. But Jesus was not claiming to be a mere man; he was saying that if men were called gods, it was appropriate to call him God. Jesus was claiming to be God and the fact that the people wanted to stone him was evidence that they understood his claim to be God.

CHAPTER THIRTY-TWO

PRINCIPLES OF DISCIPLESHIP
Luke 13:22-14:35; John 10:40-42

The Jews tried to arrest him again, but he got away. He crossed the Jordan to where John had been baptizing in the early days. Many people followed him and put their trust in him there. They said to each other, "John didn't do miracles, but all of his predictions about this man have come true."

Jesus taught in the towns and villages on his way to Jerusalem. Someone asked him, "Lord, will only a few people be saved?"

He answered, "Try hard to get in through the narrow door because many will try and fail. Once the owner of the house locks the door, it will be too late. People will stand outside and plead, 'Open the door for us because we ate and drank with you, and you taught in our streets.' But the house owner will answer, 'Get away from me, you evildoers! I don't know you or where you're from.'

"You will weep and grind your teeth when you see Abraham, Isaac, Jacob, and the prophets in the kingdom of God. People will come from all over the earth to take their places, but God will throw you out. Indeed, those who are last will be first, and those who are first will be last."

***

"You should leave because Herod wants to kill you," some of the Pharisees told Jesus. Herod likely sent them because he wanted Jesus to leave the region.

Jesus replied, "Go tell that fox that I will continue to cast out demons and heal the sick today and tomorrow, and then the third day I will fulfill my purpose. I must keep going because no prophet can die outside of Jerusalem."

"O Jerusalem, city that kills the prophets and stones those sent to you. I have wanted to gather your children together like a hen gathers her chicks under her wings, but you wouldn't let me. Now your house is desolate and you won't see me again until you say, 'Blessed is the one who comes in the name of the Lord.'"

***

One Sabbath, Jesus was eating in the home of a prominent Pharisee, and everyone was watching, hoping to find a reason to accuse him. There was a man suffering from edema, so Jesus asked the Pharisees and experts in religious law, "Is it lawful to heal on the Sabbath or not?" When they remained silent, Jesus touched the man, healed him, and sent him home.

Then he turned to the crowd and asked, "If your son or your cow fell into a well on the Sabbath, wouldn't you immediately pull him out?" But they had nothing to say.

When Jesus noticed that they were all trying to sit near the head of the table, he told them, "When someone invites you to a meal, don't head for the best seat. If someone more distinguished than you arrives, the host will tell you to give up your spot. Then you will be embarrassed and have to sit at whatever seat is left. Instead, you should sit at the foot of the table and then your host will come tell you to sit in a more dignified place. You will be honored in front of the other guests. Everyone who exalts himself will be humbled, and everyone who humbles himself will be exalted."

Jesus turned to his host and said, "When you throw a party, don't invite your friends, relatives, and rich neighbors, because they will pay you back. Invite the outcasts of society because God will reward you for inviting those who couldn't repay you."

A man who heard this said, "Blessed is the man who will share in the kingdom of God."

Jesus replied, "A certain man was preparing a banquet and invited many people. When the banquet was ready, he sent his servant to get his guests.

"But the guests all made excuses. One needed to check on a new field, another wanted to try out his new oxen, and another had just been married.

"The servant came back and told his master they all declined the invitation. His master was upset and told the servant to invite the outcasts of society. The servant told him that they already had, and there was still room. So, his master told him to find whoever they could to fill his house and that the men he originally invited wouldn't get even a single bite of the food he had prepared."

Jesus turned to the crowd following him and said, "If anyone wants to follow me, you must love me more than you love your parents, spouse, children, siblings, and even your own life. If you don't, then you cannot be my disciple. You also cannot be my disciple unless you pick up your cross and follow me.

"If you want to build a tower, you first sit down and figure out how much it will cost to make sure you have enough money to finish. If you only complete the foundation and cannot finish the rest, everyone will make fun of you because you couldn't finish what you started.

"A king who wants to go to war first figures out if he has the strength to fight against the other king. If he doesn't, he sends a delegation to ask for a peace treaty. In the same way, you must give up everything if you want to be my disciple.

"Salt is good, but if it loses its flavor, how will you make it salty again? Flavorless salt is useless and you throw it out. Whoever can hear me should listen to what I say."

CHAPTER THIRTY-THREE

FURTHER PARABLES
Luke 15:1-17:10

A large group of tax collectors and other notorious sinners were crowding around Jesus to listen to him. The Pharisees and teachers of the religious law complained bitterly when Jesus ate with them, angry that Jesus even associated with such wicked people.

Then Jesus told this parable: "If you had 100 sheep and lost one in the wilderness, wouldn't you leave the 99 and look for the lost one? Once you found it, you would joyfully carry it home on your shoulders and throw a party. In the same way, there is more joy in heaven when a lost sinner repents than when 99 righteous people don't sin.

"Or suppose a woman has ten valuable silver coins and loses one. She will light a lamp and clean out the house until she finds it. Once she finds it, she calls her neighbors over to celebrate because she found her lost coin. In the same way, God's angels rejoice whenever a sinner repents."

Jesus continued, "There was a man with two sons, and the younger son told his father to give him his share of the inheritance now. His father agreed and so he divided his property.

"A few days later, the younger son took everything he had and left for a distant country, where he spent all his money on wild living. Around the time he ran out of money, there was a terrible famine and he began to starve. He found a job with a local farmer feeding pigs, and he became so hungry that even the slop he was feeding the pigs looked good.

"After a while, he came to his senses and said, 'All the hired men at home have plenty to eat, but I'm stuck here, hungry. I should go home and apologize to my father and beg him to take me back as a servant.'

"The younger son headed home, and while he was still a long way off, the father saw him coming. His heart broke with compassion, and he ran to his son, threw his arms around his neck, and kissed him. His son said to him, 'Father, I have sinned against heaven and you, I am no longer worthy of being called your son.'

"But his father told his servants, 'Quick! Bring my son the finest robe, put a ring on his finger, and shoes on his feet. Go kill the fattened calf because we're going to celebrate my lost son's safe return.'

"The oldest son heard the party from the fields, so he asked one of the servants what was happening. The servant told him, 'Your brother just came back and your father is throwing a party because he's safe.'

"The oldest son got angry and refused to go to the party. His father came out to ask him to come in but he said, 'I've always worked hard for you and never disobeyed you, but you have never even given me a goat so I could celebrate with my friends. But when your son comes back after wasting all your money on prostitutes, you kill the fattened calf for him!'

"The father replied, 'My dear son, you have always been with me, and everything I have is yours. We're celebrating because your brother was dead, but is alive again; he was lost, but now is found.'"

***

Then Jesus said to his disciples, "The manager of a rich man's possessions was accused of wasting his boss's wealth. The rich man called him in to give an account for his work.

"The manager thought to himself, 'What am I going to do if I'm fired? I'm too weak to dig ditches, and I'm too proud to beg.'

"Then he had an idea that would make sure he had a place to stay when he was fired. So, he called in everyone who owed his boss money to discuss their bills. If they owed 800 gallons of olive oil, he made it 400. If they owed 1,000 bushels of wheat, he made it 800.

"The rich man commended the dishonest manager for his shrewdness, and worldly people are far shrewder than the godly are. I tell you, use worldly wealth to make friends so that you will be welcomed into eternal dwellings once it is gone.

"Whoever is trustworthy with a little will be trustworthy with a lot, and whoever is dishonest with a little will be dishonest with a lot. If you haven't been able to handle worldly wealth, why should you get heaven's riches? If you aren't faithful with someone else's property, why should God trust you with your own property?

"No one can serve two masters because you will hate one and love the other, or you will devote yourself to one, and despise the other. Therefore, it's impossible to serve both God and money."

The Pharisees, who loved money, sneered at Jesus, and he told them, "You may justify yourselves before men, but God knows your hearts. God detests what the world values.

"The Law and the Prophets were your guides up until the coming of John the Baptist. Now I preach the kingdom of God and many people are forcing their way into the kingdom. But heaven and earth will disappear before a single part of the Law fails.

"Whoever divorces his wife and marries another woman is committing adultery; anyone who marries a divorced woman is committing adultery.

***

"There was a well-dressed rich man who lived a life of luxury. A beggar named Lazarus used to sit at his gate, longing to eat what fell from the rich man's table. He was covered with sores and the dogs used to come and lick his wounds. Finally, Lazarus died and the angels carried him to Abraham's side. The rich man also died, but he went to Hades and was constantly in torment.

"From a distance, he saw Lazarus at Abraham's side and begged, 'Father Abraham, have pity on me, and send Lazarus to give me a drop of water because I'm in agony.'

"But Abraham replied, 'During your life, you had everything you wanted, and Lazarus had nothing; now he is in comfort, and you are in agony. Besides, no one can cross the great chasm that separates us.'

Then the rich man said, 'Then send him to my family to warn my five brothers so they don't end up in this place of torment when they die.'

"Abraham said, 'They have Moses and the Prophets to warn them.'

"The rich man replied, 'But if they see someone come back from the dead, they will repent.'

"Abraham answered, 'If they don't listen to Moses and the Prophets, they won't listen to someone from the dead either.'"

Hell

Hell is the unpopular concept of a place of eternal punishment and suffering for those who reject Jesus' life and ministry. Jesus talked about hell more than any other figure in the Bible. Scripture describes it as a fiery furnace where there will be weeping and gnashing of teeth, sorrow, torment, unquenchable fire, darkness, and destruction. Popular culture often depicts hell as a mildly warm place where all the "bad kids" hang out and do whatever they want, but this is not the picture the Bible paints.

Some believe that a loving God would never condemn people to an eternal punishment like this, but God's wrath is a part of his nature that we cannot ignore. If God allows sin to go unpunished, then he is no longer holy. If we put our trust in Jesus, then his death pays the debt of our sin. We cannot pick and choose which of God's attributes we like and ignore the others.

Many people wonder what will happen to those who never hear the gospel and never have an opportunity to come to faith. The Bible does not explicitly address what happens in these cases, but we know that God will do the right thing because he is good, righteous, and just.

***

One day, Jesus told his disciples, "Stumbling blocks will come, but woe to the person who causes someone to stumble. It would be better to be thrown in the sea with a large millstone tied around the neck than to cause someone to sin, so watch yourselves.

"If another believer sins, reprimand him; if he repents, forgive him. Even if he sins against you seven times a day and asks for forgiveness, forgive him."

The disciples said to Jesus, "Increase our faith!"

Jesus answered, "If you had faith as small as a mustard seed, you could tell this mulberry tree to uproot and plant itself in the sea, and it would.

"If you have a servant who is out working in the field or looking after the flocks, he doesn't come in and sit down to eat. First, he prepares his master's food and serves him and then he can eat and drink. The master doesn't even thank the servant for doing this because he's just doing his job. In the same way, when you do what you're told to do, you should say, 'We are unworthy servants who are only doing our duty.'"

CHAPTER THIRTY-FOUR

RAISING LAZARUS
John 11

A man named Lazarus was sick in Bethany, where he lived with his sisters, Martha and Mary (the same Mary who had anointed Jesus' feet). His sisters sent word to Jesus and said, "Lazarus is sick." This was a different Lazarus than the one in the previous chapter.

When Jesus heard this, he said, "His sickness won't end in death, it's for God and the Son of God's glory." Jesus loved Lazarus and his sisters, but he stayed where he was for a couple more days before telling his disciples they should go back to Judea.

His disciples were confused and said, "Teacher, not too long ago, the Jews there wanted to kill you, and you still want to go back?"

Jesus answered, "Every day has twelve hours of daylight. While it is light, people can walk safely. But they will stumble if they walk at night because they don't have light. Our friend Lazarus has fallen asleep, but I'm going there to wake him up."

His disciples said, "If he's asleep, he will wake up." They thought Jesus meant he was literally asleep, but Jesus meant that he had died.

"Lazarus is dead," Jesus told them. "I'm glad that I wasn't there so you can trust in me. Let's go see him."

Thomas (called Didymus) said to the rest of the disciples, "Let's go die with him."

When they got to Bethany, they found that Lazarus had already been in the tomb for four days. Bethany was only a few miles from Jerusalem, and many Jews had come to console Mary and Martha on their brother's death. When Martha heard that Jesus was coming, she went out to meet him, but Mary stayed at home.

Martha said to Jesus, "Lord, my brother wouldn't have died if you had been here, But I know that God will give you whatever you ask for."

Jesus told her, "Your brother will rise again."

"I know he will rise on the last day when everyone else will," Martha replied.

Jesus said to her, "I am the resurrection and the life, those who believe in me will live, even though they die. Whoever believes in me will never die. Do you believe me Martha?"

"Yes, Lord, I believe that you are the Messiah, the Son of God." Then Martha went to Mary and told her that Jesus wanted to talk to her.

Mary got up quickly and went outside the village to where Martha had met Jesus. When the mourners saw that she was leaving, they assumed she was going to the tomb, and they followed her. When Mary got to Jesus, she fell at his feet and said, "Lord, if you would have been here, my brother would still be alive."

Deeply moved by her grief, Jesus asked, "Where is he buried?"

They led him to the grave and Jesus wept. Some of the Jews said, "See how much Jesus loved him." But others said, "If he can open the eyes of the blind, he could have healed Lazarus."

At the grave, Jesus was profoundly moved and said, "Take away the stone."

But Martha said, "Lord, it's going to stink because he's been in there for four days."

"Didn't I tell you that if you believed, you would see God's glory?" Jesus replied.

So, they rolled the stone away; Jesus looked up to heaven and said, "Father, thank you for hearing me. I know that you always hear me, but I say this out loud so that the people here will believe that you sent me."

Then Jesus shouted, "Lazarus, come out!" The dead man came out with his hands and feet wrapped in linen strips and with a cloth around his face. Jesus said, "Unwrap him and let him go."

Many of the Jews who witnessed what Jesus did believed in him. But some went and told the Pharisees about this miracle.

The Pharisees got together and asked each other, "What are we doing? This man is performing many miracles, and if we let him keep going, the whole nation will follow him, and then the Romans will take away our land and freedom."

Then Caiaphas, the high priest, said, "Don't be stupid. Don't you realize that it's better for one man to die than the whole nation?" These weren't Caiaphas' own words, but he prophesied that Jesus would die for the Jews and the Gentiles so that all God's children might become one people.

From that point on, the Pharisees plotted Jesus' death. Therefore, Jesus couldn't move around publicly, so he went to the desert village of Ephraim with his disciples.

> **How God uses those who don't follow him**
>
> God still used the corrupt high priest for his purposes. God will use many different people to work out his plan, even if they are unaware of their role in his overall design. We may not understand how he does this, but that's part of what makes him God.

CHAPTER THIRTY-FIVE

TEACHING ON THE WAY TO JERUSALEM
Matthew 19:1-20:34; Mark 10; Luke 17:11-19:28

A short while later, Jesus headed back towards Jerusalem and passed through Samaria and Galilee. As he entered a village, ten lepers cried out, "Master, have pity on us."

Jesus looked at them and said, "Go show yourselves to the priests." As they went, they were healed.

When one of them saw that he was healed, he came back and fell down on his face before Jesus, praising and thanking God.

Jesus asked, "Didn't I heal all ten? Where are the other nine? Does only this Samaritan come to praise God?" Then he said, "Stand up and go; your faith has made you well."

***

One day the Pharisees asked when the kingdom of God would come, and Jesus replied, "The kingdom of God doesn't come with visible signs. You won't be able to find it here or there because the kingdom of God is among you."

Later, Jesus talked with his disciples and said, "It won't be long until you will want to see one of the days of the Son of Man, but you won't be able to. People will tell you that he has returned to various places, but don't believe them. It will be obvious when the Son of Man returns, but first, he must suffer many things and have this generation reject him.

"When he returns, it will be just like the days of Noah. People were eating, drinking, and getting married up until the Flood came and destroyed them all.

"It will also be like the days of Lot. People went through their daily routines until the day Lot left, and then God destroyed everything with fire and brimstone.

"Things will go on as usual until the day he returns. When he comes, the person outside shouldn't go inside to pack and the man in the field shouldn't return to town. Remember Lot's wife because whoever tries to keep his life will lose it, and whoever loses his life will save it. Two people may be in one bed, and the Son of Man will take one and leave the other. Two women may be working together, and the Son of Man will take one and leave the other."

The disciples asked, "Lord, where will this happen?"

Jesus answered, "The vultures always gather around a dead animal." By saying this, Jesus meant that his return will be obvious to all.

***

One day Jesus was teaching his disciples that they should always pray. To illustrate his point he said, "There was a godless judge who didn't care about anyone. A widow from his city kept coming to him, begging him to protect her from her enemy. He ignored her for a long time, but finally, he said to himself, 'Even though I don't care about God or people, I will give this woman protection, or else she will wear me out.'

"If this godless judge does this much, won't God bring about justice for his children if they keep asking him. He won't ignore them, but he will make sure they get justice quickly. But will the Son of Man find people with faith?"

Then Jesus told a parable to some people who were self-righteous and looked down on everyone else. He said, "A Pharisee and a tax collector went to the temple to pray. The Pharisee stood up and prayed, 'God, thank you for making me better than other men, especially that tax collector. I don't rob, cheat, or lie; I fast twice a week and give a tenth of my income.'

"The tax collector went off by himself and wouldn't even look up to heaven. He beat his chest and said, "God, have mercy on a sinner like me.' God was pleased with this tax collector rather than the Pharisee because God humbles the proud and exalts the humble."

After saying these things, Jesus left Galilee and went south to the region of Judea and into the area across the Jordan River. Many people followed him, and he taught them and healed their sick.

Some Pharisees were in the crowd and they tried to trap him by asking, "Should a man be able to divorce his wife for any reason he wants?"

Jesus replied, "Haven't you read the Scriptures? They say that from the beginning, God 'made them male and female' and that 'a man will leave his father and mother and be united with his wife so that the two become one.' Therefore, they are now one flesh, and no one should separate what God has joined."

They asked, "Then why did Moses say a man could divorce his wife?"

Jesus answered, "Moses allowed divorce because of your hard hearts, but that's not how God meant it to be. I tell you that the only acceptable reason for divorce is marital unfaithfulness. Those who get a divorce and marry someone else are committing adultery."

His disciples said, "If this is how it is, it's better not to get married."

Jesus replied, "Not everyone can accept this statement, but only those that God helps. Some people are born eunuchs, others make some that way, and some choose not to marry for the kingdom of heaven. Anyone who can accept this statement should accept it."

***

One day some parents brought their children to Jesus so he could bless them, but the disciples tried to stop them. When Jesus saw what was happening, he became upset with his disciples and said, "Don't stop the children from coming to me because the kingdom of God belongs to them. Whoever doesn't have childlike faith will never get into the kingdom of God." Then he took the children in his arms, put his hands on their heads, and blessed them.

***

One day, a man ran up to him, knelt, and asked, "Good Teacher, what do I have to do to inherit eternal life?"

Jesus turned his question around, "Why do you call me good? Only God is good. If you want eternal life, you must obey the commandments."

> **Did Jesus deny his goodness?**
>
> Jesus did not deny that he was good, but he was trying to get the man to think about his statement. If he was saying that Jesus was good, then he was implying Jesus' divinity.

"Which ones?" the man inquired.

Jesus replied, "Don't murder, don't commit adultery, don't steal, don't lie, don't cheat, honor your father and mother, and love your neighbor as yourself."

The young man said, "Teacher, I've done all of these things since I was a boy. What else do I have to do?"

Jesus felt genuine love for this man as he spoke to him and said, "You only lack one thing. Sell everything you have and give the proceeds to the poor and you will have treasure in heaven. Then come follow me."

When the man heard this, he went away sad, because he was rich. Jesus watched him go and then said to his disciples, "It's tough to get into the kingdom of heaven. In fact, it's easier for a camel to go through the eye of a needle than for a rich person to enter the kingdom of God."

The disciples were amazed and asked, "Then who can be saved?"

Jesus looked at them and said, "It's impossible for men, but everything is possible with God."

Peter answered, "We've left everything to follow you! What do we get?"

> **Wealth and following Jesus**
>
> It's okay to have earthly possessions, but we cannot put them before God, which is what this man had done. Jesus didn't chase him down and make it easier to follow him because he wouldn't water down the gospel. This shocked the Jews because they equated earthly prosperity with divine favor. Neither the poor nor the rich are inherently more righteous; God is more concerned about our hearts. The disciples wondered how anyone could be saved, but Jesus was telling them that people cannot save themselves, only God can do that.

Jesus replied, "I tell you the truth, when the Son of Man sits on his glorious throne, you will sit on twelve thrones and judge the tribes of Israel. Everyone who gives up a home, family, or property for the gospel and me will receive 100 times more than what you left, including persecutions, while on earth. Then you will also receive eternal life. Those who are first will be last, and those who are last will be first.

"The kingdom of heaven is like a landowner who went out early one morning and hired workers for his vineyard. He agreed to pay them a day's wage and sent them to work. Around nine o'clock he saw some more people standing in the marketplace and he told them to go work in his field and that he would pay them a fair wage at the end of the day. He did the same thing at noon and at three in the afternoon. Finally, at about five, he found some other men doing nothing and he asked them why they had just been standing around all day. They told the landowner that no one had hired them, so he said to them, 'Go work in my vineyard too.'

"When evening came, the landowner had his supervisor pay his workers starting with the last ones first. The men hired at five got a full day's pay, so the men hired that morning expected to get much more. But they all got the same amount. These men were upset and complained that the men hired at the end of the day got just as much as they did though they hadn't worked as long.

"But the landowner said, 'I'm not being unfair to you, didn't you agree to work for a day's pay? I wanted to give the last workers as much as I paid you. Can't I do whatever I want with my money? Should you get mad because I'm generous?'

"So, the last will be first, and the first will be last."

***

Jesus walked ahead of them on the way to Jerusalem and his followers were afraid because they thought they were going to die. Then Jesus took his disciples aside and told them what would happen, saying, "All the prophecies about the Son of Man will be fulfilled when we get to Jerusalem. The Son of Man will be betrayed to the leading priests and teachers of the religious law and they will sentence him to die. They will mock him, spit on him, beat him, and kill him; but on the third day he will rise from the dead." But the disciples didn't understand him.

Then James and John's mother came to Jesus with her two sons. She knelt and Jesus asked, "What is your request?"

She replied, "Let my two sons have the places of honor in your glorious kingdom. Put one on the right and one at the left."

Jesus answered, "You don't know what you're asking. Are you able to drink the cup I drink or be baptized with my baptism?"

"We can," they answered.

Jesus said to them, "You will drink from my cup and be baptized with my baptism, but I don't have the right to say who will sit to my right or left. My Father has chosen who will sit in those seats."

When the ten other disciples heard about this, they were angry with James and John. Jesus knew what was happening, so he called them together and said, "You know that the rulers of the Gentiles revel in their authority, but it shouldn't be that way with you. Whoever wants to be a leader should be a servant, and whoever wants to become first must be everyone else's servant. In the same way, the Son of Man didn't come to be served, but to serve and give his life as a ransom for many."

***

On their way to Jericho, a great crowd followed Jesus and his disciples. A blind beggar named Bartimaeus was sitting on the side of the road with another blind beggar. When they found out that Jesus of Nazareth was passing by, they shouted, "Jesus, Son of David, have mercy on us!" The crowd tried to get them to be quiet, but they kept shouting louder and louder.

When Jesus heard them, he stopped and told the crowd to bring the men to him. They told the blind men, "Cheer up, Jesus is calling you." So, they jumped up, threw their coats aside, and came to Jesus.

Jesus asked the men, "What do you want me to do?"

The blind men replied, "Lord, we want to see."

Jesus had compassion on them and touched their eyes; instantly, they could see. Then the men followed Jesus down the road, praising God with the crowd.

Jesus entered Jericho and made his way through the town. A rich man named Zacchaeus lived there and he was one of the most influential Jews in the Roman tax-collecting business. He was too short to see Jesus through the crowd, so he climbed a sycamore tree to watch from there.

When Jesus came by, he looked up and said, "Zacchaeus, come down because I'm going to stay at your house today." So, Zacchaeus came down and welcomed him into his home. But the crowds muttered because he was going to be the guest of a sinner.

When Jesus arrived at his house, Zacchaeus stood and said, "I will give half my possessions to the poor, and if I have cheated anyone, I will pay back four times what I owe."

Then Jesus said to him, "Salvation has come to this home today because this man is a son of Abraham. For the Son of Man has come to seek and save the lost."

***

The crowds were listening to everything he said, and he told a parable because the people thought the kingdom of God was going to appear right away. He said, "A nobleman was called to a distant land to be crowned king and then return. He called ten of his servants and gave them money to invest while he was gone. But his people hated him and sent a delegation to say that they didn't want him to be their king.

"However, they made him king and he returned home. When he arrived, he sent for his servants to find out how much money they had earned.

"The first servant reported that he had earned ten times as much. His master was impressed and put him in charge of ten cities as a reward. The second servant reported that he had earned five times as much and his master put him in charge of five cities. Another servant brought the original amount of money and said, 'I hid your money and kept it safe because I know you are a hard man to deal with, taking what you did not put in, and reaping what you did not sow.'

"His master answered, "You wicked servant, if you knew I was a hard man, why didn't you at least put the money in the bank so that I could have collected it with interest? Take his money and give it to the one who earned the most.'

"His servants replied, 'But master, that servant already has plenty.'

"The man said, 'Those who have will have more given to them, and those who don't have will have everything taken from them. Bring the people who didn't want me to be king and kill them in my presence.'"

After saying these things, Jesus went ahead to Jerusalem.

CHAPTER THIRTY-SIX

TRIUMPHAL ENTRY AND THE FIG TREE
Matthew 21:1-22; Mark 11:1-25; Luke 19:29-48; John 11:55-12:50

It was almost time for the Passover celebration, and people crowded into Jerusalem for the cleansing ceremony. They kept looking for Jesus in the temple and asked each other, "Do you think he will come to the Passover?" The chief priests and the Pharisees were looking for him too and gave orders that anyone who knew where he was should report it so they could arrest him.

Six days before the Passover, Jesus arrived at Lazarus' house in Bethany. People flocked to see him and Lazarus because Jesus had raised him from the dead. Hearing this, the chief priests planned to kill Lazarus too because many of the people believed in Jesus when they heard about that miracle.

The next day, at the Mount of Olives, Jesus sent two disciples ahead of him. He said, "As you enter the village, you will see a donkey tied there with its colt beside it. Bring them to me. If anyone asks what you're doing, say, 'The Lord needs them, and will return them.'"

The two disciples found the animals tied outside of a house, just as Jesus had said. As they were untying the animals, some folks nearby said, "Why are you untying that colt?" The disciples answered as Jesus instructed and the people allowed them to take the animals. When they brought the animals to Jesus, they threw their garments over the donkey and he sat on it. This fulfilled the prophecy, "Your King is coming to you, humble and riding on a donkey."

A huge crowd of Passover visitors spread their coats on the road ahead of Jesus; others cut leafy branches in the fields and spread them on the road. As they reached the place where the road started down the Mount of Olives, his followers began to shout and sing as they walked, "Praise the Lord! Blessed is the One who comes in the name of the Lord!

Blessed is the coming kingdom of our ancestor David! Peace and glory in the highest heaven!"

Conquering kings rode on donkeys and spreading coats and palm branches on the road was what people did to show respect for their rulers. The people were half begging and half demanding him to be their king and liberate Israel. At the time, his disciples didn't realize that he was fulfilling prophecy, but after Jesus' glorification, they realized that they had seen Scripture fulfilled.

Pharisees in the crowd said, "Teacher, reprimand your followers for saying things like that."

"If they keep quiet, the stones will burst forth in praise," Jesus replied.

***

As they got closer to Jerusalem, Jesus saw the city ahead, and began to cry, saying, "I wish that you knew what would bring you peace, but now it's hidden from you. Before long, your enemies will surround you and close in on you. They will crush you and your children to the ground, and they won't leave a single stone in place, because you have rejected God's opportunity."

Those in the crowd who had seen Jesus raise Lazarus from the dead were telling others about it and many more went out to meet him when they heard of the miracle. The Pharisees said to each other, "We've lost, the whole world is following him!"

The blind and lame came to him, and he healed them in the temple. Children ran around praising God. The chief priests became indignant and said, "Do you hear what these children are saying?"

Jesus replied, "Yes, haven't you ever read the Scriptures that say, 'You have taught the children and infants to praise you.'" Then he went back to Bethany with his disciples to spend the night.

***

As they were leaving Bethany and returning to Jerusalem the next morning, Jesus was hungry. He saw a fig tree in the distance in full leaf, so he went over to see if there were any figs on it. I was too early for fruit, so there were only leaves on the tree. Jesus cursed the tree in front of his disciples, "May no one ever eat your fruit again!"

When they arrived in Jerusalem, Jesus went into the temple and immediately began driving out the merchants and their customers that thronged there, just as he had at the beginning of his public ministry. He knocked over the moneychangers' tables and benches of those selling doves, and he stopped everyone from bringing in merchandise. He said, "It is written, 'My house will be a place of prayer for all nations, but you have made it a den of thieves.'"

After that, he taught daily in the temple. The leading priests and teachers of the religious law heard about what Jesus had done and began plotting how to kill him, but they couldn't think of anything because of all the people surrounding him, hanging on his every word.

***

Some Greeks who had come to Jerusalem to worship at the Passover came to Philip, saying, "Sir, we would like to see Jesus." Philip told his brother Andrew and they both went to tell Jesus.

Jesus replied, "The time has come for the Son of Man to be glorified. I tell you the truth; unless a kernel of wheat falls to the ground and dies, it remains a single seed. But if it dies, it produces many seeds. The man who loves his life will lose it, and the man who hates his life on earth will have eternal life. Whoever wants to be my disciple must follow me because my servants must be where I am, and my Father will honor my servants. Now my soul is deeply troubled, should I ask God to save me from what lies ahead? No, because I came to bring glory to my Father's name."

Then a voice came from heaven, "I have glorified it and will glorify it again. Some in the crowd thought it was thunder and others said that an angel had spoken.

Jesus said, "This voice was for your benefit, not mine. Now it's time to judge the world, and I will drive out the prince of this world. But when

I am lifted up, I will draw everyone to myself." He said this to indicate that he would be crucified.

The crowd was confused and said, "The Scripture says the Messiah will live forever, so why do you say that the Son of Man must be lifted up? Who is the Son of Man?"

Jesus replied, "You will only have the light for a little while longer, so walk in the light before darkness overtakes you. Those who walk in the dark don't know where they are going, so put your trust in the light while it is still here, and then you will become sons of light." After he finished saying these things, Jesus hid himself away from them.

***

Despite all his miracles, most would still not trust in him. This fulfilled Isaiah's prophecy, "Lord, who has believed our message and to whom will the Lord reveal his saving power?" The people couldn't believe, and because Isaiah saw Jesus' glory he said, "He has blinded their eyes and hardened their hearts. So, their eyes cannot see, their hearts cannot understand, and they cannot turn to me so I can heal them."

Yet many people, including some of the Jewish leaders, trusted in him. None of them would confess it publicly because they were afraid that the Pharisees would kick them out of the synagogue and they loved the praise of men more than the praise of God.

Then Jesus cried out, "When someone believes in me, he also believes in the one who sent me because when you see me, you see the one who sent me. I have come to this world as a light so that those who believe in me should not stay in darkness. I don't judge people if they hear me and don't obey, because I did not come to judge the world, but to save it. But everyone who does not listen to my words will be judged by those same words on the last day. I have only said what the Father has told me to say and his command leads to eternal life."

That evening Jesus and his disciples left the city. The next morning, they passed the fig tree that Jesus had cursed and the disciples noticed that it had withered from the roots. Peter pointed it out and said, "Teacher, the fig tree you cursed has withered! How did this happen so quickly?"

Jesus answered, "Have faith in God. I tell you the truth, if you have faith and don't doubt, you can do this and more. You can even tell a mountain to throw itself into the sea and it will obey. Therefore, you will receive whatever you ask for in prayer if you believe that you have received it. But when you are praying, you must forgive anyone that you have a grudge against so that God will be able to forgive your sins too."

Every night Jesus returned to spend the night on the Mount of Olives, and every day crowds would gather to listen to him teach in the temple.

Why did Jesus curse the fig tree?

Mature fig trees often produce out of season fruit and it was likely that Jesus expected to find some of that kind of fruit on the tree. The fig tree is like Israel and the religious leaders at that time. They had the appearance of bearing fruit, but there was no actual substance to them. This was an image of Jesus' condemnation of the religious leaders.

CHAPTER THIRTY-SEVEN

OFFICIAL CHALLENGE TO JESUS' AUTHORITY
Matthew 21:23-22:14; Mark 11:27-12:12; Luke 20:1-19

Jesus continued teaching and preaching the good news in the temple, and the religious leaders came up to him and demanded, "Where did you get the authority to do what you're doing?"

Jesus answered, "I'll tell you where I get my authority if you answer this question. Was John's baptism from heaven, or was it merely human?"

They debated. "If we say it was from heaven, he will ask why we didn't believe him, but if we say it was merely human, the crowd will turn on us because they believe John was a prophet." Finally, they said, "We don't know."

Jesus replied, "Then I won't answer your question either.

"What do you think about this? A man had two sons and he told them both to go work in the vineyard. The older son said he wouldn't, but later changed his mind and went anyway. The younger son said he would go, but then he didn't. Which son obeyed his father?"

"The first," they answered.

Jesus said to them, "I tell you the truth, tax collectors and prostitutes will get into the kingdom of God before you do. John the Baptist came to show you the way of righteousness, and you didn't believe him, but the tax collectors and prostitutes did. Even after you saw this, you refused to repent and believe him.

"Here's another parable. A landowner planted a vineyard, built a wall around it, dug a winepress, and made a lookout tower. He then leased the vineyard to some farmers and went away on a long journey. At harvest time, he sent a servant to the farmers to collect his share of the profits. But the farmers grabbed him, beat him up, and sent him back empty-handed.

"The owner sent another servant, but they beat him and treated him shamefully as well; the farmers killed the next servant he sent. He sent other servants and they were all beaten or killed until only his only son was left. The owner finally sent his son, thinking the farmers would respect him.

"But when the farmers saw the son coming, they decided to kill the heir and steal his inheritance. So, they grabbed him, took him out of the vineyard, and killed him.

"What will the owner do to those wicked farmers when he gets back?"

The religious leaders answered, "He will put those men to a horrible death and rent the vineyard out to others who will give him his share of the crop after each harvest."

Then Jesus asked them, "Didn't you ever read this Scripture? 'The stone the builders rejected has become the cornerstone. This is God's doing and it is marvelous to see.' Whoever trips over that stone will be broken to pieces and it will crush them. Therefore, the kingdom of God will be taken from you and given to a nation that will produce the proper fruit."

When the delegation of officials heard Jesus, they realized that they were the farmers in the story. They wanted to arrest Jesus, but they feared the crowds' reaction; so, they left him and went away.

Then Jesus told several other parables saying, "The kingdom of heaven is like a king who threw a wedding banquet for his son. He invited many people and when the banquet was ready, he sent his servants to tell everyone that it was time to come; but they refused. So, he sent other servants to tell them to come, but they ignored them and went about their daily business. Some of the guests even mistreated and killed some of the servants.

"The king became furious and he sent his army to destroy the wicked men and burn their cities. He said to his servants, 'The wedding feast is ready, but the guests I invited aren't worthy to come; go out to the street corners and invite everyone you find.'

"So, the servants went out and brought in everyone they could find and the banquet hall was full of people. But the king came in and noticed that a man wasn't wearing the proper wedding clothes, even though he had made them available for all his guests. So, he asked him, 'Why did you come without wedding clothes, my friend?' The man was speechless, so the king had his servants tie him up and throw him into the outer darkness where there is weeping and gnashing of teeth. Many are called, but few are chosen."

CHAPTER THIRTY-EIGHT

JESUS' RESPONSE TO QUESTIONS
Matthew 22:15-23:39; Mark 12:13-44; Luke 20:20-21:4

The Pharisees and Herodians got together to come up with a way to trap Jesus. They sent some of their followers to ask him questions. One of them said, "Teacher, we know you are an impartial man of integrity and teach God's word regardless of the consequences. But tell us, should we pay taxes to the Roman government or not?"

Jesus knew their evil intent and said, "You hypocrites! Who are you trying to trick with your questions? Show me the coin used to pay the tax." Someone handed him a coin and he asked, "Whose picture and title is on this coin?"

"Caesar's," they replied.

Jesus replied, "Then give Caesar what belongs to him, and give God everything that belongs to him." Amazed by his answer, they left without saying a word because they hadn't been able to trap him.

That same day the Sadducees, who deny that there is life after death, stepped forward and asked him, "Teacher, Moses told us that if a man dies without children, his brother should marry his widow and have children for him. Once, there were seven brothers, and the oldest married a woman and died without children. The second brother also married her but died childless. This continued until she had married all seven brothers, and none of them had children; finally, she died too. Since she had married all seven of them, whom will she be married to in the resurrection?"

Jesus replied, "You don't understand the Scriptures or the power of God. Marriage is only for people here on earth. Those who rise from the dead are God's children and they will be like angels in heaven that cannot die and don't get married. But since you don't believe in a resurrection, you should read the story of Moses and the burning bush. Even though Abraham, Isaac, and Jacob had died, God said, 'I am the God of Abraham, Isaac, and Jacob.' Since he is the God of the living and not the dead, they are all alive to him. You've made a serious mistake."

When the Pharisees heard that he had silenced the Sadducees, they got together to think up another question. One of them was an expert in the Law and asked, "Teacher, what's the greatest commandment in the Law of Moses?"

Jesus replied, "'The Lord our God is the only God. Love him with all your heart, soul, mind, and strength.' The second greatest commandment is to 'Love your neighbor as yourself.' The rest of the Law depends on these two commandments.

The man who asked the question said, "Well said, Teacher. You're right when you say that there is only one God and that I should love him with all our heart, soul, mind, and strength, and that I should love my neighbor as I love myself. This is more important than all the offerings and sacrifices that the Law requires."

When Jesus saw that he had answered wisely, he said, "You're not far from the kingdom of God."

***

While teaching in the temple, Jesus asked the Pharisees, "What do you think about the Messiah? Whose son is he?"

They replied, "He is the Son of David."

Jesus responded, "Then why does David, under the inspiration of the Holy Spirit, call him Lord? David says, 'The Lord said to my Lord, "Sit at my right hand until I make your enemies a footstool under your feet."' If David called him Lord, how can he also be his son?" The crowd was fascinated; no one could answer his question. From then on, no one dared to ask him any more questions.

Then Jesus addressed the crowds and his disciples, saying, "The teachers of the religious law and the Pharisees teach from the Law so you should obey whatever they say, but don't follow their own example. They don't practice what they teach; they crush you with heavy loads and do nothing to ease the burden.

"Beware of these teachers of the religious law because they do everything for show. They love walking around in flowing robes, greetings in the marketplace, and honor in the synagogues and at banquets. But they cheat widows out of their property and cover it up by making long prayers in public. These men will face severe punishment.

"They love it when people call them 'Teacher,' but don't let anyone call you teacher because you have one teacher, and you are all brothers. Don't call anyone on earth 'Father' because God in heaven is your Father. Don't let anyone call you 'Master,' because the Messiah is the only master. The greatest among you must be a servant because God will exalt those who humble themselves and humble those who exalt themselves.

"Woe to you teachers of the religious law and Pharisees. You hypocrites won't enter the kingdom of heaven, and you don't let others in either.

"Woe to you teachers of the religious law and Pharisees. You hypocrites travel all over to make a single convert and then you make him twice the son of hell that you are.

"Woe to you blind guides. You say that swearing by the temple is meaningless, but swearing by the temple gold is a binding oath. You blind fools, which is greater, the gold, or the temple that makes the gold sacred? You also say that swearing by the altar is meaningless, but swearing by the offering on the altar is a binding oath. But which is greater, the offering, or the altar that makes the offering sacred? When you swear by the altar, you swear by everything on it; when you swear by the temple, you swear by the one who dwells in it; and when you swear by heaven, you swear by God's throne and by him."

"Woe to you teachers of the religious law and Pharisees. You hypocrites give a tenth of everything, but you ignore the important parts of the Law like justice, mercy, and faithfulness. It's good that you tithe, but you need to do the more important things too. Blind guides, you strain out a gnat, but swallow a camel.

"Woe to you teachers of the religious law and Pharisees. You hypocrites carefully clean the outside of a cup, but inside you are filthy and full of greed and self-indulgence. You blind Pharisees should wash the inside of the cup, and then the outside will be clean too.

"Woe to you teachers of the religious law and Pharisees. You hypocrites are like whitewashed tombs, beautiful on the outside, but full of death and uncleanness. On the outside you look righteous, but you are full of hypocrisy and wickedness on the inside.

"Woe to you teachers of the religious law and Pharisees. You hypocrites build tombs for the prophets and decorate the graves of the righteous. You say that you wouldn't have done what your ancestors did if you would have been alive when they were. But you testify against yourselves that you are the descendants of the men who killed the prophets. Go ahead and finish what your ancestors started.

"You snakes and brood of vipers! How will you escape the judgment of hell? I am sending you prophets, wise men, and teachers and you will kill them, beat them, and chase them from town to town. Then you will be guilty of murdering all the prophets, from righteous Abel to Zechariah, whom you murdered between the temple and the altar. You are responsible for the death of every prophet of God. I tell you the truth, all this judgment will come upon this generation.

"O Jerusalem, Jerusalem, city that kills the prophets, and stones God's messengers. I have often wanted to gather your children together, just like a hen protects her chicks under her wings, but you resisted. But now your house is desolate because you will not see me again until you say, 'Blessed is the one who comes in the name of the Lord.'"

***

While he was in the temple, Jesus sat down and watched the crowd drop their offerings into the collection box. Many rich people put in large amounts, but a poor widow came and put in two coins worth less than a penny. Jesus called his disciples over and said, "I tell you the truth, this poor widow has put in more than everyone else because they gave out of their surplus, but she gave everything she had."

CHAPTER THIRTY-NINE

OLIVET DISCOURSE
Matthew 24:1-25:46; Mark 13; Luke 21:5-38

As Jesus was leaving the temple grounds, his disciples pointed out the various buildings and commented on the beautiful stonework and decorations. Some of the stones were 37 feet long, 12 feet high, and 18 feet deep. One of them said, "Teacher, look at these magnificent buildings and the massive stones."

But Jesus replied, "A time is coming when not a single stone of these buildings will be left on another; they will be completely demolished."

***

Later, Jesus sat on the slopes of the Mount of Olives across from the temple. Peter, James, John, and Andrew came to him and asked, "When will this happen and how will we know it's about to happen?"

Jesus told them, "Don't let anyone deceive you because many will come in my name, claiming to be the Messiah, and saying that the time is here. Don't listen to them. Don't be afraid when wars break out all over the place, because these things must happen, but the end won't come right away. Nations will go to war with each other and there will be famines, earthquakes, epidemics, terrifying things, and miraculous signs in the heavens. But all these things are only the beginning of the horrors to come.

"Watch out, because before all this, they will hand you over to the courts, and they will beat, persecute, and kill you in the synagogues and prisons. They will accuse you before governors and kings of being my followers.

"But when they arrest you and put you on trial, don't worry about how you will answer your accusers, because I will give you the right words and wisdom that will confound your opponents. This will be your opportunity to tell the world about me. But know that everyone will hate you because you are my followers and even your family and friends will betray you. They will kill some of you, but not a hair of your head will perish.

"Many false prophets will appear and lead many people astray. Sin will be everywhere, and many will have their love grow cold, but those who endure to the end will be saved. The whole world will hear the good news about the kingdom, and then the end will come.

"You will see 'the abomination that causes desecration' that Daniel described. When you see Jerusalem surrounded by armies, you will know that its destruction is near, and those in Judea will flee to the hills. Those outside their house shouldn't go inside to pack and those in the field shouldn't even go back to get a coat. The people in Jerusalem should escape and those outside the city shouldn't enter it for shelter. These will be days of God's vengeance and the fulfillment of Scripture. They will brutally kill people or take them as captives to other nations and the Gentiles will trample Jerusalem down until the age of the Gentiles ends.

> **What is the desecration that Daniel described?**
>
> There are different views of how we should interpret this portion of Scripture. Some believe that these events already happened with the destruction of the temple in 70 A.D. Others think that this is referring to a future event that has not happened yet. A third possibility is that it refers to both, just as Jesus fulfilled many Old Testament prophecies about the Messiah and will finish their fulfillment at his second coming.

"It will be horrible for pregnant women and nursing mothers and you should pray that you don't have to run in the winter or on the Sabbath. These days of distress will be worse than any in history or any to come; unless God relents, he will destroy the entire human race. But he will shorten those days for the sake of his chosen ones.

"Then if people tell you they know where the Messiah is, you should ignore them; if someone says the Messiah is out in the desert or hiding in some secret place, don't bother to go and look. Because many false Messiahs and prophets will arise and perform miracles in an attempt to deceive God's chosen ones. Beware, because I have warned you. But when the Son of Man comes, it will be like lightning, which lights up the entire sky. Just as vultures gather near a carcass, know that these signs indicate that the end is near.

"After those horrible days end, 'The sun will be dark, the moon won't give light, the stars will fall from the sky, and the planets will shake.'

"There will be strange events in the skies and signs in the sun, moon, and stars. On the earth, the nations will be in turmoil and perplexed by the roaring seas and strange tides. People will be afraid of what's happening and there will be great mourning because the heavens will shake. Then everyone will see the Son of Man coming in the clouds with power and great glory. He will send his angels out with the sound of a mighty trumpet and they will gather his chosen ones from all over the earth. When you see these things start to happen, lift your heads, because your salvation is near.

"Learn a lesson from the fig tree: when its buds are tender and it sprouts leaves, you know that summer is close. When you see the things I'm telling you about, know that his return is near. I tell you the truth, the generation living when this happens will not pass away until all these things happen. Heaven and earth will disappear, but my words will remain forever.

"No one knows when these things will happen, not even the angels or myself; only the Father knows. But when I return, it will be just like it was in Noah's day. Before the Flood, people enjoyed parties and weddings until the day Noah got into the ark. People didn't know what was happening until the Flood came and swept them all away; that's how it will be when the Son of Man returns. Two men will be in the field and God will take one and leave the other; two women will be working together and God will take one and leave the other.

"Don't weigh down your hearts with alcohol and the worries of life because the Son of Man's return will come suddenly. Always stay alert and pray that you might be able to escape everything that's about to happen and stand before the Son of Man. It will be like a man who goes on a trip and leaves his servants in charge of his house. They don't know when the owner will come back, so they must constantly keep alert and watch for his return.

> ### When will Jesus come back?
>
> The short answer is that we don't know. There are many books and teachers who claim to know when he will come back based on many different metrics. Jesus promises that he will come back when we are least expecting it and that many will be surprised by his arrival. Our job is to be prepared and use signs of the times to renew our faith and keep us close to God. The fact he did not know his return's exact date is a sign of his humanity, not a limitation of his divinity.

"Know that if a homeowner knew a thief was coming, he would not allow that thief to break into his house. Always be ready because the Son of Man will come when you least expect it.

"Who is a faithful, sensible servant that the master can put in charge of managing his household and feeding his family? The servant will receive a reward if the master finds him doing a good job and the master will put him in charge of the entire house. But if the servant thinks that the master won't be back for a while and begins abusing his authority, then the master will return when least expected. The master will tear him apart and throw him out with the hypocrites where there will be weeping and gnashing of teeth.

"The kingdom of heaven will be like ten bridesmaids who took their lamps and went out to meet the groom. Five were foolish and took their lamps out without bringing extra oil, but five were wise and brought extra oil. But the groom took longer than expected and they all fell asleep.

"They were awakened at midnight with news that the groom had come. The bridesmaids woke up and trimmed their lamps and the foolish ones begged the wise ones to give them some of their oil. But the wise ones said, 'If we give you some, then there won't be enough for both of us. Go buy some of your own oil.'

"But the groom arrived while they were out buying oil and the wise bridesmaids went into the wedding feast and they locked the door behind them. The five foolish bridesmaids came and begged to be let in, but the groom said, 'I don't know you.' So, keep watch, because you don't know when I will return.

"The Son of Man's coming will be like a man going on a journey who entrusted his property to his servants. He gave five bags of gold to one, two bags to another, and one bag to the last; then, he left. The man who received the five bags of gold put it to work and earned five more bags. The servant with two bags of gold did the same and earned two more bags. But the man who received one bag of gold dug a hole in the ground and hid his master's money.

"After a long time, their master returned to settle accounts with them. The first servant brought the ten bags of gold and said, 'Master, you gave me five bags of gold, and I've doubled them.'

"His master was pleased and said, 'Well done, good and faithful servant. Since you've been faithful with a few things, I'll put you in charge of many things. Let's celebrate together.'

"Next came the servant with two bags of gold, and he showed his master that he had doubled his money. The master said, 'Well done, good and faithful servant. Since you've been faithful with a few things, I'll put you in charge of many things. Let's celebrate together.'

"Then the servant with the one bag of gold came and said, 'Sir, I know you're a hard man who harvests where you haven't planted seed, so I was afraid and hid your money in the earth. Here it is.'

"But the master was furious and said, 'You wicked, lazy servant. If you think I'm a hard man, you should have put my money in the bank to earn some interest. Take his money and give it to the man who earned five bags of gold. Those who receive a lot will have even more, and those who don't receive much will have it taken away. Throw this worthless servant into the outer darkness, where there will be weeping and gnashing of teeth.'

"When the Son of Man comes with his angels in his glory, he will sit on his glorious throne in heaven. All the nations will come before him and he will separate them just like a shepherd separates the sheep from the goats. He will put the sheep on his right and the goats on his left. Then the King will say to those on his right, 'Come, you that my Father has blessed, inherit the kingdom prepared for you from the world's foundation. For you fed me when I was hungry, gave me a drink when I was thirsty, invited me in when I was a stranger, clothed me when I was naked, cared for me when I was sick, and visited me in prison.'

"Then the righteous will answer, 'Lord, when did we ever see you in these states?'

"Then the King will tell them, 'Whatever you did for the least of my brothers and sisters, you were doing for me.'

> **Heaven**
>
> Heaven is the place that God is preparing for those who place faith in Jesus and follow him. There are many misconceptions about heaven. We will not become angels and float around on clouds playing harps. We will have a physical body and live for eternity with God. We will not struggle with sin and everything broken will be made right as God had intended from creation. Our minds cannot comprehend how amazing this place will be and we lack the language to describe it accurately. John saw a vision of heaven and he had to use descriptive language to compare how tremendous it will be. For example, he writes that the streets will be paved with gold. This is one of the most valuable substances on earth, and in heaven, it is a common construction material.

"Then the King will turn to those on the left and say, 'Away with you cursed ones, go into the eternal fire prepared for Satan and his demons. You didn't feed me when I was hungry, you didn't give me a drink when I was thirsty, you didn't invite me in when I was a stranger, you didn't clothe me when I was naked, you didn't care for me when I was sick, and you didn't visit me when I was in prison.'

"Then they will reply, 'Lord, when did we ever see you hungry, thirsty, a stranger, naked, sick, or in prison?'

"He will answer, 'Whatever you didn't do for the least of my brothers and sisters, you refused to do for me.' Then they will go away into eternal punishment, and the righteous will go to eternal life."

CHAPTER FORTY

ARRANGEMENTS FOR BETRAYAL
Matthew 26:1-16; Mark 14:1-11; Luke 22:1-6

After saying these things, Jesus told his disciples, "The Passover celebration and the Feast of Unleavened Bread starts in two days, and the Son of Man will be betrayed and crucified."

At this time, the leading priests and teachers of the religious law met at the home of Caiaphas, the High Priest. They were trying to figure out how to capture Jesus and put him to death, but they agreed not to do it during the Passover because it would cause a riot.

Meanwhile, Jesus was having dinner in Bethany at the home of Simon, the leper. Martha served them the meal and Lazarus sat at the table with Jesus. Then Mary brought in a beautiful, large jar of expensive perfume and poured it over his head. She also anointed Jesus' feet and wiped them with her hair, and the whole house was full of the fragrance.

Some of the disciples became indignant and scolded her, but Mary was only worried about Jesus. Judas Iscariot, who would later betray him, said, "What a waste of money, she could have sold that perfume for a small fortune and given it to the poor." But Judas didn't really care about the poor; he just wanted to steal from the disciples' funds because he was the one who took care of the finances.

But Jesus replied, "Why are you bothering her? You will always have the poor with you, and you can help them whenever you want to, but I won't be here much longer. She has done what she could to prepare my body for burial. I tell you the truth, her story will be told wherever they preach the good news."

***

Then Satan entered Judas Iscariot, and he went to the leading priests and captains of the temple guard to discuss the best way to betray Jesus. He asked them how much they would pay him and they agreed on 30 pieces of silver (five weeks' wages). From then on, he looked for an opportunity to betray Jesus so that they could arrest him when the crowds weren't around.

CHAPTER FORTY-ONE

THE LAST SUPPER
Matthew 26:17-35; Mark 14:12-31; Luke 22:7-38; John 13

On the first day of the Feast of Unleavened Bread, the day that Jews sacrificed the Passover lamb, Jesus sent Peter and John ahead to prepare the Passover meal. They asked him, "Where do you want us to go?"

Jesus replied, "As soon as you enter Jerusalem, you will meet a man carrying a pitcher of water, follow him to the house where he's staying. Tell the owner that my time has come and that we will eat the Passover meal at his house. Then ask him where the guest room is and he will show you a large upstairs room that's already set up for us. Prepare for us there." They went into the city and found everything just as Jesus described.

That evening Jesus sat down with the twelve disciples and said, "I have looked forward to eating this Passover with you because I won't eat it again until the kingdom of God comes."

Then they began to argue with each other about who would be the greatest in the coming kingdom. Jesus told them, "In this world, rulers order people around and still call themselves 'friends of the people.' But with you, the greatest should be like the least, and the leader should be like a servant. Normally, the master sits at the table and the servants serve him, but I am here as your servant. You have stood by me in my trials, so I grant you the right to eat and drink at my table in the kingdom just as my Father has given me a kingdom. I tell you the truth, you will sit on thrones and judge the twelve tribes of Israel."

Jesus knew that he had authority over everything and that it was time for him to leave the world and return to his Father, so he decided to show his disciples the full extent of his love. So, he got up from the table, took off his robe, wrapped a towel around his waist, and poured water into a basin. He began to wash the disciples' feet and dry them with the towel around his waist. Most roads in the First Century were unpaved and people walked everywhere in sandals. This meant that their feet were covered with whatever they encountered in the road, including feces. Washing feet was the lowest job one could imagine and it was shocking for Jesus to take on this task.

When Jesus came to Peter's feet, Peter asked, "Lord, why are you washing my feet?"

Jesus replied, "You don't understand what I'm doing now, but someday you will."

Peter protested, "You will never wash my feet."

Jesus answered, "Unless I wash your feet, you have no part with me."

Peter said, "Then don't just wash my feet, but my hands and head as well."

Jesus replied, "A person who has had a bath only needs to wash his feet to be entirely clean. You are clean, but not everyone here is." Jesus said this because he knew that Judas was going to betray him.

When he finished washing their feet, he put his clothes on, sat back down, and asked, "Do you understand what I was doing? You rightly call me 'Teacher' and 'Lord' because that's what I am. I've set an example for you because if I am your teacher and Lord and I have washed your feet, then you should wash one another's feet as well. I tell you the truth, no servant is greater than his master, and no messenger is greater than his sender. God will bless you if you do these things.

"I'm not saying these things to all of you, because I know who I have chosen. But this fulfills the Scripture, 'He who shares my bread has turned against me.' I'm telling you this before it happens so that you will believe I am the Messiah. I tell you the truth, whoever accepts my messengers accepts me; whoever accepts me accepts the one who sent me."

While they were sitting around the table, Jesus was troubled and said, "I tell you the truth, one of you who is eating with me will betray me."

They were very sad, and one by one, they asked, "It's not me, is it?"

Jesus replied, "It's one of you who is dipping his bread with me that will betray me. I must die because it is part of God's plan, but it will be terrible for the one who betrays me. It would be better if he had never been born."

Then Peter motioned for John to ask whom he meant and Jesus said, "It's the one I give this bread to after I dip it in the dish." Then Jesus dipped a piece of bread and gave it to Judas Iscariot.

Judas looked at Jesus and asked, "It's not me, is it teacher?"

Jesus told him, "It's you, go do what you have to do quickly."

No one else there understood what Jesus meant. Most thought that Jesus had sent Judas to buy food or give something to the poor because he was their treasurer and a respected disciple. So, Judas left and went out into the night.

Once Judas was gone, Jesus said, "It's time for the Son of Man to enter his glory so that God may be glorified. I will only be with you for a little longer and then I must leave you. You will look for me, but you cannot come where I am going. So, I give you a new commandment, that you should love one another. I love you, so you should love one another, and this will prove that you are my disciples."

Peter asked him, "Lord, where are you going?"

Jesus replied, "You cannot follow me now, but you will follow me later."

Peter asked, "Why can't I follow you now? I'm ready to die for you."

Jesus told them, "All of you will desert me tonight because Scripture says, 'God will strike the shepherd and the sheep of the flock will scatter.' But after I rise from the dead, I will go to Galilee to meet you. Peter, Satan has demanded to sift you like wheat, but I have prayed for you so that your faith won't fail. Once you have turned back, you should strengthen your brothers."

But Peter declared, "Even if everyone else leaves you, I won't. I'm ready to go to jail and even die for you."

Jesus replied, "Will you really die for me? I tell you the truth, before the rooster crows twice, you will deny that you know me three times."

"I will never disown you, even if I have to die," Peter insisted. Everyone else agreed.

Then Jesus asked, "Did you lack anything when I sent you out without money, a bag, or extra clothes?"

"No," they answered.

Jesus said, "Now you should take your money and baggage; and if you don't have a sword, sell your clothes and buy one. It's time to fulfill the Scripture that says, 'He was counted with the sinners.' Every prophecy about me must be fulfilled."

The disciples replied, "We have two swords."

Jesus said, "That's enough."

As they were eating, Jesus took a loaf of bread and asked God to bless it. After praying, he broke it in pieces and gave it to his disciples, saying, "Take it and eat, because this is my body; do this to remember me." Then he took a cup of wine, thanked God for it, and said, "Each of you drink this because it is my blood and it is poured out for the forgiveness of sins. This cup is the New Covenant in my blood, do this to remember me. I tell you the truth, I won't drink wine again until I drink it with you in my Father's kingdom."

> **The Last Supper as a marriage covenant**
>
> The breaking of bread and sharing of the cup of wine was like a Jewish marriage proposal. When a man proposed to a woman, he would take a cup of wine and say the same words Jesus said to his disciples. Jesus was telling his followers that he loved them and was asking them if they would love him in return.

CHAPTER FORTY-TWO

THE UPPER ROOM CONTINUED
Matthew 26:30; Mark 14:26; Luke 22:39; John 14:1-18:1

"Don't worry, you trust God; now trust me. My Father's house has many rooms and I'm going there to prepare a place for you. If I prepare a place for you, I will come back to bring you there. Then you will always be with me and you know the way to get there."

Thomas said, "Lord, how can we know how to get there if we don't know where you're going?"

Jesus answered, "I am the way, the truth, and the life; the only way to the Father is through me. If you really knew me, you would know my Father too; but now you know him and have seen him."

Philip said, "Lord, show us the Father and we will be satisfied."

Jesus replied, "Philip, don't you know me after all the time we've spent together? If you've seen me, you've seen the Father, so why do you ask me to show you the Father? Do you think I'm lying? My words aren't my own; they come from my Father because he lives in me and is working through me. Believe that the Father is in me and that I am in the Father, or at least believe the miracles I have shown you. I tell you the truth, whoever believes in me will do what I have done, and even more because I am going to the Father. If you ask for something in my name, it is like asking for something because it is what I would want. I will do whatever you ask in my name so that it may glorify my Father.

"If you love me, you will obey me. Then I will ask the Father to send you the Holy Spirit to be your counselor. The world doesn't accept him because they cannot see him and don't know him, but he will live within you. I promise that I won't leave you as orphans because I will come to you. Soon the world won't see me anymore, but you will still see me, and we will both live. Then you will know that I am in the Father, you are in me, and I am in you. Those who obey me love me and my Father and I will love them and show myself to them."

Judas (not Iscariot) said, "Lord, why are you going to reveal yourself to us, but not to the world?"

Jesus answered, "If you love me, you will obey me; if you don't love me, you won't obey. If you obey, my Father will love you and we will live with you. Remember that these words aren't mine; they are the Father's. I've told you all these things, but the Holy Spirit will complete your education and remind you of what I've said.

"I give you my peace, but it's not like the world's peace, so don't be afraid. Remember that I'm leaving, but I will come back to you. You should be glad that I'm going back to the Father because the Father is greater than I am. I've told you this beforehand so that you might believe. I don't have much time left to tell you things, because the Prince of the World is coming. He has no power over me, but I must do what the Father has commanded so that the world will learn that I love the Father.

"I am the true vine and my Father is the gardener. He cuts off every branch that doesn't bear fruit, and he prunes the other branches so that they will bear more fruit. You're already clean because I've spoken to you. Remain in me and I will remain in you because a branch cannot produce fruit if it is cut off from the vine. In the same way, you cannot bear fruit unless you remain in me.

"I am the vine and you are the branches; those who remain in me will bear much fruit. You cannot do anything on your own because you would be like a useless branch that withers and is tossed in the fire. If you remain in me, ask for whatever you want, and I will give it to you. You glorify my Father if you bear much fruit and prove that you are my disciples. If you do not bear fruit, you are not one of my disciples.

"Just as my Father loves me, I love you, so stay in my love. If you obey me, you will remain in my love, just like I've obeyed my Father and stayed in his love. I've told you things to bring you joy to the fullest. Therefore, I command you to love each other just like I've loved you. There is no greater love than to lay down your life for someone. You are my friends if you obey me. I don't call you servants anymore because a master doesn't tell his servants what he's doing, but I call you friends because I've told you what my Father is doing. Remember that you didn't choose me, but I chose you to bear lasting fruit. Then the Father will give you whatever you ask for in my name. I command you to love each other.

"Remember that if the world hates you, it's because it hated me first. The world would love you if you belonged to it, but since I chose you out of the world, it hates you. A servant is not greater than his master, so if they persecuted me, they will persecute you; if they obeyed me, they will obey you. They will treat you this way because they don't know the one who sent me. If I hadn't spoken to them, they would be ignorant of their sin, but now they have no excuse. Whoever hates me hates my Father too. If they hadn't seen my miracles, they'd be innocent, but now they've seen these miracles and hated me and my Father. But this fulfills their Law, which says, 'They hated me for no reason.'

"When I send you the Counselor, the Spirit of truth, he will tell you about me. Then you must tell others about me because you've been with me from the beginning.

"I've told you these things so that you won't fall away. Know that they will kick you out of the synagogues and people will think that they are serving God when they kill you. They only do such things because they don't know the Father or me. I've warned you about this now to remind you later; I didn't tell you at first because I was there to protect you.

"Now I am going to the one who sent me and none of you asks me where I'm going. My words bring you grief, but it's good that I'm leaving. If I weren't, the Holy Spirit wouldn't come to you. When I send the Holy Spirit to you, he will convict the world of its unbelief, God's righteousness, and the coming judgment and condemnation.

"I have a lot more to tell you, but you can't handle it right now. When the Spirit of truth comes, he will guide you into all truth. He won't be speaking on his own behalf; he will only tell you what he's heard. He will tell you what's coming and will bring glory to me by telling you what is mine. Everything that the Father has is mine, and that's why I told you that the Spirit will tell you what's mine.

> **Who is the Holy Spirit?**
>
> The Holy Spirit is the third person of the Trinity. He is the promised helper that lives in the hearts of everyone who follows Jesus. The Holy Spirit exists to glorify Jesus and help us better bring him glory and honor. When people put their faith in Jesus, the Holy Spirit lives within them.

"Soon, you won't see me anymore, but you will see me after a while."

Some of the disciples were confused and said to each other, "What does he mean we won't see him and then we will see him and that he's going to the Father? What does he mean after a while? What is he talking about?"

Jesus realized that they wanted to ask him questions, so he said, "Did I confuse you? I tell you the truth, you will weep and mourn while the world rejoices, but your grief will turn to joy when you see me again. A woman in labor forgets her pain because of her joy when her child is born. In the same way, this is your time of grief, but you will rejoice when I see you again, and no one will take away your joy. Then you won't need to ask me for anything because my Father will give you whatever you ask for in my name. You haven't asked for anything in my name, but now, ask and you will receive; then you will rejoice.

"I've spoken to you in parables, but a time is coming when I will tell you plainly about my Father and then you will ask the Father in my name. I'm not saying I will ask the Father on your behalf because the Father loves you, and you love me and believe that I came from God. Now I must return to him."

Then the disciples said, "We understand you now that you're not speaking in parables. We understand that you know everything and don't need anyone to tell you anything; thus, we know that you came from God."

"Finally, you trust me," Jesus answered. "But very soon you will all scatter to your own homes. You will all leave me alone, but I'm not alone because my Father is with me.

"I've told you these things to give you peace. You will have trouble in the world, but take heart, because I have overcome the world."

After saying this, Jesus looked to heaven and prayed, "Father, the time has come. Glorify your Son, so that he may glorify you. You've given me authority over all people so that I might give eternal life to all those you've given me. Eternal life comes from knowing you and me, the Messiah, the one you sent. I've glorified you by finishing the work you've given me, so Father, bring me into the glory we shared at the beginning of the world.

"I've told these men about you because you gave them to me. They have obeyed your word and now they know that everything I have is a gift from you. I gave them your words, and they accepted them; they know I came from you, and they believed my words. I pray for them because they belong to you. We share everything and they've brought me glory. Now I'm coming home to you, but they will remain in the world. Holy Father, I don't pray that you take them out of the world, but protect them by the power of your name so that they may have unity. I've kept them safe while I was here, and the only one I lost was the one that the Scriptures said was doomed to destruction.

"Now I'm coming to you, but I say these things to them so that they might have joy. I've given them your word, and the world hates them because they're not from this world, and neither am I. Purify them and make them holy by teaching them your words. Just as you sent me into the world, I'm sending them into the world, and I give myself to you that they might also be entirely yours. I'm also praying for those who will believe them, and I pray that they will have unity and the world will believe that you sent me.

"I've given them the glory that you've given me that they may have the same unity that we do. Cause them to have complete unity so that the world will know that you sent me and love them.

"Father, I want them to be with me so that they can see the glory you've given me because you loved me before the beginning of the world. Righteous Father, the world doesn't know you, but I do; and these disciples know that you've sent me. I've revealed you to them and will continue to reveal to them so that they may know the love that you have for me."

They sang a hymn and went out to the Mount of Olives across the Kidron Valley.

CHAPTER FORTY-THREE

GARDEN OF GETHSEMANE
Matthew 26:36-56; Mark 14:32-52; Luke 22:40-53; John 18:2-12

Then Jesus brought them to an olive grove called Gethsemane, and told them, "Pray that you won't fall into temptation. Sit here while I go over there and pray." Then he took Peter, James, and John with him and he was distressed. He told them, "I'm sorrowful to the point of death, stay here and watch with me."

He went about a stone's throw away and fell facedown, praying, "Daddy, Father, you can do all things. If possible, please take this cup of suffering from me; but not my will, but your will be done." An angel from heaven came to strengthen him and he prayed so fervently that his sweat fell to the ground like great drops of blood.

Jesus returned to his disciples and found them sleeping. "Peter," he said. "Are you asleep? Couldn't you stay awake and watch for me for an hour? Stay awake and pray so that temptation won't overwhelm you. The spirit is willing, but the flesh is weak."

Again, he stepped away and prayed, "Father, if I must drink this cup, your will be done." He came back to his sleeping disciples; they had nothing to say. So, he went back a third time and prayed the same thing.

When he returned, they were still asleep, exhausted from grief, so he said to them, "Why are you still sleeping and resting? Enough! It's time for the Son of Man's betrayal into the hands of sinners. Let's go, my betrayer is here."

As he said this, Judas Iscariot arrived with a mob. Judas knew where they were meeting because Jesus had gone there with his disciples many times. The leading priests and Pharisees had sent a battalion of Roman soldiers and temple guards with Judas with blazing torches, lanterns, and weapons. Judas told them that he would kiss Jesus and that they should take him away.

Jesus realized what was going to happen, so he stepped forward and asked, "Who are you looking for?"

"Jesus of Nazareth," they replied.

Jesus told them, "I'm the one you're looking for." As he said this, they all fell backward to the ground because of the authority of his words. Then he asked them again, "Who are you looking for?"

Again, they replied, "Jesus of Nazareth."

Jesus said, "I told you that I'm the one you seek. Since you want me, let these others go." He said this to fulfill his statement, "I have not lost a single one of those you gave me."

Jesus said to Judas, "Friend, do what you came for."

Judas stepped forward and as he kissed him, he said, "Greetings, Teacher!"

But Jesus said, "Judas, how can you betray the Son of Man with a kiss?" Then the temple guards grabbed Jesus and arrested him.

When the other disciples saw what was happening, they exclaimed, "Lord, should we fight? We have the two swords!" Without waiting for an answer, Peter drew a sword and cut off the right ear of Malchus, the high priest's servant.

Jesus looked at Peter and said, "Put away your sword, because those who live by the sword will die by the sword and I must drink from the cup that the Father has given me." Then he touched the place where Malchus' ear had been and healed him. "Don't you realize that if I ask the Father, he will give me thousands of angels to protect us? But if I did, how would we fulfill the Scriptures that say it must happen this way?"

Then Jesus turned to the leading priests and captains of the temple guard and said, "Am I a dangerous criminal leading a rebellion? Is that why you've come to arrest me with swords and clubs? Why didn't you arrest me in the temple when I was teaching every day? But this is the time that darkness reigns and all of this fulfills the words of the prophets."

Meanwhile, all his disciples ran away. There was a young man (likely Mark) wearing a linen nightshirt following behind them, and when the mob tried to grab him, he left his clothes behind and ran away naked.

CHAPTER FORTY-FOUR

JESUS' TRIAL WITH THE JEWS
Matthew 26:57-68; Mark 14:53-65; Luke 22:54, 63-65; John 18:13-23

First, the mob took him to Annas because he was the high priest Caiaphas' father-in-law. Even though Caiaphas had replaced Annas, many still viewed Annas as the real high priest. It was Caiaphas who had told the Jewish leaders that it was better for one man to die for the nation than to have the entire nation perish.

Inside Annas' house, they began asking Jesus about his followers and his teaching. Jesus replied, "I've spoken openly in the synagogues and the temple. Everyone has heard me clearly, so why are you asking me these questions? Ask the people who heard me, they all know what I said."

One of the temple guards hit Jesus in the face and demanded, "Is that any way to answer the high priest?"

Jesus answered, "Tell me if I've said something wrong. But if I've told the truth, why did you hit me?"

Then Jesus' accusers took him to Caiaphas' house to stand before the teachers of the religious law and the other Jewish leaders.

The leading priests and Sanhedrin (group of Jewish elders) were seeking witnesses who would lie about Jesus so that they could kill him. Even though they found many people to lie, their testimony contradicted each other. Finally, they found two men to say, "He said, 'I will destroy this temple of God and rebuild it in three days.'" But even then, they couldn't agree on their testimony.

The high priest stood up before the crowd and addressed Jesus, "Aren't you going to defend yourself against what these men are saying?" Jesus just remained silent. Finally, the priest demanded, "In the name of the living God, tell us whether or not you are the Messiah, the Son of God!"

Jesus replied, "I am, and in the future, you will see the Son of Man sitting at God's right hand and coming back on the clouds of heaven."

Outraged, the high priest tore his clothes and shouted, "Blasphemy! We don't need any more witnesses. You all heard his blasphemy! What's your verdict?"

"Guilty!" they shouted. "He must die!"

They blindfolded Jesus and some spit on him and punched him. "Tell us who hit you, Messiah," they jeered. They continued to beat and insult him as they led him away to the courtyard.

CHAPTER FORTY-FIVE

PETER'S DENIALS
Matthew 26:69-27:10; Mark 14:66-72; Luke 22:54-71; John 18:15-27

Meanwhile, Peter and John followed along far behind because they wanted to see what was going to happen to Jesus. John knew the high priest Caiaphas, so John was allowed into the courtyard with Jesus. Peter stood anxiously just outside the gate. John got the woman at the gate to let Peter in, and together they warmed themselves around a fire, with the guards and household servants.

A servant girl who worked for the high priest stared at Peter in the firelight and said, "You are one of Jesus' followers."

But Peter denied it in front of everyone, saying, "Woman, I don't know what you're talking about." Then he went out into the entryway.

Later, one of Malchus' relatives, who served the high priest asked, "Didn't I see you in the olive grove with Jesus of Nazareth? You are definitely one of them." But Peter denied it, and immediately a rooster crowed.

Peter denied it again with an oath, saying, "I don't even know him."

A little later, some other people came over to him and said, "You must be one of them because of your Galilean accent."

Peter began to call down curses on himself and he swore to them, "I swear to God that I don't know him." A rooster crowed a second time and at that moment, Jesus turned and looked at Peter. Suddenly, Peter remembered Jesus' words, and he left the courtyard, weeping bitterly.

Very early in the morning, the leading priests, the teachers of the religious law, the other leaders, and the whole Sanhedrin met again to discuss how to persuade the Romans to put Jesus to death.

They brought Jesus out, demanding, "Tell us if you are the Messiah."

Jesus replied, "You won't believe me if I tell you and you won't answer if I ask you a question. But from now on, the Son of Man will sit at God's right hand."

They all shouted, "Are you the Son of God?"

Jesus answered, "You are right to say that I am."

They said to each other, "We don't need other witnesses, we heard him say it ourselves."

Judas realized that they condemned Jesus to die, and he was sorry. So, he took the 30 pieces of silver back to the leading priests and said, "I've sinned because I've betrayed an innocent man."

But they retorted, "We don't care, that's your problem." So, Judas threw the money onto the temple floor and went out and hanged himself. The leading priests picked up the money and said, "It's against the Law to put it in the treasury because it's blood money." After discussing what to do with it, they decided to buy the Potter's Field and make it a cemetery for foreigners. After that, they called it the Field of Blood. This fulfilled Jeremiah's prophesy "They took the 30 pieces of silver that Israel paid for him and purchased the Potter's Field as the Lord directed."

CHAPTER FORTY-SIX

JESUS BEFORE PILATE
Matthew 27:11-26; Mark 15:1-15; Luke 23:1-25; John 18:28-19:16

Jesus' trial with Caiaphas ended in the early hours of the morning and the Sanhedrin bound him and took him to Pilate, the Roman governor. His accusers waited outside because they didn't want to defile themselves and be unable to participate in the Passover feast. So, Pilate went out and asked, "What's your charge against this man?"

They replied, "We wouldn't have brought him here if he weren't a criminal."

"Then go judge him by your own laws," Pilate said.

The Jewish leaders answered, "But only the Romans can execute him." This statement fulfilled Jesus' prediction about how he would die. Then the Jewish leaders made their case, saying, "This man has been trying to ruin our people by telling them not to pay their taxes and claiming to be the Messiah, a king."

Pilate turned to Jesus and asked, "Are you the King of the Jews?"

Jesus answered, "Are you asking me yourself, or did others tell you about me?"

Pilate replied, "I'm not a Jew; it was your own people and their priests that brought you here. What have you done?"

Jesus answered, "I'm not an earthly king; otherwise, my servants would have fought to prevent my arrest. My kingdom is not of this world."

"So, you are a king," Pilate said.

Jesus said, "You're right when you say that I am a king and that's why I was born. I came to bring truth to the world and everyone who loves the truth will recognize that I speak the truth."

"What is truth?" Pilate asked. Then he went out to the people and said, "He's not guilty of any crime. I find nothing wrong with this man."

The mob became desperate and said, "But he's stirred up trouble all over Judea, from Galilee to Jerusalem."

Jesus remained silent while the Jewish leaders accused him of many crimes. Pilate was surprised and said, "Don't you hear them? You should answer these charges." But Jesus said nothing.

After listening to their charges, Pilate asked if Jesus was a Galilean. When he found out that Jesus was, Pilate sent him to Herod Antipas because he was in Jerusalem, and Galilee was under Herod's authority.

Herod was delighted to see Jesus because he had heard about him and wanted to see him perform a miracle. He asked him many questions, and the leading priests and teachers of the religious law made many accusations, but Jesus refused to answer any of them. Herod and his soldiers mocked and ridiculed Jesus; they put a royal robe on him and sent him back to Pilate. That day Herod and Pilate became friends, where they had previously been enemies.

Every Passover, the governor would release one prisoner the crowd wanted. This year, a notorious prisoner named Barabbas was in jail for murder during an insurrection. Pilate called the Jewish leaders together and said, "You brought me a man that you accuse of leading a revolt, but I have examined him in your presence and I find him innocent. Herod found him innocent as well, and there is no reason to put him to death. So, I will flog him and then release him. I will bring him out to you now, but know that I don't find him guilty."

When they brought out Jesus, Pilate said, "Here he is! Who do you want me to release, Barabbas, or Jesus, the Messiah?"

The leading priests and other leaders persuaded the crowds to ask for Barabbas instead of Jesus. When Pilate asked again, "Who do you want me to release to you?" the crowd shouted, "Barabbas!"

Pilate asked, "But if I release Barabbas, what should I do with the man you call the King of the Jews?"

The crowd shouted, "Crucify him!"

Pilate answered, "You crucify him, I find him innocent."

The Jewish leaders replied, "Our Law says that he should die because he called himself the Son of God."

When Pilate heard this, he was afraid and took Jesus back inside. "Where are you from?" he demanded, but Jesus was silent. Then Pilate continued, "Don't you realize that I can release or crucify you?"

Finally, Jesus said, "You wouldn't have any power unless God gave it to you, so the ones who brought me to you are the greater sinners."

Pilate tried to release him, but the Jewish leaders insisted, "You're not a friend of Caesar if you release this man because anyone who calls himself a king is rebelling against Caesar."

Pilate brought Jesus out to the mob again and sat down on the judgment seat on the platform known as the Stone Pavement. It was about noon on the day before the Passover. As Pilate was sitting on the judgment seat, his wife sent a message, saying, "Leave that innocent man alone, because I had a terrible dream about him last night."

"Here's your king!" Pilate said to the people.

"Away with him! Crucify him!" the crowd yelled.

Pilate asked, "Do you want to crucify your king?"

The leading priests shouted, "Our only king is Caesar."

Pilate demanded, "Why should I crucify him? What crime has he committed?"

But the crowd only roared louder, "Crucify him!"

Pilate demanded a third time, "What crime has he committed? There's no reason for me to put him to death, so I will flog him and let him go."

But the crowd shouted louder and louder, and Pilate realized that a riot was starting. So, he sent for a bowl of water and washed his hands, saying, "I am innocent of this man's blood, you take responsibility."

The people yelled back, "Let his blood be on our children and us."

Pilate wanted to please the crowd, so he released Barabbas and had Jesus flogged with a lead-tipped whip 39 times (this was one short of a lethal sentence). Then he sentenced Jesus to die and he gave him over to the Roman soldiers to crucify him.

Some of the governor's soldiers took Jesus into their headquarters and brought out all the other soldiers. They stripped him and put a scarlet robe on him. They also made a crown of long, sharp thorns and put it on his head, and put a stick in his right hand as a scepter. They knelt before him and mocked him, yelling, "Hail the King of the Jews!" Then they spit on him and beat him with the stick they gave him.

When they got tired of mocking him, they took off the robe, put his clothes back on, and led him away to be crucified.

CHAPTER FORTY-SEVEN

THE CRUCIFIXION
Matthew 27:27-66; Mark 15:16-47; Luke 23:26-66; John 19:16-42

On their way out, they met a man from Cyrene named Simon, and forced him to carry Jesus' crossbeam, a piece of wood weighing between 30 and 40 pounds. Then they went to a place called Golgotha, or the Place of the Skull, and great crowds followed behind. Jesus turned to some of the grief-stricken women in the crowd and said, "Don't weep for me, but weep for yourselves and your children because they will soon say that the childless are blessed. People will beg the mountains to fall on them and for the hills to bury them. If men do these things when the tree is green, what will happen when it is dry?"

The soldiers gave him some wine mixed with bitter gall; this was a painkiller given to those condemned to die. But once he had tasted it, he refused to drink it. Meanwhile, the soldiers led out two criminals that were also being executed that day.

The soldiers nailed Jesus to the cross about nine in the morning and Jesus said, "Father, forgive them, they don't know what they're doing."

Crucifixion

The Romans were experts at torture and death and one of the primary methods they used for execution was crucifixion. While this technique predates the Romans, they perfected the art. The condemned would have their hands tied or nailed to a crossbeam attached to a vertical pole. Prisoners had a small platform to stand on or had their feet nailed to the pole. Eventually, victims would become exhausted and the bodyweight would cause them to asphyxiate and die.

> When Jesus was executed, he had two spikes nailed through his wrists between his radius and ulna. He also had a spike hammered through the tops of his feet close to his ankles. He had to alternate between holding his body weight on his feet and pulling himself up with his arms to breathe. This was an excruciating way to die.

After they nailed him to the cross, the soldiers divided his clothes among the four of them. They cast lots to decide who would get his undergarment because it was a seamless robe and would be worth a small amount of money. This fulfilled the Scripture that said, "They divided my garments amongst them and cast lots for my clothing."

Then the soldiers sat around and kept watch as he hung there. They fastened a sign in Aramaic, Latin, and Greek above his head that read, "This is Jesus of Nazareth, the King of the Jews."

The leading priests went to Pilate and said, "Change it to say that he claimed to be the King of the Jews."

Pilate replied, "I've written what I've written."

Jesus' mother, his aunt, Mary (the wife of Clopas), and Mary Magdalene were standing near the cross; when Jesus saw his mother standing next to John, he said to her, "Mother, here is your son." Then he turned to John and said, "Here is your mother." From then on, John took her into his home.

***

The people who passed by mocked him, saying, "So you can destroy the temple and rebuild it in three days? If you're the Son of God, save yourself and come down from the cross!"

The leading priests and Jewish leaders also mocked Jesus, saying, "He saved others, but he cannot save himself. If he is the Messiah, he should come down from the cross so that we can all believe in him. If he trusts in God, let God come save him since he said he is the Son of God."

The soldiers also mocked him by offering him some sour wine. They called out, "If you're the King of the Jews, you should save yourself."

One of the criminals next to him scoffed, "If you're the Messiah, prove it by saving yourself and us."

But the other criminal protested, "Don't you fear God? We deserve to die, but this man is innocent." Then he turned to Jesus and said, "Remember me when you come into your kingdom."

Jesus replied, "I tell you the truth, you will be with me in paradise today."

At noon, darkness fell across the whole land for three hours. Then Jesus called out, "*Eli, Eli, lama sabachthani?*" which means, "My God, my God, why have you forsaken me?"

Some of the bystanders thought he was calling for the prophet Elijah and one of them said, "Let's see if Elijah will come save him."

Jesus knew that everything was finished, and to fulfill Scripture, he said, "I'm thirsty." Someone soaked a sponge in a jar of sour wine, put it on a hyssop branch, and held it up to his lips. These were the sponges that servants used at public toilets to clean the wealthy users' backsides and the wine was what they used to disinfect the sponges. When Jesus tasted it, he said, "It is finished! Father, I entrust my spirit into your hands!" With those words, he breathed his last and died.

> **What happened when Jesus died?**
>
> When Jesus died on the cross, God the Father was pouring out all his wrath and judgment on Jesus instead of us. A sacrifice means something set aside from everyday life as a gift to make things right between two parties, like parents will sacrifice money, time, and privacy to raise happy, healthy children. Jesus had lived a perfect life and was the perfect sacrifice for all past, present, and future sins that people would commit to make things right between God and man. Jesus willingly went to the cross because he loves us and wants us to spend eternity with him, rather than be separated from him in judgment.

At that moment, the thick veil hanging in the temple was torn in two, from top to bottom and there was a great earthquake. Many tombs opened and the bodies of many holy people came back to life. These people went into Jerusalem and many people saw them.

The Roman soldiers handling the execution were terrified. When the captain of the guard saw how Jesus died, he said, "Certainly this was a righteous man; truly he was the Son of God!"

When the crowd saw what had happened, they beat their breasts and went home in despair. Many women who had been with Jesus since Galilee were watching from a distance. Among them were Mary Magdalene, Mary (the mother of James the younger and Joseph), Salome, and Zebedee's wife (the mother of James and John).

This all happened on Friday, the day before the Sabbath, and this Sabbath was going to be special because it was also the Passover. The Jews didn't want the bodies to hang overnight, so they asked Pilate to break their legs and take them down. The soldiers broke the two criminals' legs, but when they came to Jesus, they saw he was already dead, so they didn't break his legs. However, John saw them put a spear in his side, and blood and water flowed out. These things fulfilled the Scripture that reads, "None of his bones will be broken" and, "They will look on the one they pierced."

> **Did Jesus really die?**
>
> The Romans were experts at death, and if they declared Jesus to be dead, he was undoubtedly dead. If they declared victims to be dead when they were not, they forfeited their own lives, so there was tremendous motivation to be accurate with their judgments. When people die, the water in the blood begins to separate, so this is a sign that Jesus really was dead.
>
> There are theories against the resurrection that Jesus did not really die, but none of these are realistic when we look at the brutality he suffered. There is no way that he could have gone through everything that he did and then convinced his disciples that he had risen from the dead. He would have been very weak from blood loss and barely able to stand if he had just revived in the cool of the tomb.

As evening approached, Joseph of Arimathea, a member of the Sanhedrin, gathered his courage and asked Pilate for Jesus' body. Joseph was a secret disciple of Jesus because he was afraid of the Sanhedrin. He was waiting for the kingdom of God and disagreed with the actions of the other religious leaders. Pilate verified that Jesus was dead and gave Jesus' body to Joseph.

***

Nicodemus, the man who had come to Jesus at night, came with Joseph and brought 75 pounds of embalming ointment made from myrrh and aloes. They wrapped Jesus in linen cloth with the spices according to the Jewish burial custom. Joseph owned a new tomb in a nearby garden and they put Jesus' body there and rolled a large stone over the entrance.

Mary Magdalene and the other Mary were watching where they buried Jesus, and then they went home and prepared more spices and ointments to embalm him. But they rested on the Sabbath in obedience to the Law.

The next day the leading priests and Pharisees went to see Pilate and told him, "That deceiver we just killed once said, 'After three days I will rise again.' We ask that you guard the tomb until the third day so that the disciples won't be able to steal the body. If they do, their lies will be worse than his."

Pilate replied, "Take a guard and make the tomb as secure as you know how." So, they put a seal on the stone and posted guards to protect it.

Who killed Jesus?

Multiple parties are responsible for his death and we cannot pin it on one person or people group. The Romans are the ones who carried out the execution and were guilty. The Jews rejected him as Messiah and were also responsible. Jesus died for our sins as well, so we bear the guilt for his death too. Finally, God is the one who is ultimately responsible, and if Jesus had not wanted to die, he would not have. He chose to go to the cross because of his love for us.

CHAPTER FORTY-EIGHT

THE RESURRECTION
Matthew 28:1-15; Mark 16:1-11; Luke 24:1-12; John 20:1-18

The next evening, when the Sabbath had ended, Mary Magdalene, Mary, James' mother, and Salome bought spices to anoint Jesus' body. Early Sunday morning, while it was still dark, there was a great earthquake because an angel of the Lord rolled away the stone and sat on it. The guards shook with fear and became like dead men when they saw him because his face shone like lightning and his clothing was as white as snow.

> **Three days in the grave?**
>
> Some people object that Jesus only spent about 36 hours in the grave (Friday evening to Sunday morning) and not the three days that Scripture claims. However, in Jewish accounting of time, any part of a day counted as a day. He was in the grave Friday evening, Saturday, and Sunday morning, thus making three days.

Not long after that, Mary Magdalene came to the tomb and found the stone rolled away. She ran and found Peter and John and said, "They've taken the Lord's body out of the tomb and I don't know where they've put him."

Peter and John ran to the tomb and John got there first. He looked in and saw the linen cloth on the ground, but he didn't go in. Peter arrived, went inside, and saw the linen cloth on the ground and Jesus' head covering folded on the side. Then John went in and believed because he finally understood that Scripture had said that the Messiah would rise from the dead.

Peter and John both went home, but Mary, who had followed them, lingered outside the tomb. She cried as she looked in the tomb and she saw two men sitting where Jesus had been. One of them asked her, "Why are you crying?"

She replied, "Because they've taken away my Lord and I don't know where they've put him."

She looked over her shoulder and saw Jesus standing there, but she didn't recognize him. He asked Mary, "Why are you crying? Who are you looking for?"

She thought he was the gardener so she said, "Sir, if you've taken him away, tell me where you've put him, and I'll go get him."

Jesus said, "Mary."

She recognized his voice, turned to him, and exclaimed, "Teacher!"

Jesus said, "Don't cling to me because I haven't returned to the Father yet. Go find my brothers and tell them that I'm returning to our God and Father."

Mary Magdalene, the woman that Jesus had cast seven demons from, was the first to see the risen Lord. She went and found the other disciples and told them that Jesus was alive. They didn't believe her and continued to weep and grieve. Despite their unbelief, she insisted that she had seen the Lord, and she gave them his message.

Meanwhile, as the new day was dawning, the other women went out to the tomb with the spices. On the way they talked about who would roll the stone away. When they got to the tomb, they saw that the large stone covering the entrance was already rolled away. They were puzzled when they entered the tomb and couldn't find the body. They saw two men in dazzling robes and the terrified women bowed before them.

One of the men said, "Don't be afraid. You're looking for Jesus of Nazareth, but he isn't here because he's risen from the dead. Don't you remember that he told you that the Son of Man would be betrayed, crucified, and rise on the third day? Come look where they put his body and then tell his disciples and Peter that he has risen and is going ahead of them to Galilee. You will see him there just as he said before his death." They then recalled that Jesus had indeed said this.

The bewildered women ran from the tomb, trembling, yet elated. They were too frightened to talk, and they rushed to find the disciples and give them the angels' message. As they went, Jesus met them and said, "Greetings." Then they ran to him, touched him, and worshipped him. Jesus said, "Don't be afraid! Go tell my brothers that I will meet them in Galilee.

> **Jesus and women**
>
> Women were not treated well during the First Century. Jesus did much to change and elevate the status of his female followers as evidenced by listing the women who helped in his ministry and saw his crucifixion. He also made his first appearances to women, giving them an elevated position in the resurrection story.

As the women entered the city, some of the men who had been guarding the tomb went to the leading priests and told them what had happened. The religious leaders decided to bribe the soldiers, telling them to say that the disciples came while they were asleep and stole the body. They also said, "We'll stand up for you if the governor hears about you falling asleep." The soldiers agreed and the story became widespread among the Jews.

The women who went to the tomb, Mary Magdalene, Joanna, Mary, the mother of James, and several others, rushed back to tell everyone what happened. They told the disciples their story, but they didn't believe them because it sounded like gibberish. However, Peter ran back to the tomb and saw the linen wrappings. Then he went home again, wondering what had happened.

> **Did Jesus really rise from the dead?**
>
> Many have tried to discredit Jesus' resurrection because they don't like the implications. This is the crucial component of Christianity, and if he did not rise from the dead, then our faith is worthless. Jesus

appeared multiple times to multiple people, ate food, and had his followers touch his physical body.

People present many arguments that try to deny the resurrection, although it is interesting that none of Christianity's early opponents tried to refute it. When we examine the various attempts to explain away the resurrection, none of them hold water. The first hypothesis is that the disciples stole the body. However, this does not explain why the disciples would later die for their faith (people do not die for what they know is a lie).

Another view is that the Roman or Jewish authorities stole the body. However, this view does not make sense because these authorities had nothing to gain by stealing the body. The authorities could have stopped the resurrection story by producing his body.

A third possibility is that the disciples went to the wrong tomb. Again, the authorities could produce Jesus' body to stop the resurrection story. Also, Joseph of Arimathea, the tomb's owner, would not have gone to the wrong tomb.

Another view is that Jesus never really died, but rather fainted and then revived in the tomb. However, if Jesus, weakened by blood loss and lack of food and water, could get himself out of the 75 pounds of burial wrappings, move the stone by himself, and get past the guard, he would not inspire great confidence in his disciples. Furthermore, the Romans were experts at putting people to death, and they knew Jesus was dead.

A final theory is that Jesus' followers had a group hallucination. However, 500 people do not have the same hallucination at once, hallucinations do not suddenly stop (Jesus left after 40 days), and hallucinations only come from what is already in the mind (the disciples did not believe that Jesus would resurrect). If the hallucination theory is true, then the authorities could have produced the body and stopped the disciples' story from spreading. When we look at the evidence, which even the harshest critics agree with, the only option that makes sense is that Jesus physically rose from the grave.

CHAPTER FORTY-NINE

RESURRECTION APPEARANCES
Mark 16:12-15; Luke 24:13-43; John 20:19-21:25; I Corinthians 15:5-6

That same day two of Jesus' followers were walking to Emmaus, a village about seven miles from Jerusalem. As they were walking, Jesus joined them, but God kept them from recognizing him.

Jesus asked, "What are you talking about?"

They stopped walking, looking heartbroken. One of them named Cleopas replied, "You must be the only person in Jerusalem who doesn't know what's happened over the last few days."

"What things?" Jesus asked.

They replied, "The things that happened to Jesus of Nazareth, the prophet who did wonderful miracles and was a mighty teacher. We had hoped that he would redeem Israel, but our leaders sentenced him to death and crucified him. It's the third day since his death and some of our women have told us that they were at his tomb and couldn't find his body this morning. Some of our friends went to the tomb and found it just like the women said, but they couldn't find his body."

Then Jesus said, "You foolish men, why don't you believe what the prophets wrote? Didn't the prophets say that the Messiah must suffer all these things before he could enter his glory?" Then Jesus explained to them what the Scriptures said about him. Still, the men did not recognize Jesus.

They were getting close to Emmaus, and Jesus acted like he would go further, but they begged him to stay because it was evening. So, Jesus stayed with them.

When they sat down to eat, he took a loaf of bread, gave thanks, broke it, and gave it to them. Suddenly they recognized him, but he disappeared. They turned to each other and said, "Didn't our hearts burn within us while he explained the Scriptures to us?"

They got right up and ran back to Jerusalem, where the other followers of Jesus were meeting behind closed doors, fearing the Jewish leaders. When the two followers arrived, they told the disciples, "The Lord has risen and appeared to Peter." Then they told the story of how Jesus had come to them and how they had recognized him when they broke bread together.

Just as the two men were finishing their story, Jesus himself appeared and said, "Peace be with you." The whole group was frightened because they thought they were seeing a ghost. But Jesus continued, "Why are you scared and why do you doubt? Look at my hands and feet, and here is my side. Touch me, because a ghost doesn't have a body like I do."

They still didn't believe it because they were in shock. Jesus rebuked them for not trusting him and asked, "Do you have anything to eat?" They gave him a piece of broiled fish and watched him eat it.

When they finally realized that it really was him, they were euphoric. Jesus said, "Peace be with you. Just as the Father sent me, I am sending you." Then he breathed on them and said, "Receive the Holy Spirit. If you forgive anyone's sins, they are forgiven; if you don't forgive them, they aren't forgiven."

***

Thomas was not with the disciples when Jesus came, and they told him, "We've seen the Lord!"

But he replied, "I won't believe it unless I see the scars and touch them."

They were meeting all together a week later and this time, Thomas was with them. Although the doors were locked, Jesus appeared in their midst and said, "Peace be with you."

Then he turned to Thomas and said, "See my hands and my side and touch them. Stop doubting and believe."

Thomas exclaimed, "My Lord and my God!"

> **Did people think Jesus was God?**
>
> Yes, and there are many examples of him receiving worship from his followers. Jesus would not have allowed them to do this if he were not God. Other New Testament writers also claimed that he was God and all of this would be blasphemy and a capital crime if they were not 100% sure.

Jesus said, "You trust because you have seen me, but blessed are those who believe even though they haven't seen me."

***

A little while later, Peter went fishing in the Sea of Galilee with Thomas, Bartholomew, James, John, and two other disciples. They went out and caught nothing all night. At dawn they saw a man standing on the beach and he called out, "Friends, have you caught any fish?"

"No," they replied.

Jesus said, "Throw your net on the right-hand side of the boat, and you'll catch some." They did, and they were unable to pull in the net because there were so many fish.

John realized that the man on the beach was Jesus and he turned to Peter and said, "It's the Lord!" Peter put on his coat (he had stripped for work), jumped into the water, and swam to shore. Since they were only about 100 yards out, the others stayed in the boat and pulled the net to the shore. When they landed, Jesus was cooking fish on a fire, along with some bread.

"Bring some of the fish you just caught," Jesus said. Simon dragged the net onto the shore, and although there were 153 large fish, the net was not torn by their weight.

"Let's have some breakfast," Jesus said, serving out the bread and fish. None of the disciples asked if he was really Jesus because they were all sure.

After breakfast, Jesus asked Peter, "Peter, do you love me more than these?"

Peter answered, "Yes, Lord, you know that I love you."

Jesus said, "Feed my lambs."

Jesus repeated the question, "Peter, do you love me?"

Peter replied, "Yes, Lord, you know I love you."

Jesus said, "Take care of my sheep."

Once more Jesus asked, "Peter, do you love me?"

Peter was sad that Jesus asked him a third time and said, "Lord, you know all things, and you know that I love you."

> **Why did Jesus keep asking Peter if he loved him?**
>
> Throughout this exchange, Jesus and Peter are using different words for love. Jesus is using the word *agape*, which is an unfailing love that the Father has for us. Peter was using *phileo*, which is brotherly love, or affection that's not nearly as deep. However, the third time Jesus switched and used the same word that Peter had been using.

"Then feed my sheep. I tell you the truth, when you were young, you dressed yourself and went where you wanted, but when you are old, you will stretch out your hands, and someone else will dress you and take you where you don't want to go." Jesus said this to indicate how Peter would glorify God in his death. Then he said, "Follow me."

Peter turned and saw John following them and asked, "Lord, what about him?"

Jesus replied, "What difference does it make to you if I want him to stay alive until I return?" The rumor spread that John wouldn't die, but Jesus had only said that it didn't matter to Peter if he wanted John to stay alive.

"I told you that everything in the Law, the Prophets, and the Psalms must come true." Then he opened their minds so that they could understand the Scriptures and he said, "They wrote that the Messiah must suffer, die, and rise again on the third day. Preach this message to all the nations, beginning in Jerusalem, because you are witnesses of these things.

"Now I will send the Holy Spirit that my Father promised. But stay here in Jerusalem until you are clothed with power from heaven."

CHAPTER FIFTY

FINAL INSTRUCTIONS
Matthew 28:16-20; Mark 16:15-20; Luke 24:44-53; Acts 1:3-12

During the 40 days after his crucifixion, he appeared to his disciples, proving that he was alive and talking to them about the kingdom of God. One time he appeared to more than 500 of his followers at one time, and another time, he appeared to his half-brother James.

In one of these meetings, they were eating a meal, and he told them, "Don't leave Jerusalem until the Father sends the Holy Spirit. John baptized with water, but I will baptize you with the Holy Spirit in a few days."

The disciples kept asking him, "Are you going to free Israel and restore our kingdom?"

Jesus replied, "The Father sets those dates, and they're not for you to know. But when the Holy Spirit comes upon you, you will receive power and will tell people about me in Jerusalem, Judea, Samaria, and to the ends of the earth."

Then Jesus led them to Bethany, lifted his hands, and blessed them, saying, "I've been given complete authority on heaven and earth. Go into the entire world and preach the good news to everyone you meet. Make disciples of all the nations, baptizing them in the name of the Father, the Son, and the Holy Spirit. Teach them to obey everything that I've commanded you and know that I'm with you always, even to the end of the age."

While he was blessing them, he went up into the sky while they were watching, disappeared into a cloud, and sat down at God's right hand.

His disciples were staring at the sky when two white-robed men appeared and said, "Men of Galilee, why are you standing here, staring at the sky? Jesus has gone back to heaven, and someday he will return in the same way he left." Then they worshipped Jesus and joyfully walked the half-mile back to Jerusalem.

Jesus' Resurrection Appearances

Mary Magdalene	At the empty tomb, early Sunday morning. Physically touched Jesus.
Mary and the other women	Outside the tomb after hearing he had risen. Physically touched Jesus.
Peter	Saw the burial clothing in the empty tomb.
Two disciples	On the road to Emmaus. Jesus ate a meal with them.
Ten disciples (not Thomas)	Appeared amid their meeting. Saw his wounds, touched him, and watched him eat.
Eleven disciples	Saw wounds and Jesus invited Thomas to touch him.
Seven disciples	Came on the shore while they were fishing. They watched him eat food.
All disciples	Gave the Great Commission.
500 believers at one time	Paul reports the largest appearance to many people.
James	Jesus' half-brother
All disciples	Jesus' ascension. Ate a meal with him.
Paul	Jesus taught Paul individually after conversion.

After that, the disciples spent their time in the temple, praising God. Then they went out preaching the good news everywhere and God confirmed their words with many miracles.

The Second Coming

The first time that Jesus came to earth, he was a suffering servant who died and rose again to pay for our sins. He will come back a second time as a conquering king who will judge his enemies and rule forever with those who have put their faith in him. There is a lot of controversy about when he will return and the events surrounding his return, but the most crucial piece for us is that he is coming back and this should be a source of encouragement and comfort to us. With much of the world's chaos around us, it is easy to believe that his return is right around the corner, but every generation since Jesus ascended into heaven believed they would witness his return. He could come back tomorrow, 100 years from now, or 1,000 years from now.

Spread of the Church

Reorganized Concise Paraphrased Bible

Book V

By: Obadiah Paulus

MAP OF THE SPREAD OF THE CHURCH

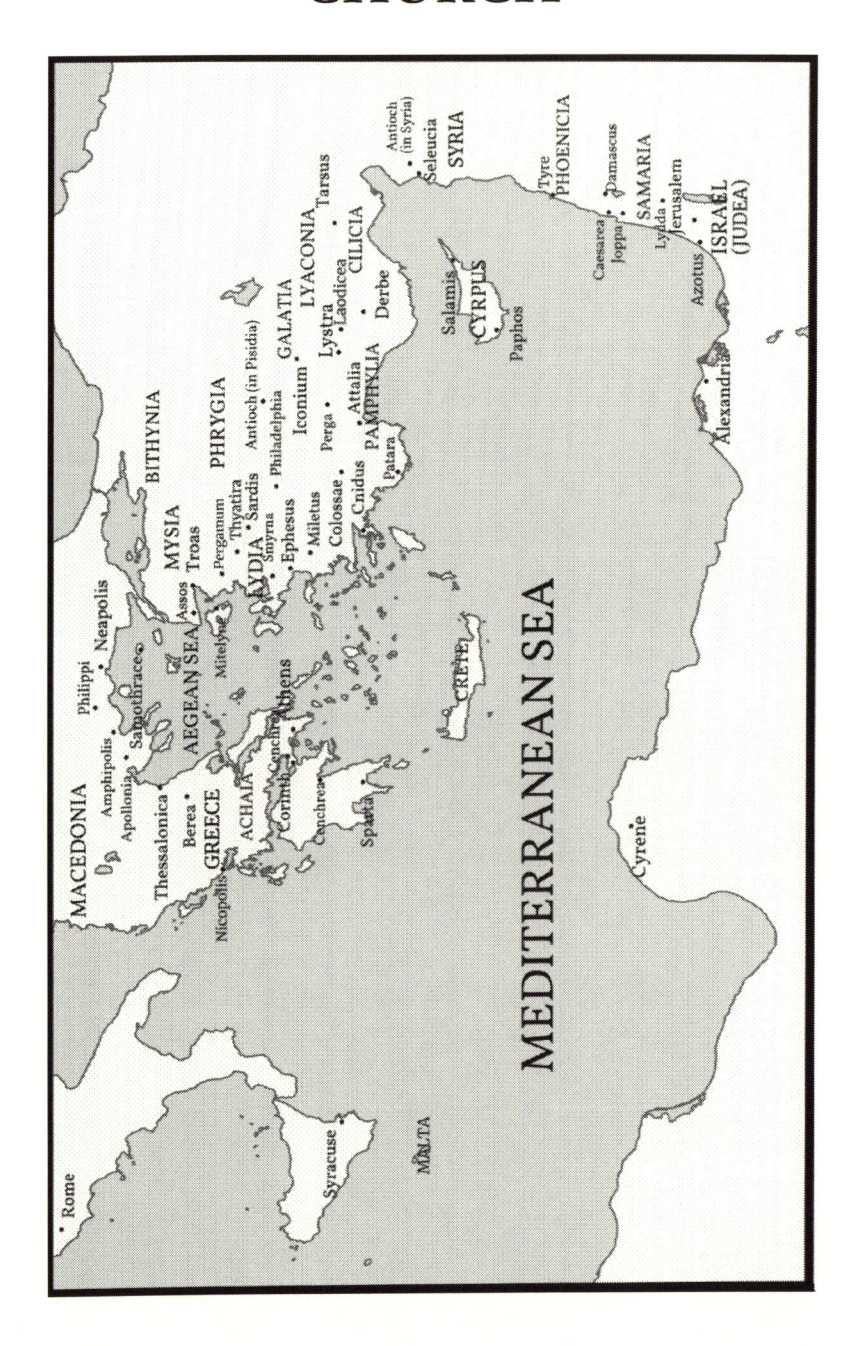

TABLE OF CONTENTS

CHAPTER 1: Beginning of the Church	203	
CHAPTER 2: First Conflict with Jewish Leaders	207	
CHAPTER 3: Ananias and Sapphira and Persecution	210	
CHAPTER 4: Stephen Martyred	213	
CHAPTER 5: Philip and the Ethiopian Eunuch	217	
CHAPTER 6: Saul's Conversion	219	
CHAPTER 7: Peter and Cornelius	221	
CHAPTER 8: The New Gentile Church	225	
CHAPTER 9: Paul's First Missionary Journey	228	
CHAPTER 10: Paul's Second Missionary Journey	233	
CHAPTER 11: Paul's Third Missionary Journey	238	
CHAPTER 12: Holy Living and the Second Coming	242	
CHAPTER 13: Clarification on Jesus' Return	246	
CHAPTER 14: Paul's Response to Corinthian Problems	249	
CHAPTER 15: Marriage and Questionable Things	255	
CHAPTER 16: Spiritual Gifts and the Resurrection	260	
CHAPTER 17: Justification by Faith in Christ	268	
CHAPTER 18: Paul's Ministry and Collection for the Saints	274	
CHAPTER 19: Paul's Defense of His Ministry	280	
CHAPTER 20: The Problem of Sin	283	
CHAPTER 21: Salvation Through Faith	287	
CHAPTER 22: Results of Salvation	291	
CHAPTER 23: Jews and Gentiles	296	
CHAPTER 24: A Transformed Life	299	
CHAPTER 25: Paul's Arrest	303	
CHAPTER 26: Paul Transferred to Caesarea	307	
CHAPTER 27: Paul's Journey to Rome	311	
CHAPTER 28: Our Riches in Christ	314	
CHAPTER 29: Rejoice in the Lord	321	
CHAPTER 30: Christ's Supremacy	326	
CHAPTER 31: Reconciliation with Onesimus	330	
CHAPTER 32: True and Practical Religion	332	
CHAPTER 33: Proper Living During Suffering	338	
CHAPTER 34: Superiority of Christ	342	
CHAPTER 35: Superiority of the New Covenant	348	

CHAPTER 36: Exhortations	352
CHAPTER 37: Leading a Church	357
CHAPTER 38: Stay Strong	363
CHAPTER 39: Finish Your Ministry	365
CHAPTER 40: Steadfast in Christ	369
CHAPTER 41: Warning Against False Teaching	373
CHAPTER 42: Jesus Came in the Flesh and Gives Eternal Life	375
CHAPTER 43: John's Second and Third Letters	381
CHAPTER 44: John's Vision and Letters to the Churches	383
CHAPTER 45: The Seven Seals and the First Five Trumpets	388
CHAPTER 46: The Sixth and Seventh Trumpets	394
CHAPTER 47: The Great Dragon and Bowls of Wrath	396
CHAPTER 48: Judgment of Babylon	402
CHAPTER 49: The Final Battle	404
CHAPTER 50: The New Jerusalem	407
EPILOGUE: What's the Point?	410

CHAPTER ONE

BEGINNING OF THE CHURCH
Acts 1:13-2:47

After Jesus ascended to heaven, the disciples returned to Jerusalem and entered the Upper Room to pray with the women who followed him. One day Peter stood up in their midst (about 120 people total) and said, "Brothers and sisters, the Scriptures had to be fulfilled about Judas betraying Jesus. He was one of us and shared in our ministry and now we must appoint someone to take his place. It should be one of the men who has been with us throughout Jesus' whole ministry, from his baptism until his ascension, so that he can tell people of all that Jesus said and did."

They put forward Joseph (also known as Barsabbas or Justus) and Matthias as potential candidates. Then they prayed and asked God to show them who should take Judas' place and then cast lots. The lot fell to Matthias and he became an apostle with the other eleven.

> **What is an apostle?**
>
> In the First Century, an apostle was a messenger sent to bear the message of the sender. With the commissioning of the Holy Spirit, Jesus' eleven remaining disciples and Matthias became apostles. Jesus' remaining disciples were Peter, James (Zebedee's son), John, Andrew, Philip, Bartholomew, Matthew, Thomas, James (Alphaeus' son), Thaddeus, and Simon. Thomas, Later, Paul became an apostle through Jesus' commissioning as well.

When the day of Pentecost came, the believers gathered in the Upper Room, and a mighty rushing wind filled the entire house. Tongues of fire rested upon them, and the Holy Spirit filled them, giving them the power to speak in other languages.

There were devout Jews from all over the region who had come to Jerusalem to worship; they came together when they heard the mighty, rushing wind. They were amazed when they saw a group of Galileans speaking in languages that the crowd understood as their native tongues. Some wondered what this meant, but others mocked them, thinking that they were drunk.

What is Pentecost?

Pentecost is the Greek name for Shavuot, the spring festival for the Jewish harvest. This was the seventh Sabbath (50 days) after Jesus' death just before Passover. Passover was the Jewish festival where the Jews commemorated God leading them out of Egypt.

Peter stood up with the other eleven apostles and said, "These men are not drunk; it is only nine in the morning! This is a fulfillment of the prophet Joel who said that God would pour out his Holy Spirit in the latter days and that his people would have visions and prophesy. He will show mighty wonders and save all who call upon his name.

"Men of Israel, Jesus of Nazareth, who did signs and wonders in your midst, was crucified by godless men to fulfill God's predetermined plan. God raised him from the dead because death couldn't hold him down. Our former king, David, said that he saw him seated on high. This gave him hope because God will not allow him to undergo decay. God made him know the paths of life and he rejoiced in his presence.

"David died, was buried, and we know where his tomb is. The Lord had promised that David would have a descendant to sit upon the throne forever, and he prophesied about the Resurrection and that Jesus would not undergo decay. Jesus rose from the dead and we are all witnesses of this fact. Now God has exalted him to the right hand of God and he has poured out the Holy Spirit on us as you have seen.

"David did not ascend to heaven, but he says, 'God said to my Lord to sit at his right hand until he makes his enemies a footstool beneath his feet.' God has made Jesus, whom you crucified, both Messiah and Lord."

> **What does Christ mean?**
>
> Christ is the Greek word for Messiah, the promised Savior of Israel and the world. The name Jesus Christ means Jesus the Messiah. The Old Testament promised that the Messiah would be God in the flesh and would eventually deliver Israel and bless the world.

Peter's message convicted the people and they asked Peter and the other apostles what they should do. Peter told them, "Every one of you should repent and be baptized in the name of Jesus Christ for the forgiveness of sins so that you may receive the Holy Spirit. This promise is for everyone who hears the message and God calls to himself." He continued to preach to them and give them evidence that they need to repent for salvation. About 3,000 of them believed and the apostles baptized them that day.

> **What is baptism? How does it work?**
>
> Baptism is the public act where we identify with Jesus' death, burial, and Resurrection. It is an outward act that is a public profession of what God has done in our hearts. This is like a married person wearing a wedding ring. The literal translation for the Greek word for baptism is to dip or immerse. Baptism should be one believer fully submerging another believer who is proclaiming their faith in Christ.
>
> Jesus commanded baptism, so it is a requirement, but it does not save us. The Bible is clear that God saves us through our faith, by grace, and there is no physical action necessary. Believers who understand their decision should be baptized to identify their internal faith.

The newly born church devoted themselves to the apostles' teaching, fellowship, sharing meals, and prayer. Everyone was in awe and the apostles performed many signs and wonders amongst them. All the people were together and shared all their possessions, selling belongings so that they could give money to whomever had need. They met daily in the temple and shared their meals with glad and generous hearts, praising

God, and gaining favor with all the people. God added people to their number every day.

> **What is the church?**
>
> The church is more than just a building where Christians meet on Sundays. The church is a group of people who worship Jesus as Lord and Savior and gather. This is the way that Jesus has chosen to spread the good news of his death, burial, and Resurrection to the world around us. The church exists on two levels, the universal and the local. The ultimate purpose is to glorify God, and it helps people know, grow, and go in Christ for God's glory.

CHAPTER TWO

FIRST CONFLICT WITH JEWISH LEADERS
Acts 3:1-4:35

One day, Peter and John were on their way to the temple for afternoon prayers when they saw a disabled man who begged at the temple entrance every day. He saw the two men coming and expected to receive some money from them, but Peter looked at him and said, "I don't have any money, but I will give you what I have. In the name of Jesus Christ, stand up and walk!"

Peter took him by the hand, pulled him to his feet, and immediately God healed his legs, and he could walk. He jumped around, praising God, and all the people who saw him were full of wonder and amazement because they recognized him as the lame beggar who daily sat at the temple gates.

The people all gathered around. Peter said, "Why are you amazed as if we made this man walk by our power? The God of our fathers has glorified Jesus, whom you crucified and rose again from the grave, and Jesus has made him well. Faith in Jesus is what made this man well even though you rejected Jesus when Pilate tried to set him free. I know that you acted in ignorance, but God foretold that this would happen. Therefore, repent from your sins so that he may forgive you and refresh you with the Holy Spirit.

"Moses said that a prophet like him would arise from you and that you should listen to him and that whoever does not listen would be destroyed. All of the prophets spoke about Jesus, and now God has raised him up to bless you by turning all of you from your wickedness."

As the disciples spoke to the people, some of the religious leaders came to listen and grew very annoyed upon hearing the teaching about Jesus and his Resurrection from the dead. This message went against their core beliefs and undermined their authority. The religious leaders arrested Peter and John and held them in jail overnight. But many more people believed and their number came to about 5,000.

The next day, the religious leaders gathered with the high priest and members of his family. They had Peter stand in their midst and asked him on what authority he did these things. Peter was filled with the Holy Spirit and he replied, "If we are on trial for a good deed that we did for a disabled man and you want to know how he was healed, listen to me. By the name of Jesus Christ of Nazareth, whom you crucified, and God raised from the dead, is this man healed and able to stand before you. Even though you rejected Jesus, he has become the cornerstone, and there is salvation with no one else but him, for there is no other name under heaven that can save us."

> **Prescriptive vs. descriptive**
>
> As we read through the Bible, we must remember that the authors wrote these books to a historical people group. While many parts of Scripture apply to our lives, we must differentiate which parts are prescriptive and descriptive.
>
> Descriptive passages describe what happened and we can draw instruction from the reason beneath the event. For example, when Peter and John healed this man, it is a description of what happened. While God still has the power to heal, not everyone we tell to "be healed" will experience healing. This is a descriptive passage of what occurred. We can use this to teach us that the power to heal is from God.
>
> Prescriptive passages tell both the original audience and us what is true or what we should do. For example, when Peter tells the people that "there is salvation with no one else but him," that is prescriptive for us as well. Generally, material from the book of Acts is descriptive, while material from the letters is prescriptive. However, there are exceptions to this rule.
>
> To know whether a passage is prescriptive or descriptive, we must determine how the original audience would understand the text. While this book has added boxes to help with this process, it will require study beyond this text's scope. One thing we can do is to look at all

> of Scripture to see if there is information that helps us determine if the message is for all people or just the original audience.

The religious leaders were astonished because they realized that these uneducated men had been with Jesus. They could not say anything to oppose Peter and John because they saw the formerly disabled man standing in front of them. They sent them out of the council and talked with each other to decide what they should do because there was no denying that a miracle had taken place. They called Peter and John back in and told them to no longer preach in the name of Jesus.

But Peter and John replied, "You decide if we should listen to you rather than God, but we cannot stop preaching what we have seen and heard." The leaders threatened them, but could not find a reason to punish them because all the people were praising God for what had happened. The man who was healed had been unable to walk for over 40 years.

After their release, Peter and John went to their friends and told them what the chief priests had said to them. When the people heard it, they lifted their voices and said, "Sovereign Lord, maker of heaven and earth, our father David wondered why the Gentiles raged and plotted in vain against the Lord and his anointed. The people of Jerusalem, Herod, Pilate, and the Gentiles fought against Jesus and the plan that you made. See the threats that they have made against us and give us boldness and power to heal through your servant, Jesus." While they were praying, the place where they gathered shook, and they were all filled with the Holy Spirit and continued to speak the Word of God with boldness.

All the people who believed were of one heart and soul, and they shared all their possessions with each other and had all things in common. The apostles were performing great acts and were testifying of what Jesus had done. There was not a needy person among them because many of them were selling their possessions and laying it at the apostles' feet.

CHAPTER THREE

ANANIAS AND SAPPHIRA AND PERSECUTION
Acts 4:36-5:42

At this time, a follower named Joseph, also known as Barnabas (which means son of encouragement), sold a field and brought the proceeds to the apostles. A man named Ananias and his wife Sapphira also sold a piece of property. They brought a portion of the profit to the apostles but said that they gave the entire amount. Peter said to Ananias, "Why has Satan filled your heart and convinced you to lie to the Holy Spirit? While you owned the property, it was in your hands, and you could do whatever you wanted with it. Why are you trying to convince us that you have done some great thing? You have not just lied to us; you have lied to God!" When Ananias heard these words, he fell down and died, and everyone was terrified. The young men took his body to bury him.

> **The Holy Spirit is God**
>
> This is one of the clearest places where the Bible establishes the Holy Spirit as the third person of the Trinity. Peter tells Ananias that he has not just lied to them, but by lying to the Holy Spirit, he has lied to God. See the note in Chapter 42 of The Life of Jesus for more information on the Holy Spirit and Chapter 8 of The Life of Jesus for more information about the Trinity.

Three hours later, Sapphira came in, not knowing what had just happened. Peter asked her if they had brought the full profit to the apostles, and she said that they had. Then Peter said, "Why have you and your husband agreed to lie to us? The men who buried your husband are outside and now they will bury you!" Then she fell down and died as well. The young men took her out and buried her with her husband. The congregation was very afraid.

> **Why was God so harsh?**
>
> From our perspective, it seems like God overreacts to Ananias and Sapphira's lie to the church. Some might even say they accomplished much good while only telling a "white lie." God was so harsh because the church was just starting, and he needed to communicate how much he hated sin so that his followers understood how important the church was. He acted this way with the Hebrews when they first came out of Egypt as well.
>
> Some don't like that God has wrath, but that is a part of his nature that we cannot ignore. God's reaction to Ananias and Sapphira's lie is what he should do anytime we sin. However, he rarely punishes our sin the moment we commit it. If God allows sin to go unpunished, then he is no longer holy. If we put our trust in Jesus, then his death pays the debt of our sin. We cannot pick and choose which of God's attributes we like and ignore the others.

***

The believers gathered regularly at Solomon's porch in the outer courts of the temple where any person could enter. While there, they performed many great signs and wonders. All the people spoke well of them, but many were afraid to join them. But people continued to join their numbers every day. They brought many sick people in the hopes that Peter's shadow would even fall upon them and the apostles healed them all.

The high priest and Sadducees were jealous, so they arrested the apostles and threw them into prison. But in the middle of the night, the angel of the Lord freed them and sent them back to the temple to preach the gospel. At daybreak, they went into the temple and preached the good news to anyone who would listen.

When the high priest came in, he called for the soldiers to bring the apostles out of prison. However, the jailors reported that the doors were locked, but that their cells were empty. The high priest was perplexed, and then some people said they were preaching the gospel just as they had previously. The officials asked the apostles to speak to them but were afraid to bring them in by force because they thought the people would riot.

The high priest asked them why they were continuing to preach when they had been commanded not to, and Peter answered, "We must obey God rather than men. The God of our fathers raised Jesus, whom you crucified, and has exalted him to his right hand as the Lord and Savior to bring Israel to repentance. We are witnesses of these things, and so is the Holy Spirit, whom God has given to those who obey him."

Furious, the council wanted to kill them all, but a Pharisee named Gamaliel stood up and said, "Men of Israel, be careful what you do with these men. Remember how Theudas claimed to be somebody and about 400 men followed him. But once he died, they scattered, and it came to nothing. Then Judas from Galilee arose during the census. Some people followed him, but then his followers scattered once he died. Leave these men alone, because if this is not from God, this movement will fizzle out. But if this is from God, you will not be able to stop them, and you may even end up fighting against the Lord!"

The council took his advice, beat the apostles, and then let them go, commanding them to stop preaching about Jesus. The apostles left, rejoicing that they had been worthy to suffer for the name of Jesus. They continued preaching every day about Jesus and kept meeting from house to house.

CHAPTER FOUR

STEPHEN MARTYRED
Acts 6:1-8:2

As the number of Christians increased, some Jewish believers complained because they felt the church was overlooking them in the daily distribution of food. The twelve apostles gathered and decided that it would be best for them to use their time preaching the gospel and praying. So, they advised the people to choose seven men who were full of the Holy Spirit to take over the church's day-to-day operations.

The people liked this idea, so they chose Stephen, Philip, Prochorus, Nicanor, Timon, Parmenas, and Nicolas, men full of the Holy Spirit. They presented them to the disciples who prayed for them and commissioned them into service. Thus, the Word of God continued to spread rapidly in Jerusalem, and several Jewish priests came to faith.

Stephen, one of the men appointed to serve, was full of God's grace and performed great wonders and signs before the people. However, Jews from the Synagogue of Freedmen opposed Stephen and began to argue with him; but they could not stand against the wisdom that the Spirit gave him.

Finally, they persuaded some men to give false testimony that Stephen had blasphemed against God and Moses. The Jews stirred up the people to grab Stephen and bring him in front of the Sanhedrin (Jewish ruling council). The false witnesses said, "This man never stops speaking against the holy place and our laws. He keeps saying that Jesus of Nazareth will destroy the temple and change the customs that Moses handed down to us." After hearing these accusations, the Sanhedrin stared at Stephen and saw that his face was like an angel's.

The high priest asked Stephen, "Are these charges true?"

Stephen replied, "Brothers and fathers, listen to me! God appeared to our father Abraham when he was still in Mesopotamia and told him to leave his home and people and go to the land God would show him. So, after his father died, Abraham left home for the land where we now live. God never gave him an inheritance here, but the Lord promised Abraham that his descendants would inherit the land, even though Abraham was childless at the time. God told him that his descendants would spend 400 years in slavery, but eventually, he would punish their captors and bring Abraham's people into the Promised Land to worship him. Then God gave Abraham the covenant of circumcision.

"Eventually, Abraham became the father of Isaac, and he circumcised his son on the eighth day. Isaac became the father of Jacob, and Jacob became the father of the twelve Patriarchs, including Joseph. Joseph's brothers were jealous of him and they sold him into slavery in Egypt. But God was with him and rescued Joseph from his troubles. He gave Joseph wisdom and allowed him to gain Pharaoh's favor, eventually becoming ruler over the land and the palace.

"Then, a famine struck the land, bringing great suffering, and our ancestors could not find any food. When Jacob heard that there was food in Egypt, he sent his sons to buy some. On their second visit, Joseph told his brothers who he was, and Pharaoh learned about Joseph's family. Joseph brought the 75 members of his family to Egypt, where they all eventually died. Our ancestors carried their bodies out of Egypt and buried them in the tomb Abraham had purchased.

"As the time came for God to fulfill his promises, our people had multiplied, and a new king who did not know Joseph came to power. He oppressed our ancestors and forced them to kill their newborn babies. During this time, Moses was born, and his family hid him for three months. When Moses' mother placed him in the Nile, Pharaoh's daughter found him and adopted him. He learned all the wisdom of the Egyptians and became mighty in word and deed."

Stephen continued, "At age 40, Moses visited his people and saw an Egyptian mistreating one of the Israelites, so Moses killed the Egyptian. Moses thought the Israelites would realize that God was using him to deliver them from the Egyptians, but he was wrong. The next day, he tried to intervene in a fight between two Israelites, but one of them pushed him away and said, 'Who made you ruler and judge over us? Are you going to kill me like you killed the Egyptian yesterday?' When Moses heard this, he fled to Midian, where he lived as a foreigner. Eventually, he had two sons.

"After 40 years in the desert, an angel appeared to Moses in a burning bush near Mount Sinai. Astounded, he went to get a better look, and the Lord spoke to him from the flames, 'I am the God of your fathers, Abraham, Isaac, and Jacob. Take off your sandals because you are standing on holy ground. I have seen the suffering of my people in Egypt and heard their groans; now, I am sending you back to Egypt to lead them to freedom.' Moses was terrified, but he returned to Egypt and led his people out, performing signs and wonders in Egypt, at the Red Sea, and in the wilderness over the next 40 years.

"Moses told the Israelites that God would raise up a prophet like him from within them. He received God's Words on Mount Sinai and brought them to our ancestors. But they refused to obey; instead, they rejected Moses and turned their hearts back to Egypt. They told Aaron, Moses' older brother, to make a god to lead them because they weren't sure what had happened to Moses. They made a golden calf into an idol, brought it sacrifices, and reveled in their hands' work.

"God turned away from them and let them worship the sun, moon, and stars. Therefore, the prophets wrote, 'Did you bring me sacrifices and offerings the 40 years you were in the wilderness? You have taken up the false gods of the local people, so I will send you into exile beyond Babylon.'

"The Lord directed Moses to build the tabernacle according to God's specifications and our ancestors carried it with them in the wilderness. Joshua took the tabernacle with them as God drove the nations of the Promised Land out before the Israelites. It stayed there until the time of David, who enjoyed God's favor and asked to build the Lord a permanent home. However, David's son Solomon built the temple even though the prophets tell us that no building can house God, no created thing can contain him.

"You stubborn people! Your hearts and ears are not able to hear God!" Stephen continued, "You are just like your ancestors, always resisting the Holy Spirit. They persecuted every prophet and even killed those that predicted the coming of Christ. Now, you have betrayed and murdered him; you have received the Law, but you have not obeyed it!"

When the Sanhedrin heard this, they were furious and raged against Stephen. But he was full of the Holy Spirit, and he looked to heaven, seeing God's glory and Jesus standing at the right hand of God. He said, "Look, I see heaven opened and the Son of man standing at the right hand of God!"

This was the last straw, and the Sanhedrin covered their ears and rushed at him, screaming at the top of their lungs. They hated that he proclaimed that Jesus was the Messiah. They dragged him out of the city and threw him to the ground. The men threw their coats at the feet of a young man named Saul, signifying that he approved their actions. Then they began to throw stones at Stephen. While they were stoning him, he prayed, "Lord Jesus, please receive my spirit and do not hold this sin against them." Then he died.

Stephen's murder started widespread persecution against the church in Jerusalem, and all the believers scattered throughout Judea and Samaria. Godly men buried Stephen and the church mourned for him. Meanwhile, Saul made war against the church, going house to house, and arresting anyone who claimed to believe in Jesus.

CHAPTER FIVE

PHILIP AND THE ETHIOPIAN EUNUCH
Acts 8:3-40

Those who had scattered preached the gospel wherever they went. Philip went to Samaria and preached there and the people listened to his message when they saw the signs he performed. He healed the lame and paralyzed and cast out many shrieking demons, and the people rejoiced.

For some time, a man named Simon had impressed people by practicing sorcery throughout Samaria. He claimed to be a great man, and all the people listened to him and proclaimed that he was the Great Power of God. They had followed Simon for a long time, but when they believed Philip's message, they were baptized. Even Simon believed, was baptized, and followed Philip everywhere.

When the apostles in Jerusalem heard that the Samaritans had believed the gospel, they sent Peter and John. When the men arrived, they prayed that the believers would receive the Holy Spirit because although the people had been baptized, they had not yet received the Spirit. When they laid their hands on the people and prayed, the believers received the Holy Spirit. Simon saw this, and he offered Peter and John money, begging for the same power.

Peter answered, "May your money die with you because you thought you could buy God's gift! You have no part of this ministry because your heart is not right. Repent from your sin and pray that God would forgive you for having such a thought. I can see that you are still full of bitterness and a slave to sin!"

Simon replied, "Pray for me that nothing you've said will happen to me." Peter and John continued to testify about Jesus and returned to Jerusalem, preaching the gospel.

***

An angel of the Lord told Philip to head south along the desert road from Jerusalem to Gaza. As he started out, he met a eunuch who was a treasurer for the Ethiopian queen. This man had gone to Jerusalem to worship, and on his way home was sitting in his chariot, reading the prophet Isaiah's words. The Holy Spirit told Philip to go up to the chariot.

Philip ran up to the eunuch and asked him if he understood what he was reading. The eunuch answered, "How can I understand unless someone explains it to me?"

Philip sat down with the man and the eunuch was studying the passage that reads, "He was led like a sheep to slaughter, and as a lamb is silent before its shearer, he did not speak. In his humiliation, he was deprived of justice. Who can speak of his descendants, for his life was taken from him?"

The eunuch asked Philip, "Is the prophet talking about himself or someone else?"

Philip began with that passage and explained the good news about Jesus. As they traveled along the road, they saw some water, and the eunuch asked what kept him from baptism. They stopped the chariot and Philip took the eunuch down to the water and baptized him.

When they came up out of the water, the Holy Spirit took Philip away; and although the eunuch did not see him any longer, he went on his way rejoicing. Philip immediately appeared in Azotus and he traveled on to Caesarea, preaching as he went.

CHAPTER SIX

SAUL'S CONVERSION
Acts 9:1-31

Meanwhile, Saul was still breathing murderous threats against the Lord's disciples. He went to the high priest and asked him to send word to Damascus' synagogues to give him permission to arrest any professing Christians and bring them back to Jerusalem. As he neared Damascus, a bright light from heaven flashed around him. He fell to the ground and heard a loud voice saying, "Saul, Saul, why are you persecuting me?"

Saul replied from his knees, "Who are you, Lord?"

The voice from heaven answered, "I am Jesus, whom you are persecuting! Now get up and go into the city where I will tell you what to do." Saul's traveling companions stood by him, speechless because although they heard the sound, they did not see anyone speaking.

Saul got up from the ground and opened his eyes, but he couldn't see anything. So, his friends took him by the hand and led him to Damascus. Once he was there, he did not eat or drink anything for three days.

There was a believer in Damascus named Ananias whom the Lord told in a vision, "Go to Judas' house on Straight Street and ask for Saul of Tarsus because he is there praying. He saw you in a vision come place hands upon him to restore his sight."

Ananias replied, "Lord, I have heard many reports about this man and all the damage he has done to Christians in Jerusalem. Now, he has come here with authority from the chief priests to arrest anyone who trusts in your name."

But the Lord insisted, "Go! I have chosen him to proclaim my name to the Gentiles, their kings, and the people of Israel. I will show him how much he must suffer for me."

Ananias obeyed and went to Judas' house. He put his hands on Saul, saying, "Brother Saul, the Lord Jesus appeared to you on the road here;

now he has sent me so that you can regain your sight and be filled with the Holy Spirit." Immediately, something like scales fell off Saul's eyes, and he could see again. Saul got up and was baptized; he ate and regained his strength.

He spent several days with the believers in Damascus and immediately started to preach in the synagogues that Jesus was the Son of God. The people were stunned because they recognized Saul as the one who persecuted the church and arrested Christians. Yet Saul continued to grow more powerful and baffled the Jews in Damascus by proving that Jesus was the Messiah.

After a while, some of the Jews conspired to assassinate Saul because they were angry Saul proclaimed Jesus as the Messiah. They kept watch day and night at the city gates, so that they could catch and kill him. Saul learned of the plan, and one night, his followers lowered him over the wall in a basket so he could escape.

Saul traveled to Jerusalem, and when he arrived, he tried to join the other disciples. But they refused because they didn't believe he was a true follower of Jesus. Barnabas took Saul under his wing and stood up for him, telling the other brothers about Saul's experience on the road to Damascus and how he had preached the gospel.

Saul stayed in Jerusalem and freely moved about the city, fearlessly preaching Jesus. He debated the Jews, and eventually, they plotted to kill him. When the other believers discovered this, they sent him to his home city of Tarsus. After Saul's departure, the church enjoyed a time of peace and growth. They lived in fear of the Lord and the Holy Spirit strengthened and encouraged them.

CHAPTER SEVEN

PETER AND CORNELIUS
Acts 9:32-11:18

Peter traveled about the country, visiting the Christians in Lydda. While he was there, he found a man named Aeneas who had been paralyzed for eight years. Peter looked at him and said, "Jesus Christ heals you. Get up and roll up your mat." Immediately, he got up and picked up his mat. All the people in Lydda and Sharon saw him and turned to the Lord.

In Joppa, there was a disciple named Tabitha who was always doing good and helping the poor. She died from an illness, and the other Christians washed her body and placed her in an upstairs room. Joppa was near Lydda, so when the believers heard that Peter was there, they sent two men who urged him to come at once.

Peter went with them and entered the upstairs room. The widows stood around the room, weeping and holding out articles of clothing that Tabitha had made. Peter sent them all out of the room and then knelt and prayed. Turning towards her, he said, "Tabitha, get up." She opened her eyes, saw Peter, and sat up. Peter took her by the hand and brought her to other believers and presented her alive. Word of this miracle spread throughout Joppa and many people trusted in the Lord. Afterward, Peter stayed in Joppa with a man named Simon.

***

At Caesarea, there was a centurion in the Italian Regiment named Cornelius. He and his family were devout and feared God, giving generously to the needy and praying regularly. One day, at about three in the afternoon, he saw an angel who called to him. Surprised, Cornelius said, "What is it, Lord?"

The angel answered, "Your prayers and gifts to the poor have come before the Lord as a memorial offering. Send men to Joppa to bring back a man named Peter, who is staying with a man named Simon." When the angel left, Cornelius called two soldiers, including one of his attendants, and told them what the angel had said. He sent the men to Joppa to bring back Peter.

Around noon the following day, Peter was praying on the roof as the two men approached Simon's house. While lunch was prepared, Peter fell into a trance. He saw heaven open and something like a large sheet coming down by its four corners. It contained all kinds of animals, including both clean and unclean birds and reptiles. A voice told him to get up and eat, but Peter protested that he had never eaten anything unclean.

> **Unclean food**
>
> In the Old Testament, God gave the Jews many rules about what they could eat. Forbidden food was considered unclean. Most of the foods that God declared unclean were because they were difficult to prepare healthily. God used the laws about unclean food as an analogy for people. The Jews considered Gentiles (non-Jews) unclean, but God was showing his people that all people were worthy of his love.

The voice spoke to him, "Don't call anything unclean that the Lord has made clean." This vision happened three times and then the sheet went back into heaven. While Peter wondered what the vision meant, Cornelius' men arrived at Simon's house and asked for Peter. As he continued to ponder, the Holy Spirit told him to go with the men without misgivings.

Peter went down and asked the men why they had come. The two soldiers told him, "We have come from Cornelius, a God-fearing centurion who is respected by all the Jewish people. An angel had told him to send for you so that he can hear what you have to say."

Peter invited them into the house as his guests. The next day, Peter went with the men and some of the other believers from Joppa. Cornelius, along with many of his friends and family, was expecting them. When Peter arrived, Cornelius bowed down to worship him, but Peter said, "Stand up, I'm just a man like you."

Peter saw the gathered people and said, "You all know that it is unlawful for a Jew to visit or associate with anyone from another nation, but God has shown me that I should not call any person common or unclean. So, here I am. Why did you send for me?"

Cornelius answered, "Four days ago, I was praying around three in the afternoon when I saw a man in bright clothing who told me that God had heard my prayers and that I should send for you in Joppa. Now that you are here, we have all gathered to hear what God has told you to say."

Peter opened his mouth and said, "Now I understand that God does not show partiality, and he accepts anyone who fears him and does what's right. You all know the good news that God sent to Israel, proclaiming peace through Jesus Christ. How, beginning with John's baptism, God anointed him with the Holy Spirit and power; he went around doing good and healing those under the Devil's control because God was with him. We are all witnesses of what Jesus did amongst the Jews in both the country and Jerusalem. They crucified him, but on the third day, God raised him from the dead, and he appeared to those that he chose to be his witnesses. Not everyone saw him, but we ate and drank with him after his Resurrection.

"Jesus commanded us to preach to the people and testify that he has been appointed by God to judge the living and the dead. All the prophets spoke of him and wrote that all who trust in him have their sins forgiven."

While Peter was still speaking, the Holy Spirit fell on his audience. The circumcised believers with Peter were amazed that the Gentiles had the Holy Spirit as they heard them speak in tongues and praise God. Peter said, "They have received the Holy Spirit, just as we have, surely we cannot keep them from being baptized." Then Peter commanded them to be baptized. The new believers asked Peter to stay with them for several days.

The apostles and other Christians in Judea heard that the Gentiles had received the Word of God. So, when Peter returned home, the circumcised believers criticized him for eating with uncircumcised men. But Peter told them the entire story of his vision and visit to Cornelius in Caesarea. He argued that if God had given them the same gift, they couldn't stop it. When the other believers heard this, they had no further objections, and they glorified God, saying, "God has granted life-giving repentance to even the Gentiles."

CHAPTER EIGHT

THE NEW GENTILE CHURCH
Acts 11:19-12:25

The believers who had scattered during the persecution after Stephen's death traveled throughout the known world, spreading the message only to Jews. But some men from Cyrene and Cyprus went to Antioch (a Gentile city in Syria) and preached to them as well. The Lord's hand was with them, and many people believed and turned to the Lord.

This report came to the church in Jerusalem and they sent Barnabas to Antioch. When Barnabas arrived, he was glad to see God's grace, and he encouraged the people of Antioch to remain strong in their faith and purpose. He was a good man, full of the Holy Spirit and faith, and he helped lead many people to the Lord.

Barnabas went to Tarsus to look for Saul and brought him back to Antioch. They stayed with the new church for a year, teaching many people. Antioch was the first place that believers were called Christians; it was meant to be an insult, like "little Christs."

During this time, some prophets came to Antioch from Jerusalem. One of them, named Agabus, stood up and foretold the famine during the reign of Claudius (around 45 A.D.). Thus, the Antioch Christians determined to send support and relief to those living in Judea. After collecting what they could, they sent it to the elders in Jerusalem with Saul and Barnabas.

***

Around that time, King Herod began violently persecuting the church by arresting some of them. He had James, John's brother, executed. When Herod saw that this made the people happy, he arrested Peter during the Festival of Unleavened Bread. Herod imprisoned Peter intending to bring him to trial after Passover; he put him under 16 soldiers' care to ensure there was no chance that he could escape. While Peter was in jail, the church prayed for him.

On the night Herod was going to bring Peter out to trial, he was chained to two soldiers with two others standing watch at the door. Suddenly, an angel appeared in the cell along with a bright shining light. The angel woke Peter by hitting him in the side and said, "Get up and get dressed quickly." The chains fell off Peter's hands, and he quickly put on his clothes, sandals, and cloak.

Peter followed the angel, not knowing if what was happening was real or a dream. Peter followed the angel past the two soldiers guarding the prison to the iron gate to the city. The gate opened for them on its own, and they walked out and then down the street when the angel suddenly left them.

When Peter finally realized what was happening, he said, "Now I know the Lord has rescued me from Herod and everything the Jews expected to happen."

He hurried to Mary's house, the mother of John Mark (a believer who wrote the book of Mark), where many believers had gathered to pray. He knocked on the door and a servant named Rhoda answered. She recognized his voice, but in her joy, she ran to tell the others instead of letting him in. They told her that she was out of her mind and that it was only Peter's angel. Peter kept knocking, and when they finally let him in, the believers were astonished. Peter motioned for them to be quiet and then he told them how the Lord had led him out of prison.

When morning came, the soldiers were frantic over what had become of Peter. After Herod searched for Peter and could not find him, he questioned the guards and then ordered their execution. Peter left for Caesarea and spent time there.

***

Herod was angry with the people of Tyre and Sidon and forbade food exports to them. The people persuaded Blastus, the king's chamberlain, to give them an audience with Herod because they depended on royal provisions of food. On the appointed day, Herod put on his robes and gave a speech to the gathered masses.

When he finished, the people roared in approval and chanted, "The voice of a god and not a man!" Immediately, an angel of the Lord struck

Herod down because he did not give God the glory; worms ate his insides, and he died.

***

The gospel continued to spread and more people believed. Once Saul and Barnabas had finished their work, they returned to Antioch from Jerusalem, bringing John Mark along with them.

CHAPTER NINE

PAUL'S FIRST MISSIONARY JOURNEY
Acts 13-15

At the church in Antioch, there were prophets and teachers: Barnabas, Simeon (also called Niger), Lucius of Cyrene, Manaen (a member of Herod the tetrarch's court), and Saul. They worshipped the Lord and fasted, and the Holy Spirit told them to send Barnabas and Saul on a special mission. After more fasting and prayer, they laid their hands on Barnabas and Saul and sent them off.

After being set apart by the Holy Spirit, Saul and Barnabas went to Seleucia with John Mark, and together they sailed for Cyprus. When they arrived at Salamis, they preached in the synagogues. They made their way through the whole island as far as Paphos and came across a Jewish false prophet named Elymas (also known as Bar-Jesus), who practiced the magic arts. A local governor, Sergius Paulus, an intelligent man, called for Saul and Barnabas to hear the Word of God. But the magician tried to stop them because he wanted to keep political power.

Saul (who was now going by Paul) looked at Elymas and said, "You son of the Devil! You are the enemy of righteousness, full of evil and lies! When will you stop perverting God's ways!? Now his hand is on you and you will be completely blind for a time!" Immediately, mist and darkness fell upon Elymas, and he stumbled around, looking for someone to guide him. When Sergius Paulus saw what had happened, he believed, astonished by the Word of the Lord.

***

After this, Paul and his companions sailed from Paphos to Perga in Pamphylia. John Mark left them, but the rest continued to Antioch (in Pisidia). One Sabbath, they went to the synagogue and sat down. After the reading of Scripture, the leaders asked them if they had any word of encouragement.

Paul stood up, quieted the crowd, and said, "Men of Israel and those who fear God, listen to me. The God of Israel chose our fathers and made them great while they were in Egypt and then led them out with his power. God put up with them in the wilderness for 40 years before driving out seven Canaanite nations and gave them the land as an inheritance.

They lived there for 450 years and God gave them judges until the prophet Samuel. Then our ancestors asked for a king, and God gave them Saul, a Benjamite, for 40 years. When God removed Saul, he raised up David, the son of Jesse, a man after God's heart who would do his will. From this man's offspring, God brought Israel a Savior in Jesus, as he promised. Before Jesus came, John the Baptist preached a baptism of repentance to all Israel. As John was finishing his ministry, he testified that he was not the Messiah and was unfit to untie the Savior's sandals. Fellow Israelites and God-fearing Gentiles, he has sent us this message of salvation.

"The people of Jerusalem and their rulers did not recognize the Savior or understand their prophets that they hear every Sabbath; they fulfilled the prophets' message by condemning the Messiah to death. Even though he hadn't committed any crime, Pilate had him crucified. When they had fulfilled all the prophecies about him, they took him off the cross and buried him in a tomb. But God raised Jesus from the dead and he appeared for many days to his followers who now testify about him.

"Now we bring you the good news of what God promised our fathers, that he fulfilled by raising Jesus from the dead. The second Psalm promised, 'You are my Son and I am your Father.' God raised him from the dead to not rot; God gave him the holy blessings promised to David. After David served God's purpose, he died, and his body rotted; but the same is not true of Jesus.

"Now, I proclaim to you the forgiveness of sins through Jesus, and he can free you from everything that the Law couldn't. Beware that what the prophets warned doesn't come true about you, that he will do an amazing work in your time and you won't even know it if someone told you about it."

As the people left, they begged that Paul and Barnabas would come back the next week to tell them more. They encouraged the Jews and converts to continue in God's grace.

The next Sabbath, almost the entire city came out to hear God's Word. But when the Jews saw the crowds, they were jealous and began to contradict and revile Paul and Barnabas. But the men spoke out boldly, "You needed to hear God's Word first. But since you think you are unworthy of eternal life, we are turning to the Gentiles. God has commanded us to be a light to the Gentiles so that we can spread salvation to the whole earth."

When the Gentiles heard this, they rejoiced and glorified God, and as many as he appointed to eternal life believed.

The Word of the Lord spread throughout the region. But the leading men and women stirred up the people, persecuted Paul and Silas, and drove them out of the city. Paul and Silas shook the dust off their feet and went to Iconium and the Holy Spirit filled the disciples with joy.

***

In Iconium, Paul and Barnabas went to the synagogue and preached so effectively that many Jews and Gentiles accepted the gospel. But the unbelieving Jews stirred up the Gentiles and poisoned their minds against these new ideas. Paul and Barnabas stayed there for a long time, preaching boldly about God's grace, and performing miracles by his power.

The city was divided; some sided with the Jews and some with Paul and Barnabas. When they learned they were to be stoned, Paul and Barnabas fled to Lystra and Derbe, where they preached the gospel throughout the region.

In Lystra, they met a man disabled since birth. As he listened, Paul looked at him, saw that he had the faith for healing, and said in a loud voice, "Stand on your feet!" Immediately, he jumped up and began walking.

When people saw this, they cried out in their native language, "The gods have come down to us as men." They called Barnabas Zeus and Paul

Hermes because he was the primary speaker. The temple of Zeus was near the city gates and the local priest brought out garlands and oxen to sacrifice.

When Paul and Barnabas realized what was happening, they tore their garments and rushed into the crowd, crying out, "Men, why are you doing this? We are humans, just like you! We bring you good news so that you would turn away from these false gods to the living God who created everything. In the past, he allowed people to do their own thing, but he did not leave himself without witness, he gave you rains and fruitful seasons of harvest, satisfying you with good things." Even with this, they barely stopped the people from offering them sacrifices.

Some Jews from Iconium and Antioch (in Pisidia) came to Lystra and incited the crowds to stone Paul and leave him for dead outside the city. But as the disciples gathered around him, Paul got up and went back into town.

The next day, he and Barnabas left for Derbe. While there, they preached the gospel and made many converts. Then they returned to Lystra, Iconium, and Antioch, strengthening and encouraging the believers. They appointed elders in each church and taught them that they must face many trials as they entered the kingdom of God.

Paul and Barnabas continued their journey through Pisidia, Pamphylia, Perga, and Attilla before they returned to Antioch. They gathered the church together and told them all that God had done during their travels, and they stayed there for quite some time.

***

Some men came to Antioch from Judea, teaching the new Christians must be circumcised to be saved. Paul and Barnabas debated with them, and eventually, they decided to send some men to Jerusalem to ask the apostles and other elders about this issue. As they passed through Phoenicia and Samaria, they told the believers how the Gentiles had come to faith, and everyone rejoiced together.

***

When they arrived in Jerusalem, the church welcomed them, and the men from Antioch told them everything that had been happening. Some of the Pharisees who had become believers stood up and protested that all Christians need to be circumcised to keep Moses' Law. Peter gathered the apostles and elders to discuss the matter.

After much debate, Peter stood up and said, "Brothers, you know that God decided that the Gentiles would believe the gospel when I preached to them. God knows the heart, and he bore witness to their faith by giving them the Holy Spirit, just like he gave to us. He made no distinction between them and us because he cleansed their hearts by faith. Now, why are you testing God by putting a yoke on these brothers that none of us have been able to bear? We believe that they will be saved by the grace of God alone, just as we will."

Then Paul and Barnabas told them everything God had done through them with the Gentiles. Once they finished, James said, "We have heard how God visited the Gentiles to make a people for his name. The prophets agree with this when they write that God said, 'I will return to rebuild the fallen tent of David, so that the rest of the world may call on the Lord and be saved.'

Therefore, I think we should not make it any harder for Gentiles who turn to God. We should write a letter telling them to stay away from things polluted by idols, sexual sin, meat from strangled animals, and blood. For the Law of Moses has been proclaimed in every city and is preached every Sabbath in the synagogues."

The church in Jerusalem sent Paul, Barnabas, Judas Barsabbas, and Silas to the church in Antioch with a letter summarizing their decision. The people rejoiced in the message; they rejoiced because of its encouragement. Judas Barsabbas and Silas strengthened the church with many words and then returned to Jerusalem. But Paul and Barnabas stayed in Antioch, preaching the gospel with many others.

CHAPTER TEN

PAUL'S SECOND MISSIONARY JOURNEY
Acts 16-18

After a while, Paul told Barnabas that he wanted to go back through the cities where they had preached to see how the believers were doing. Barnabas and Paul argued about bringing John Mark with them; finally, they separated. Barnabas went with John Mark to Cyprus while Paul went through Syria and Cilicia with Silas.

Paul and Silas traveled through Derbe to Lystra, where they met a disciple named Timothy, who had a believing Jewish mother and a Greek father. He had a good reputation with the churches in Lystra and Iconium because of the work he had done there. Paul wanted to bring Timothy with them, so Paul circumcised him so it wouldn't be an issue with the Jews who knew his father was a Greek. Even though it wasn't necessary, Paul wanted to avoid the arguments. They delivered the apostles' letter to the churches they visited, strengthening their faith and increasing their numbers.

***

The Holy Spirit forbade them to preach in Asia, so they went through Phrygia and Galatia. They attempted to go to Bithynia, but the Spirit did not allow them, so they went to Troas. One night, a vision appeared to Paul of a Macedonian man urging him to help them. Paul concluded that God wanted him to preach the gospel in Macedonia, so they went there. Luke began traveling with Paul at this time.

They made their way to Philippi, sailing through Samothrace and Neapolis, staying there for many days. One Sabbath day, they went outside the city gate to the river, where a group of women had gathered to pray. One of the women named Lydia was from Thyatira; she sold expensive goods and worshipped the Lord. God opened her heart to believe and she was baptized along with the rest of her household. After this, she urged Paul and Silas to stay at her house as her guests.

One day, on their way to the place of prayer, they met a servant girl who communicated with demons and had made her masters lots of money by fortune-telling. She followed them, crying out, "These men are servants of the Highest God and they proclaim the way of salvation!" She kept this up for many days.

Eventually, Paul became so annoyed that he turned to the girl and said, "I command you in the name of Jesus Christ to come out of her!" The evil spirit left her.

When her masters saw that their potential to profit was gone, they seized Paul and Silas and dragged them into the marketplace before the city leaders. The men accused Paul and Silas of disturbing the city and advocating breaking Roman law. The crowd joined in with some of the leaders, tearing Paul and Silas' clothes off, and ordering some soldiers to beat them. After many blows, they threw Paul and Silas into the city's highest security jail cell.

Around midnight, Paul and Silas were singing praises to God loud enough for all the jail to hear. Suddenly, there was a great earthquake, all the prison doors opened, and the shackles fell off the prisoners. When the jailer saw this, he drew his sword to kill himself, thinking that the prisoners had escaped. But Paul cried out, "Don't hurt yourself; we are all here!"

The jailer called for lights and fell down in fear at Paul and Silas' feet. He brought them out and asked, "What must I do to be saved?"

Paul and Silas replied, "Trust in the Lord Jesus and he will save you and your household." They continued to share the good news with them and the jailer believed. Within the hour, he was baptized, and then he tended to Paul and Silas's injuries and gave them food to eat. He celebrated with his family that he had believed in Jesus.

In the morning, the city leaders gave the order to set Paul and Silas free. When the jailer tried to let them go, Paul said, "They publicly beat two Roman citizens without a trial and then threw us in prison; now they want to let us out secretly? No, they need to let us out themselves!"

The police reported Paul's words to the city leaders, and they were afraid when they found out that Paul and Silas were Roman citizens. The leaders went to them, apologized, and begged them to leave the city. Paul and Silas left the jail and went to visit with Lydia. After encouraging the other believers there, Paul and Silas left the city.

***

They passed through Amphipolis and Apollonia on their way to Thessalonica, where there was a synagogue. For three consecutive Sabbaths, Paul went into the synagogue, to reason with the Jews. He explained from the Scriptures that the Messiah must suffer and die and that it was Jesus. Some Jews were convinced and joined Paul and Silas, including many devout Greeks and leading women.

But the Jews were jealous; they formed a mob with some worthless men, set the city in an uproar, and attacked one of the members of Jason's house where Paul and Silas were staying. When the mob discovered Paul and Barnabas weren't there, they dragged Jason and some of the believers before the city authorities yelling, "These men have turned the world upside down and now they've come here to stay with Jason. They are breaking Caesar's laws by claiming that Jesus is king!" Hearing this threw the crowd into an uproar. Jason posted bond and they let them go.

As soon as it was night, the church sent Paul and Silas to Berea, where they went to the synagogue. These Jews were nobler than those in Thessalonica; they heard the Word with gladness, daily examining the Scriptures to see if this message was true. Many people believed, including many influential Greek women and men.

But when the Jews from Thessalonica heard that Paul had gone to Berea, they came there too and stirred up the crowds. The brothers immediately sent Paul away by boat, leaving Silas and Timothy to stay. Paul sailed as far as Athens and sent the ship back for Silas and Timothy, while Paul remained.

***

While Paul was waiting for them in Athens, he saw that the city was full of idols, which provoked his spirit. He reasoned with Jews and devout Greeks in the synagogue and whoever would listen to him in the marketplace. Some of the philosophers gathered to listen to Paul. Some thought he was insane, and others saw him as a preacher of foreign gods because he proclaimed Jesus and the Resurrection.

So, Paul stood up in the Areopagus (a local meeting place) and said, "Men of Athens, I see that you are very religious. I've seen your objects of worship; I even saw a plaque to the unknown god. I proclaim to you the God you don't know. The God who made heaven, earth, and everything in it does not live in man-made temples, nor is he served by humans as if he needs anything since he made everything. He made all the nations of the earth from one man, and he set forth their allotted times and boundaries so that they might search for God and find him. He is not far from us because, 'in him, we live, move, and have our life' and even as some of your poets have said, 'we are his children.'

"Being God's children, we should not think of God as gold, silver, stone, or anything else that can be made by human hands or from our imagination. God has overlooked our times of ignorance, but now he commands all people everywhere to repent because he will one day judge the world by the righteousness of Jesus, whom he raised from the grave."

When he spoke of resurrection, some mocked, but some desired to hear him again. Paul left them, but some people believed, including an Athenian aristocrat named Dionysus and a woman named Damaris.

After this, Paul left Athens and went to Corinth. He met a Jew named Aquila, who had recently come from Italy with his wife Priscilla because Claudius had kicked all Jews out of Rome. They were tentmakers by trade, so Paul stayed and worked with them. Every Sabbath, he went to the synagogue and reasoned with both Jews and Greeks. When Silas and Timothy arrived, Paul devoted himself exclusively to preaching the Word, testifying that Jesus was the Messiah. When the Jews opposed him, he shook out his coat in protest and said, "Your blood be on your heads! I am innocent. From now on, I will only preach to the Gentiles."

He left there and went to the house of Titius Justus, a man who worshipped God and lived next to the synagogue. Crispus, the synagogue leader, believed in the Lord, along with his entire household, gave him a place to preach, and many people believed and were baptized.

One night, the Lord spoke to Paul in a vision and said, "Don't be afraid, keep speaking because I am with you and will protect you; I have many people in this city." So, Paul stayed there for 18 months, teaching the Word of God.

***

But when a man named Gallio became a trusted advisor to the governor of Achaia, the Jews made a united attack against Paul. They brought him to court, accusing him of breaking the Law by teaching people to worship God.

When Paul opened his mouth to defend himself, Gallio said, "Jews, if this were a matter of some vicious or actual crime, I would listen. But since this is an issue of your Law, figure it out yourselves. I refuse to be the judge of such things." He kicked them out of court, and the Jews grabbed Sosthenes, the new head of the synagogue, and beat him in front of the court. But Gallio paid no attention.

Paul eventually left for Syria with Priscila and Aquila. When he arrived at Cenchrea, Paul cut his hair because he was keeping a vow. When they arrived in Ephesus, he left his companions and went to the synagogue to reason with the Jews. They begged him to stay longer, but he declined, saying, "If God wills, I will return."

When he got to Caesarea, he greeted the church and then proceeded on to Antioch. He spent some time there and then went on through the regions of Galatia and Phrygia, strengthening the believers.

A Jew named Apollos, a native of Alexandria, came to Ephesus. He spoke well and knew the Scriptures. Apollos had learned the way of the Lord and being fervent in spirit, he taught accurately about Jesus, but he only knew about John's baptism. He boldly preached in the synagogue, but when Priscila and Aquila heard him, they took him aside and better explained the gospel. When Apollos wanted to go to Achaia, the church encouraged him and wrote letters to support his mission. When he arrived, he helped those who had believed by the grace of God. He powerfully refuted the Jews by proving that Jesus was the Messiah.

CHAPTER ELEVEN

PAUL'S THIRD MISSIONARY JOURNEY
Acts 19-20

While Apollos was in Corinth, Paul traveled in-land until he came to Ephesus, where he found a group of about twelve believers. He asked if they had received the Holy Spirit and they answered that they didn't know about it. When Paul heard this, he asked about their baptism, and they told them that they only knew of John's baptism. So, Paul said, "John preached a baptism of repentance telling people to believe in Jesus, who came after John. Upon hearing this, they were baptized in the name of the Lord Jesus. Paul laid his hands on them, the Holy Spirit filled them, and they began speaking in tongues and prophesying.

Paul went into a synagogue and spent three months boldly proclaiming the gospel, trying to persuade people about the kingdom of God. But some people were stubborn and refused to believe. They even maligned the faith to others in the congregation; so, Paul took the believers and taught them daily in the hall of Tyrannus. They met for about two years, and eventually, all the Jews and Greeks in Asia heard the gospel.

God was doing amazing miracles through Paul; even the handkerchiefs and aprons he had touched were able to heal people and cast out demons. There were seven sons of a Jewish high priest named Sceva who were traveling around casting out demons. They saw that the name of Jesus had power over evil spirits. They tried to cast out a demon in "the name of Jesus whom Paul proclaims."

But the demon possessing the man replied, "I know Jesus, and I recognize Paul, but who are you?" Then the possessed man jumped on the seven men and gave them such a beating that they ran out of the house naked and bleeding. This story became known to all the residents of Ephesus; they were frightened and spoke highly of the Lord.

Many new believers publicly confessed their sins and many who had practiced magic arts brought their books and publicly burned them. The total value of their books was worth the annual wages of about 160 people. The Word of the Lord continued to increase.

***

After this, Paul decided to go through Macedonia and Achaia on his way to Jerusalem and eventually Rome. Before leaving, he sent Timothy and Erastus to Macedonia and stayed a little longer in Asia.

Before Paul could leave, there was another controversy. A silversmith named Demetrius, who made shrines to Artemis, met with his fellow craftsmen. He said, "Men, you know that we have made lots of money from making shrines to Artemis, but Paul is preaching all over the world that any god people can make is not worthy of worship. We run the risk of losing our profession and having the temple of Artemis and our beloved goddess becoming irrelevant."

This made the craftsmen furious and they began crying out, "Great is Artemis of the Ephesians!" The city was in chaos, and a mob dragged Gaius and Aristarchus (two Macedonians traveling with Paul) into the local theater.

Paul wanted to go into the theater to defend himself and his friends, but the other disciples and some of the locals urged him not to. There was a lot of confusion and most people didn't even know why they were there. Some Jews prompted a man named Alexander to come forward and he tried to calm the crowd down to explain the situation. But when the people recognized that he was a Jew, they chanted, "Great is Artemis of the Ephesians!" for about two hours.

Finally, the town clerk was able to settle the people down, and he said, "Men of Ephesus, everyone knows that we Ephesians are the keepers of Artemis' temple and the sacred stone that fell from the sky. Since this is common knowledge, don't do anything rash. You have brought these men here even though they haven't committed any crimes against our goddess. So, if Demetrius or the craftsmen want to file a complaint, let them do it in court. We are in great danger of being accused of rioting today and we really don't have a reason for this commotion." Then he dismissed the crowd.

Once things calmed down, Paul encouraged the other believers and then left for Macedonia. He encouraged the local churches as he passed through until he reached Greece. Paul stayed there for three months until he uncovered a plot against him. Retracing his steps through Macedonia, he sent several of his companions ahead of him to Troas and caught up with them after the Feast of Unleavened Bread.

***

One Sunday, the church gathered in an upper room to eat together, and Paul talked with them until late in the evening. Around midnight, a young man named Eutychus was sitting in a third-floor window, and he fell into a deep sleep. As Paul went on, Eutychus fell out of the window and died when he hit the ground.

Paul went out, bent over the young man, and then told the crowd that he was okay because his life was still in him. Paul took communion and continued to talk with people until he left in the morning. The people welcomed Eutychus back and were very comforted.

Paul went to Assos and then boarded a ship to Mitylene. While there, he called for the elders of Ephesus to come to him because he wanted to get to Jerusalem by Passover. When they arrived, Paul said to them, "You know how I lived with you from the first day I arrived. I served the Lord with humility and tears and how the Jews plotted to destroy me. You know how I kept teaching you anything profitable from house to house. I preached to everyone I could about repentance toward God and faith in the Lord Jesus.

"Now I'm headed to Jerusalem, and I don't know what will happen except that the Holy Spirit has told me that I will face imprisonment and persecution everywhere I go. However, I don't value my life; I only want to finish the race and ministry given to me by Jesus, to share the gospel of God's grace.

"I know that I will never see any of you again. I am innocent of everyone's blood because I never shied away from preaching the gospel. Watch out for yourselves and the church that God has made you elders of because he bought it with his blood. After I leave, savage wolves will come in to attack the church, and men from your midst will come to draw away believers. Therefore, be alert! Remember that for three years,

I never stopped warning each of you with tears. Now I commend you to God and the Word of Grace, which can build you up and give you an inheritance with those who are holy.

"I never took anything from anyone; instead, I worked to provide for myself. In everything I've done, I've shown you that by working hard and helping the weak, we remember the words of Jesus, 'it is more blessed to give than receive.'"

After saying this, he knelt and prayed for them all. There were many tears, and they all hugged Paul, sad that they would never see him again. Then they accompanied him to his ship.

CHAPTER TWELVE

HOLY LIVING AND THE SECOND COMING
I Thessalonians 1-5

> **Paul's first letter to Thessalonica**
>
> The first letter to the Thessalonians was the first letter written to a congregation during the spread of the church. Paul founded the church during his second missionary journey when he had the vision of a Macedonian man asking for his assistance. The church was in its infant stages and Paul (along with Silas and Timothy) wrote within a year or two after leaving. Paul sent Timothy back to Thessalonica to check on them and this letter was Paul's response to Timothy's report.
>
> Thessalonica was the capital of Macedonia, located on a harbor with a significant highway. The church was a mix of Jews and Gentiles. It struggled in its infancy because some of the Thessalonian Jews were so set against Christianity that they had started a riot during Paul and Timothy's first visit.
>
> Timothy's report was mostly good, although the church was unsure of their standing in Christ and matters of Jesus' Second Coming. Paul wrote to them about holy living as believers and instructed them on Christ's return.

We always thank God for you when we pray because of the work your faith and love have produced and your endurance in the hope of our Lord Jesus Christ. We know that he chose you because the gospel came to you with power, the Holy Spirit, and deep conviction. You imitated our lives as we imitate the Lord and now many believers follow your example in suffering. We don't need to tell others about you because news has spread about your faith and service to God.

Our visit to you was productive after our suffering in Philippi because, with God's help, we preached boldly. Our appeal to you is not a mistake or deceit; on the contrary, we speak as God has approved us to preach the gospel. We aren't trying to please men or seek their approval; God is our witness that we didn't use flattery or a mask to cover our true intentions. As apostles, we could have asserted our authority over you; but instead, we cared for you as a mother cares for her children. We loved you so much that we shared our lives with you as well as the gospel.

You remember our toil and hardship as we worked without stopping so that we wouldn't be a burden to anyone while we preached. You and God know how holy, righteous, and blameless we were; how we treated you like a father treats his children, encouraging, comforting, and urging you to live a life worthy of God who called you.

We continually thank God because you accepted our teaching as God's Word. You imitated God's churches in Judea and suffered the same things they were experiencing at the hands of those who killed the Lord Jesus. These oppressors displease God and oppose humanity to keep us from preaching and saving people. They are heaping guilt upon themselves until God pours out his wrath on them at the end.

We are apart from you for a while, and we've tried to visit you, but Satan stood in our way. You are our hope, joy, and the crown of glory that Jesus will give us when he comes again. When we couldn't stand it anymore, we sent Timothy to you to strengthen and encourage your faith so that our trials wouldn't unsettle you. We were destined for this and we told you this would happen. We were afraid that Satan had tempted you and that our work might have been in vain.

Now that Timothy has returned to us, he has brought good news to us about your faith and love and given us pleasant memories of our time with you. During our persecution, your faith encouraged us since you are standing firm in the Lord. We cannot thank God enough because of the joy you give us. We continuously pray for you that we might see you again and strengthen your faith. May he cause your love to overflow for others just as our love overflows for you. May he strengthen your hearts so that you will be blameless and holy before our God and Father when Jesus comes again.

***

As for other matters, we instructed you how to please God, just as you have been. Now we ask you to go even further because God wants you to be holy, avoid sexual immorality, and control your body in an honorable manner. Don't live in lust like the pagans who don't know God and take advantage of each other. God has called you to holiness and not impurity; anyone who ignores this is ignoring the Holy Spirit.

I don't need to tell you anything about brotherly love. God has already taught you this and you are already doing it. Keep going and aspire to live quietly, minding your own business, and doing your work as we showed you. Then you may behave properly and live independently.

We want to inform you about those who have died so that you don't grieve like others who don't have hope. Since we believe Jesus died and rose again, we think that he will bring them with him. The Lord declares that those who are still alive when Jesus returns will not precede those who have died.

Jesus will descend from heaven with a commanding cry, the voice of an archangel, and God's trumpet. The dead in Christ will rise first and then those who are still alive will join with them in the clouds to meet the Lord. Then we will be with him forever. Encourage each other with these words.

The Day of the Lord will come like a thief in the night when people least expect it. But you are not in the dark, you are children of the light and should not be surprised by his return. Stay awake and be sober because people sleep and get drunk in the dark. Since we belong to the Lord, be sober, put on faith and love as a breastplate, and the hope of salvation as a helmet.

God did not appoint us to suffer wrath, but for salvation through Christ; he died for us so that we can live with him whether we are dead or alive. Encourage and build each other with these words.

Respect those who work hard at caring for you in the Lord. Esteem them with love because of their labor. Warn those who are idle and disruptive, encourage the fainthearted, help the weak, live in peace, and be patient with everyone. Do not repay evil with evil, but do good to everyone. Always rejoice, pray without ceasing, and give thanks in every circumstance because this is what God wants from you. Do not despise prophecy, but test everything; hold onto good, and abstain from evil.

> **How does prayer work?**
>
> See the box in Chapter 29 of The Life of Jesus for more information on how prayer works.

May the God of peace sanctify you so that your whole body, soul, and spirit may be blameless when Jesus comes again. God who calls you is faithful and he will do it. Pray for us and greet all the brothers and sisters warmly. Read this letter to the church and may the grace of our Lord Jesus Christ be with you.

CHAPTER THIRTEEN

CLARIFICATION ON JESUS' RETURN
II Thessalonians 1-3

> **Paul's second letter to Thessalonica**
>
> Paul, Silas, and Timothy wrote this second letter to the church in Thessalonica within a year of the first. There was some confusion about Christ's return and they wrote to clarify some of these points. Someone had circulated a forged letter from Paul after his first letter leading some church members to believe that the Second Coming was imminent. Some of these believers had become fanatics and Paul found it necessary to correct their misconceptions.

We always thank God for you because of your faith and love for each other continue to grow. Therefore, we boast about your perseverance in faith and afflictions. All of this is evidence of God's righteous judgment, and as a result, you will be worthy of God's kingdom.

When our Lord Jesus comes from heaven in blazing fire with his mighty angels, he will repay those who trouble you and give you relief. He will punish those who do not know God or obey his gospel. They will suffer eternal punishment away from the glory of God's power on the day he comes for glorification in his holy people because you believed our message. So, we always pray that God would make you worthy of his calling and accomplish every good work of faith by his power. Then you may glorify our Lord Jesus' name according to his grace.

Do not let the teaching that allegedly comes from us that Jesus has already returned unsettle or alarm you. Don't be deceived, that day will not come until the man of lawlessness, the son of destruction comes. He opposes and exalts himself against every so-called god or object of worship, even claiming to be God himself. I told you this when I was with you and you know that God is holding him back until the right time.

> **Who is "the man of lawlessness"?**
>
> The "man of lawlessness" that Paul writes about is the Antichrist that will come just before Jesus comes again. He will be a man who denies God and seeks to lead people away from devotion to the Lord.

When the lawless one comes, he will do miracles that serve the lie and do evil until the Lord Jesus destroys him when he returns. God will allow him to deceive people so that those who didn't believe the truth will face condemnation.

We should always thank God for you because he chose you as the first fruits of salvation by the Spirit and faith. He called you through our gospel so that you may obtain the glory of our Lord Jesus Christ. So, stand firm in what we taught you. Then our God and Father who loves and comforts us through the hope of grace may comfort your hearts and establish you in every good work and word.

***

Finally, pray for us that the gospel may continue to spread rapidly, just as it did with you. Pray that he would deliver us from wicked people; the Lord is faithful and will strengthen you and protect you from Satan. We know that you are doing what we command and will continue to obey. May the Lord direct your hearts to God's love and Christ's perseverance.

In the Lord Jesus Christ's name, we command you to stay away from every idle believer who is disruptive and does not follow our teaching. Just as we were not idle when we were with you and did not eat anyone's food without paying for it. We worked nonstop so that we wouldn't be a burden to any of you. We had every right to compensation, but we did this as an example because anyone unwilling to work should not eat.

We have heard that some of you are idle and disruptive; they are not busy, they are busybodies. We urge such people to settle down and earn their keep. Don't tire of doing good, and refuse to associate with idle and disruptive believers so that they might be ashamed. They are not your enemies; warn them as brothers or sisters.

May the Lord of peace always be with you and grant you grace and peace.

> **Jesus' Second Coming**
>
> The Bible talks about Jesus' Second Coming in multiple places. Jesus speaks to his followers about it in his final instructions to his disciples, Paul writes about it in his two letters to the Thessalonians, and John writes about in Revelation.
>
> The first time that Jesus came to earth, he was a suffering servant who died and rose again to pay for our sins. He will come back a second time as a conquering king who will judge his enemies and rule forever with those who have put their faith in him. There is a lot of controversy about when he will return and the events surrounding his return. However, the most crucial piece for us is that he is coming back; this should be a source of encouragement and comfort. With much of the world's chaos around us, it is easy to believe that his return is right around the corner; every generation since Jesus ascended into heaven has believed the same. He could come back tomorrow, 100 years from now, or 1,000 years from now.

CHAPTER FOURTEEN

PAUL'S RESPONSE TO CORINTHIAN PROBLEMS
I Corinthians 1-6

> **Paul's first letter to Corinth**
>
> Paul wrote to the Corinthian church in conjunction with Sosthenes, one of Paul's co-workers. The two men had a long-standing relationship with the church. Paul founded the church during his second missionary journey between 49 and 52 A.D. There is a lost letter to the Corinthians that Paul wrote, asking the church to dissociate from professing believers who lived sinful lives. Paul wrote this surviving letter in 55 A.D. from the city of Ephesus during his third missionary journey. He wrote it in response to a message that the church had sent to him.
>
> Corinth was located on the Isthmus of Greece between the Aegean and Mediterranean Seas, about 50 miles west of Athens. Nearly 400,000 people lived in Corinth. There was a lot of travel and trade through the city and people could find every imaginable vice there.
>
> Corinth was a pagan city with a reputation for extreme wickedness. It was a cosmopolitan city made up of retired soldiers, freemen, Jews, and people from all over the region. It was a mainly Gentile church with little background in Judaism, as evidenced by some of the members' extreme behavior. Paul wrote about the nature and unity of the church. He dealt with issues ranging from factions, worldly wisdom, unethical conduct, marriage and celibacy, idols, female leaders, communion, spiritual gifts, and the Resurrection.

Grace and peace to you from God, our Father, and the Lord Jesus Christ. I always thank God because of his grace for you in Jesus. He has enriched you in both speech and knowledge just as Christ confirms his testimony in you. Therefore, you do not lack any spiritual gift as you eagerly await our Lord's return. God has called you into fellowship with his Son and he is faithful.

I ask that you agree with each other so that there are no divisions and that you are united in thought and purpose. Chloe's people made it clear that there are quarrels among you, and each of you claim to follow Paul, Apollos, Peter, or Christ. Is Christ divided? Was Paul crucified for you, or were you baptized in the name of Paul? I thank God that I didn't baptize very many of you. For Christ didn't send me to baptize, but to preach the gospel plainly so that Christ's cross might not be powerless.

The message of the cross sounds foolish to those on the road to destruction, but to believers, it is God's power. He will destroy the wisdom of the wise and set aside the cleverness of the clever. There is no wise man, scholar, or debater who can stand before God. The world's wisdom doesn't lead to God, so he was pleased to save those who believe through the foolishness of our preaching. Jews ask for miracles, and Greeks seek wisdom, but we preach Christ crucified. The cross is a stumbling block for Jews and nonsense to Greeks, but to everyone who has been called, Christ is the power and wisdom of God. Even God's foolishness is wiser than us and his weakness is stronger than our strength.

Consider yourselves; the world wouldn't call many of you wise, powerful, or noble. But God chose the foolish things of the world to shame the wise and the weak to shame the strong. He chose the lowly and despicable things of the world, to nullify that which is important so that no one can boast before God. He is the source of your life in Jesus Christ, who has become our wisdom, righteousness, holiness, and redemption. Therefore, whoever boasts should boast in the Lord.

When I came to you, I did not have eloquence or superior wisdom as I preached the gospel. While I was with you, I decided to know nothing except Jesus and his crucifixion. I came to you in weakness, fear, and trembling. My message and preaching didn't consist of wise and persuasive words, but with a demonstration of the Spirit's power so that your faith would not rest on men's wisdom, but on God's power.

We speak wisdom to the mature, but not the wisdom of the world or the world's rulers because they are becoming irrelevant. We speak God's secret wisdom that he predestined for our glory; the wisdom which none of the world's rulers have understood. If they had, they would not have crucified Jesus.

No eye has seen, no ear has heard, and no one has ever imagined all that God has prepared for those who love and trust him. But the Lord has revealed them to us through his Spirit, for the Spirit searches everything, even the depths of God. Who can know what a person is thinking except that man's spirit? In the same way, no one knows God's thoughts except his Spirit. We have not received the world's spirit, but God's so that we may understand what he has graciously given us.

We speak in words taught by the Spirit, not human wisdom, and we explain spiritual matters to spiritual people. But those who do not have the Spirit do not accept the things from God, for they seem foolish to them, and they cannot understand them because that requires spiritual judgment. But those who have the Spirit judge all things, but no one judges them. We cannot know all that God knows, but we understand these things because we have the mind of Christ.

I could not address you as spiritual men, but only as worldly, mere infants in Christ. I gave you milk instead of solid food because you weren't ready for it; you're still not prepared because you are still worldly. Where there is jealousy and strife, you are worldly and acting like mere people. When you take sides with Paul or Apollos, you are acting like mere people. Apollos and I are only servants who preached the gospel to you. I planted, Apollos watered, but God was causing the growth. Neither the one who plants nor the one who waters are anything, but only God who causes the growth. The one who plants and the one who waters have the same purpose, and each will receive a reward according to their work. For we are God's workers and you are his field or building.

By God's grace, I laid a foundation as an expert builder, and someone else is building on it. But we should be careful how we build because no one can lay a foundation other than Jesus Christ. Regardless of what we use to build with, God will test our work with fire on the day he returns. If our work remains, we will receive a reward. If our work burns up, we will suffer loss, although God will save us by the skin of our teeth. We are his temple and he lives within us; if anyone destroys this temple, God will destroy him because his temple is sacred.

Don't be deceived; if you think you are wise by the world's standards, you should become a "fool" so that you may become wise. For the world's wisdom is foolishness to God. Scripture tells us that the Lord knows that the thoughts of the wise are worthless; therefore, do not boast about spiritual leaders! Everything belongs to you: Paul, Apollos, Peter, the world, life, death, the present, and the future. It all belongs to you, and you belong to Christ, and Christ belongs to God.

We are Christ's servants, and God has entrusted his truth with us; we must be faithful. I don't care if you judge me, my conscience is clear; it is the Lord who judges me. Wait for the Lord to come, and he will bring everything to light, including the heart's hidden motives; then, we will all receive our praise from God.

I have applied these things to myself and Apollos for your benefit so that you would not become proud and arrogant towards each other. None of us are any better than each other; we have received everything we have from God, so we should not boast. You have already become rich and are beginning to reign; we wish to reign with you.

But it seems like God has put us, apostles, at the end of the line, like those condemned to die in the gladiator arena. We are fools for Christ, but you are wise; we are weak, but you are strong; we have no honor, but you do. We are hungry and thirsty, dressed in rags, mistreated, and homeless. We work hard with our own hands; when people curse us, we bless; when persecuted, we endure; when slandered, we answer with kindness. We have become the scum of the earth, the trash of the world.

I don't want to shame you, but to warn you as my children. Even if you have countless other guides in Christ, I am your father. Imitate me, that is why I sent you Timothy, to remind you what I have taught in every church. I have heard that some are arrogant as if I am not coming, but I will come to find out about their power if the Lord wills. Because the kingdom of God does not consist in talk, but power. You choose if I should come with a spirit of discipline or love and gentleness.

***

I've heard that there is sexual immorality among you that not even the pagans tolerate, a man sleeping with his step-mother. You are proud of your tolerance, but you really should mourn! Kick this man out of your church; even though I'm not there, I've already judged him. With the power of our Lord Jesus, hand him over to Satan so that while God destroys his body, he will save the man's soul.

Your pride is not good; don't you know that a little yeast leavens the whole lump of dough? Get rid of the yeast (pride), so that you may be a new, unleavened batch as you already are. Christ, our Passover Lamb, has already been sacrificed; observe the rest of the festival with the unleavened bread of sincerity and truth and not the old bread of malice and wickedness.

> **What did Paul mean?**
>
> Paul was using the analogy of yeast in bread to show that their pride would spread and affect their entire lives. He ties this in with the Jewish Passover Feast that commemorated God delivering the Israelites from Egyptian slavery.

I wrote to you in my previous letter not to associate with sexually immoral people. I didn't mean everyone who is wicked, greedy, cheaters, nor idolaters; otherwise, you would have to leave the world. But do not associate with anyone who claims to be a believer and practices these things; don't even eat with them. If God will judge the outside world, shouldn't you judge those in the church?

If any of you have a dispute with another believer, don't take it to court; settle the matter amongst yourselves. God's people will one day judge the world, can't you decide trivial issues? One day, you will judge angels. Can't you figure things out without having the church's name dragged through the mud? The fact that you can't settle disputes is shameful; it is better to be wronged or cheated. Instead, you cheat and wrong each other.

Sinners will not inherit the kingdom of God. Don't be deceived; the sexually immoral, idolaters, adulterers, homosexuals, thieves, the greedy, drunkards, slanderers, and swindlers will not inherit the kingdom. That's what some of you were, but now you are washed, sanctified, and justified in our Lord Jesus Christ's name and by the Holy Spirit.

All things are permissible, but not everything is good for you; don't let anything master you. People say that sex is for the body and that the body is for sex, but the body is not meant for sexual sin, the body is meant for the Lord, and the Lord is for the body. By the Lord's power, God raised Jesus from the dead, and he will raise us as well. Our bodies are members of Christ; we should not join them with a prostitute. Anyone who unites themselves with a prostitute becomes one with her because, as Moses wrote, "the two become one flesh."

Whoever unites with Christ is one with him in spirit. Run from sexual immorality; all other sins are outside the body, but sexual sin is against the body. Your bodies are temples of the Holy Spirit who lives inside you. You are not your own; God bought you with a price, so honor him with your bodies.

What is sexual immorality?

Sexual immorality is any form of sex or sexuality that is outside of marriage. This includes extra-marital sex and pornography. Our current culture is hyper-sexualized and there is temptation in every direction we turn. The answer is not to adopt the morality of the world around us, but to cling to the way God designed sex before sin entered the world. Sex is a gift from God and it is best if we practice it in the way he intended, between a husband and wife, in a committed covenant marriage. The world tells us that what we do with our bodies does not affect our souls, but this is not true.

CHAPTER FIFTEEN

MARRIAGE AND QUESTIONABLE THINGS
I Corinthians 7:1-11:1

When you wrote, you asked if it was okay for people to have sex. Since sexual immorality is happening, people should only have sex with their spouses; each should fulfill their marital duty to each other. Neither has authority over their bodies, so do not deprive each other except by mutual consent so that you can devote yourselves to prayer. Then come together again to avoid temptation. This is more of a concession than a command; I wish you were all single like me, but we all have our own gifts.

To the single and widows, I think it is better to stay single, but if you can't control yourself, it is better to marry than to burn with lust. The married should stay married, and if they divorce, they should remain single or reconcile with their ex. If anyone is married to an unbeliever, try to stay married unless they want to leave. For the believing spouse sanctifies the unbelieving spouse and they make the children holy. It's okay if the unbelieving spouse files for divorce; you are not bound in this situation because God has called you to peace. You may even end up saving your unbelieving spouse.

Let each person live the life that God has given them. Whether circumcised or uncircumcised, don't try to change it because neither one matters, only obedience to God. If you were a slave when called, try to become free, but don't worry if you can't. Regardless of your status, you are free in Christ. Whatever your situation when God called you, stay in it.

> **Slavery**
>
> The New Testament talks about slavery without condemning it, but it is essential to know that it is not like the slavery we think of in modern terms. Slavery in the First Century was a way that people who

> had nothing were able to survive and keep from extreme poverty. It had nothing to do with race, class, or national origin. We should think of it more like employment than forced labor. Some slaves were mistreated, but we should not look at this as justification for degrading fellow humans.

I don't have a specific command concerning those who are engaged, but I think you should stay as you are. Considering the current situation, I think both the married and single should stay that way; but anyone who gets married is not sinning. Married people must deal with marital issues and I want to spare you of that. Our time is short, this world is passing away; we should focus on the work we have to do for the Lord. I don't want to put a burden on you; I only want you to live a life with undivided devotion to the Lord. You will be fine whether you marry or stay single, but I think you will be happier if you stay as you are.

***

Concerning food sacrificed to idols, we know that knowledge puffs up, but love builds up. If you think you know something, you don't know everything; our knowledge should not make us proud. But whoever loves God knows himself. So, regarding food sacrificed to idols, we know that there is only one God and that they are nothing. However, because of some people's past association with idols, they believe that eating food sacrificed to idols is sinful.

> **Meat sacrificed to idols**
>
> Idols were a significant problem in the First Century and they continue to be today. Merchants in most major cities would sell the meat sacrificed to idols in the marketplace. Some Christians viewed eating this meat as participating in idol worship.

It doesn't help us or hurt us if we eat food sacrificed to idols; just be careful that you are not an obstacle to the weak. If people with a weak conscience see you eating this food, it could destroy their faith. When you hurt them like this, you hurt Christ. Therefore, if what I eat causes another believer to sin, I will never eat meat again so that I won't cause them to fall.

I am free, I have seen Jesus, and you are the seal of my apostleship. In defense to those who accuse me, we all have the right to eat, drink, and get married. Do only Barnabas and myself have to work for a living? Whoever works deserves a wage and we should get paid if we preach the gospel. If we have sown spiritual seed among you, we should be able to reap a material harvest.

Those who preach the gospel should earn a living from it. We have not made use of these rights, and I'm not begging you for a salary; I would rather die. I must preach the gospel, so I cannot boast; if I preach voluntarily, I have a reward, but if not voluntarily, I'm just doing my job. My reward is that I can preach free of charge.

Even though I'm free, I have made myself a servant to everyone, so that I may lead as many as possible to Christ. I have lived like a Jew to win the Jews; to those under the Law, I have lived under the Law; to those without the Law, I have lived like one without the Law; to the weak, I have become weak, to win as many as possible. I do everything for the sake of the gospel so that I can share in its blessings.

> ### Becoming like other groups
>
> Paul did whatever he could to make the gospel more palatable to his audience without compromising his message. Many times, when people become Christians, they withdraw from the world and lose contact with those outside the church. This is not the way it should be. We need to protect ourselves from sin, but we need to be still engaged with the world around us to tell them about the grace that Jesus offers us. Whatever your interests are, use them to bring God glory and tell similar people about God's love.

Every runner runs the race, but only one wins; run so that you might win the prize. Every athlete exercises self-control to win a perishable wreath, but we compete for an imperishable one. I discipline my body and control it so that I am not disqualified after I preach.

Our ancestors lived under a cloud, and they all passed through the sea; they were baptized into Moses in the cloud and the sea. They all ate the same spiritual food and drank the same spiritual drink that flowed from the rock of Christ. But God was not pleased with most of them and their relatives buried them in the wilderness. These things are an example for us to keep us from setting our hearts on evil as they did.

Don't be idolaters or sexually immoral as some of them were; God killed 23,000 in one day. We should not put Christ to the test like they did and snakes killed them. We should not grumble as some of them did and an angel killed them. These are all examples for us so that we wouldn't repeat their folly.

If you think you are standing, be careful that you don't fall. Nothing that is uncommon to people has tempted you; God is faithful, and he will not allow you to face any temptation beyond what you can resist. With every temptation, he will also provide a way to resist so that you can endure.

Therefore, run from idolatry. The communion we take is Christ's body and blood, and since we all share in it, even though there are many of us, we are one body. The Israelites who ate the sacrifices participated in the altar, but that doesn't mean that food offered to idols or the idol itself is anything. I don't want you to participate in what the pagans offer to demons. You cannot partake of both the Lord and demons; we are not stronger than God is.

All things are lawful, but not everything is helpful, nor does it build us up. Don't just look out for your own good, but also the good of your neighbor. You can eat whatever you find in the market without asking questions for the sake of your conscience. If someone invites you to dinner, eat whatever they serve without asking questions for the sake of your conscience. But if someone tells you that some food has been sacrificed to idols, don't eat so that you don't hurt someone else's conscience. No matter what you do, do everything for God's glory. Try not to offend anyone so that many might know God. Follow my example, as I follow Christ's example.

Questionable things

There are many things that the Bible does not prohibit us from partaking in that are problems for some people. In Corinth, one of the most significant issues was food sacrificed to idols. In modern times, we can substitute things like alcohol, tobacco, marijuana, gambling, etc. For some people, these things are sinful because they can lead to other sins. For others, they can participate without sinning. We need to decide for ourselves if we can partake in these with a clean conscience.

We also need to choose how we partake in these questionable things. If we do it in such a way that leads other believers into temptation, we must proceed with caution. Our freedom is not worth leading someone else into sin. We can be legalistic in our behavior, but we cannot apply this standard to others. While some believers may choose not to partake, they cannot force others to follow the same rule.

CHAPTER SIXTEEN

SPIRITUAL GIFTS AND THE RESURRECTION
I Corinthians 11:2-16:24

I commend you because you remember what I taught you, but I want you to understand that God is the head of Christ, Christ is the head of every man, and the husband is head of his wife. Every man who prays or prophesies with his head covered dishonors his head, but every wife who prays or prophesies with her head uncovered dishonors her head. A man should not cover his head because he is God's image and glory, but the woman is man's glory. Woman was created from man, that is why a wife should have a symbol of authority on her head. However, neither is independent of each other because just as a woman was made from man, now men are born from women, and all things are from God.

Men and women

Some use this passage to argue that men are better than women, but that is not Paul's purpose. Head coverings were a cultural sign like a wedding ring today. Men and women need each other in life and God's kingdom. Also, in other places, Paul writes about mutual submission. As believers, we must submit to each other and look out for other believers' best interests.

***

When it comes to the Lord's Supper (communion), I do not commend you. I've heard that there are divisions when you gather and I believe it because you have an unspoken hierarchy among believers. When you meet for the Lord's Supper, some have private meals and get drunk, while others go hungry. Don't you have homes where you can eat and drink? You are rejecting God and humiliating the poor. What should I say?

> **What is the Lord's Supper?**
>
> The Lord's Supper, or communion, is the Christian rite that commemorates Jesus' death, burial, and Resurrection. The night before he was crucified, Jesus shared a meal with his disciples and gave them this celebration to remember his sacrifice.

On the night Jesus was betrayed, he took bread, gave thanks, and said, "This is my body, which is for you; do this to remember me." He also took the cup and said, "This cup is the New Covenant in my blood; whenever you drink it, remember me."

As often as you eat the bread and drink from the cup, you proclaim the Lord's death until he comes. So, whoever eats the bread and drinks from the cup in an unworthy manner sins against Christ's body and blood. Examine yourself before taking the Lord's Supper, because if you don't, you are bringing yourself into judgment.

Therefore, you are weak and sick, and some of you have died. If we were more discerning, we would not come under such judgment. The Lord disciplines us when he judges us like this, so that he won't condemn us with the world. When you take the Lord's Supper, wait for each other. If you're hungry, eat at home; I will give further instructions when I come.

***

I want you to know about spiritual gifts. Once, when you were pagans, mute idols led you astray. But you must understand that no one who has the Holy Spirit can ever say Jesus is accursed, and no one can call Jesus Lord who does not have the Spirit.

There are different kinds of gifts, but the same Spirit gives them. Different types of service and works, but the same Lord who is at work through them. Each of you has a gift from the Holy Spirit for the good of the church. Some have gifts of wisdom, knowledge, faith, healing, miraculous powers, prophecy, discernment, speaking in tongues, or interpreting tongues. But all of these come from the same Spirit as he desires.

What are spiritual gifts?

The Bible teaches us that they are many different spiritual gifts, and no individual has them all. These are divine empowerment to do work so the church can function correctly. All these gifts are for building up the church and glorifying God. The Holy Spirit gives each believer gifts as he sees fit, and we all have them in different measures. All of them are necessary for both the local and universal church to function as God wants it to, and whatever gifts we have, we should use them in love. Scripture lists many spiritual gifts, including administration, teaching, prophecy, miracles, service, wisdom, knowledge, faith, discernment, tongues, interpretation of tongues, evangelism, giving, leadership, mercy, and encouragement.

Even though the body has many members, they are all one, just as it is with Christ. We were all baptized into one body and all drank from the same Spirit. But the body consists of many members. The foot isn't a hand or an ear, and it can't see, that doesn't make it any less a part of the body. If the body was only eyes or ears, it couldn't smell or walk. God put all the members of the body together as he chose so that it could work. As there are many parts, but one body, no part can tell the others that it doesn't need them. Instead, the parts that seem weaker deserve greater honor, which the seemingly greater parts don't need.

There should be no divisions among you and you should care for one another. If one member suffers, you all suffer; if one member is honored, you should rejoice; you are all individual members of Christ's body. God has appointed apostles, prophets, teachers, miracle workers, healers, servants, administrators, and those who speak in tongues. Not everyone has all the gifts but eagerly desire the greater ones.

What is prophecy?

Prophecy is not just making predictions about the future; it is also speaking on behalf of God. While God does sometimes speak through his followers to reveal what will happen, most of the time, it is

> delivering a message from God to his people. When people prophesy, it will never contradict what God has revealed in the Bible.

But I want to show you a more excellent way.

If I speak in the tongues of people but don't have love, I'm just making noise. If I have every gift, know everything, can move mountains, or become a martyr, but I don't have love, it is worthless.

Love is patient, kind, does not envy or boast, is not arrogant or rude. It does not insist on its own way, is not irritable or resentful, does not rejoice in sin, but rejoices in the truth. Love bears all things, believes all things, hopes all things, and endures all things. Love never ends. Everything else will pass away; we only know in part, but when Jesus returns, the partial will pass away. When I was a child, I spoke, thought, and reasoned like a child; but I had to put the childish away once I grew up.

Now we see as if in a fogged mirror, but when we see him face to face, then we will know everything like we are fully known. Faith, hope, and love remain, but love is the greatest of these.

> ### Love, our underlying motivation
>
> Love should be the underlying motivation for everything we do. This is not romantic love, but a choice to put the needs of others above our own.

Pursue love and earnestly desire spiritual gifts, especially prophecy. Those who speak in tongues speak to God and not to men because no one can understand them. But those who prophesy speak to everyone for their strengthening, encouragement, and comfort. Those who speak in a tongue strengthen themselves, but those who prophesy strengthen the church.

I wish you all spoke in tongues, but even more to prophesy. Those who prophesy are greater than those who speak in tongues unless there is someone to interpret. No one benefits from tongues, but you will only benefit if I bring you a revelation, knowledge, prophecy, or teaching. If a musician doesn't play specific notes on an instrument, no one will know the tune. The same is true of you, if you speak unintelligible words, no one knows what you are saying. There are many languages in the world, but if the listener doesn't understand, it is meaningless. Seek to build up the church; pray for the ability to interpret, so you are not just praying with your spirit.

If you pray with both your spirit and mind, you will be able to worship with both. How can anyone agree with your praise unless they know what you're saying? Then they can also be strengthened. I thank God that I pray in tongues, but I would much rather speak five words with my mind to instruct than many words in a tongue.

Stop thinking like children, be innocent of evil, but mature in your thinking. Tongues are a sign for unbelievers, but prophecy is for believers. If the whole church speaks in tongues, then outsiders will think you are insane. But if everyone is prophesying, then God will convict them; they will worship God and declare that he is in your midst.

What are tongues?

Tongues are one of the spiritual gifts that the Holy Spirit gives to some believers. For some, this is the ability to speak natural languages that they do not otherwise know, and for some, it is a prayer language that we speak to God. This is a mysterious gift that we don't fully understand, but it builds up the church and edifies believers. Many people with this gift use it in their private communication with God. We should not expect everyone to speak in tongues and the Bible tells us to have someone to interpret if we speak in the church.

When you meet, each of you brings a song, revelation, tongue, or an interpretation; everything must be to build up the church. Only a few of you should speak in a tongue and there must be someone to interpret. If there is no one to interpret, the one who speaks in a tongue should keep quiet and only talk to God. Two or three prophets should speak and the others should evaluate the message. If God gives a revelation to one who is sitting, then the speaker should be silent.

Prophesy one by one so that everyone can learn and be encouraged because God is not a God of disorder, but peace. Women should remain silent in church and stay in submission. If they have questions, they should ask their husbands at home.

If anyone thinks they are a prophet or have a gift from the Spirit, let them acknowledge that these aren't just my opinions, I'm writing the Lord's commands. If anyone ignores this, ignore them. Be eager to prophesy and allow tongues, but let everything be orderly.

Orderly worship

Worship services in Corinth were often chaotic. One of the more controversial teachings in the Bible is that women cannot speak in church. This was meant for the church in Corinth because some women would jump up and talk over everyone else. Women are not inferior to men and are allowed to be a part of worship services. Still, no matter what happens, church meetings need to be orderly so that outsiders don't have ammunition to speak ill of God and his congregation.

***

I want to remind you of the gospel I preached to you. It is what saves you if you hold to it; otherwise, you believed in vain. Christ died for our sins, was buried, and then rose on the third day according to the Scriptures. Then he appeared to Peter and the other apostles and then to more than 500 believers (most of whom are still living, but some have died). Then he appeared to James and the other apostles; last, he appeared to me even though I persecuted the church. But, by God's grace, I am what I am, and his grace toward me was not in vain. It was God's grace working, regardless of who preached to you.

If we preach that Christ rose from the dead, how can you say there is no resurrection? If there is no resurrection, then not even Christ has risen, then our preaching and your faith are in vain. Then we are even lying about God if he didn't rise from the dead.

If Christ has not risen, then your faith is futile, and you are still in your sins; and those who have died in Christ will remain dead. If we only have hope in this life, then we are pitiful fools. But if Christ rose from the dead, he is the first fruits of those who died.

Since death came from one man, then resurrection also comes from one man. As Adam led to our death, Jesus leads to our life. When he comes again, everyone who belongs to him will rise from the dead; then he will hand over the kingdom to God the Father after destroying his enemies. He will reign until he has put all his enemies under his feet, and the last enemy he will destroy is death. When he does this, then Christ will put himself in submission to God. If you believe there is no resurrection, then why are some of you baptized for the dead? If there is no resurrection, suffering for the gospel is worthless. We should eat and drink because we may die tomorrow.

> **Baptism for the dead**
>
> Baptism for the deceased was a First Century practice that some people performed, but it is not something that God ever commanded Christians to do. Paul referenced this as an argument to show the necessity of belief in the resurrection.

Don't be deceived; bad company corrupts good morals. Wake up from your drunken stupor and stop sinning.

Some will ask what kind of body we will have when we rise, but that's a foolish question. Seeds only grow if they die; our current bodies are like seeds that God plants. When we die, he will raise it as he determines. Every living being has its own kind of flesh; there are earthly bodies and heavenly bodies, and their splendor is different. So it will be with resurrection from the dead. We are sown perishable and raised imperishable; sown in dishonor and weakness, and raised in power and glory.

If there is a natural body, there is also a spiritual body. The first Adam became a living being; the second Adam (Jesus) became a life-giving spirit. The first is from the earth and natural; the second is from heaven and spiritual. Just as we bear Adam's image, we will one day bear Christ's.

> **Adam as a "type"**
>
> Adam was the first human God created and Paul references him as a "first" to his readers. Adam was a first for all people and Jesus was a first for all spiritual people.

Flesh and blood cannot inherit the kingdom of God, nor does the perishable inherit the imperishable. We will not all die, but we will all change in the twinkling of an eye. When the last trumpet sounds, the dead will rise imperishable. We will change; this mortal body will put on immortality, and victory will swallow up death. The sting of death is sin, and the power of sin is the Law; thanks be to God that he gives us the victory through our Lord Jesus Christ. Therefore, stand firm and don't let anything move you; give yourselves entirely to God's work knowing that it is not in vain.

***

Like I directed the Galatian churches, put aside money, and save it for when I come so that you won't have to do an additional collection. When I arrive, I will send it on to Jerusalem along with anyone you would like to send.

I hope to see you soon and spend some time with you, maybe even a whole winter, if the Lord allows. But I am staying in Ephesus until Pentecost because God has allowed me to minister there. When Timothy comes, put him at ease, for he is doing the Lord's work like I am.

Concerning Apollos, I urged him to visit you, but the time wasn't right; he will come when he gets the chance.

Watch out, stand firm in the faith, and be mature; do everything in love. Be subject to your spiritual leaders and other workers for the gospel because they have devoted themselves to serving the church. They have refreshed our spirits, give them recognition.

Let those who don't love the Lord be accursed! May he come quickly! May the Lord's grace be with you. I love you, brothers and sisters.

CHAPTER SEVENTEEN

JUSTIFICATION BY FAITH IN CHRIST
Galatians 1-6

> **Paul's letter to Galatia**
>
> The Galatian region in what is now modern-day Turkey was an area where the early church flourished. This letter is not to an individual church, but a group of local churches in the Galatian region. It was intended to be circulated to multiple congregations. Paul likely wrote this letter around 55 A.D during his time in Ephesus.
>
> In this letter, Paul writes in defense of his apostleship and against a false gospel that some were preaching. As the early church grew, one of the first issues that arose was that some taught that Christians needed to add elements to the gospel. These people were known as Judiazers, and they wanted Christians to adhere to both the Old Testament and Jesus' teachings.

I am astonished that you are so quickly deserting God's grace and turning to a different gospel. There is no other, but there are some who are trying to distort Christ's gospel. But even if an angel from heaven or we should preach a different message, let them be accursed. I am not trying to please people, but God, otherwise I wouldn't be Christ's servant.

> **Jesus is the only gospel.**
>
> Jesus is the central figure of the Christian faith. He is the ABC's and the graduate level of the faith. Some people want to add other things to the gospel for many different reasons. We must keep our focus on him rather than getting sidetracked by secondary issues. We need to reject any teaching that pulls us away from Jesus.

I am not preaching a manufactured gospel; I am teaching what Christ taught me. You know about my former life, how I violently persecuted the church, and was advancing in Judaism beyond my peers. But God, who had set me apart before birth, called me by grace to know Jesus and preach his gospel. Afterward, I didn't consult with anyone but went to Arabia, where God taught me. After three years, I went to Jerusalem and stayed with Peter for 15 days; while I was there, I didn't see any other apostles besides James. I was preaching in Syria and Cilicia while I was still unknown to the church. They praised God that I was now preaching the gospel and no longer trying to destroy the church.

Fourteen years after that first visit, I returned to Jerusalem with Barnabas and Titus to clarify what God had revealed. I only met with the church leaders so that it wouldn't become a public issue magnified by racial tensions and risk my current ministry. Even Titus, who is not a Jew, did not go along with their pressure.

While we were there, some false believers snuck in to spy on our freedom and enslave us. But we did not give them the time of day because we wanted to preserve the gospel's truth. I don't care about their reputation, and neither does God; they had nothing to add to our message. Soon it was clear that God had given me the same ministry with the Gentiles that he gave Peter to the Jews. The leaders of the church agreed to accept Barnabas and me if we kept looking after the poor.

Later, when Peter came to Antioch, I confronted him because he refused to associate with the Gentiles. He gave into the pressure from people who preached circumcision. The rest of the believers, including Barnabas, followed this hypocrisy. When I saw that this was contrary to the gospel, I called them out on it.

We may be Jews by birth and not Gentiles, but we know that faith in Christ justifies us and not the Law, which cannot make us right with God. But if we still sin, that doesn't make Christ a servant of sin. If I rebuild what I tore down, then I only prove that I'm a sinner. I died to the Law so that I might be alive to God; I have been crucified with Jesus, and it is no longer I who lives, but Christ who lives in me. I live in him by faith in the Son of God, who loved me and gave his life for me. I don't nullify God's grace because if the Law could make us righteous, then Christ died for no reason.

You foolish Galatians, who tricked you? You know Jesus was crucified, and you received the Holy Spirit by faith and not the Law. After starting with the Spirit, are you going to finish with the Law? You know that God works miracles among you by the Holy Spirit's power and not by the Law. You are Abraham's children because of the same faith that God credited to him as righteousness. Scripture prophesied that Abraham's descendants would bless the world through this faith.

Those who don't obey the whole Law are cursed, but those who live by faith will be right with God. Christ rescued us from the Law by taking our place when he was crucified. God redeemed us through Christ to receive the promise of the Spirit and fulfill the prophecies in Scripture.

No one can change the terms of a contract after the fact; in the same way, the promises made to Abraham were through a singular person and not through many. The Law that came 430 years later did not do away with the promise because the inheritance depends on the promise and not the Law.

The Law came to expose sin until Jesus came. This doesn't mean it is against God's promises; the Law merely locked everything under sin until Jesus came to give faith to everyone who believes. The Law was our guardian until Christ came to justify us; we don't need that guardian anymore. In Christ, you are all God's children; your faith and baptism are in him.

There is no longer Jew nor Gentile, slave nor free, male nor female because you are one in Christ. If you belong to Christ, then you are children of Abraham and heirs according to the promise.

Equality in Christ

Paul makes a compelling statement here that there are no longer racial, class, or gender distinctions. Some have used the Bible to justify racism, classism, sexism, and just about any other form of -ism imaginable. These are all distortions of the gospel. God views us as equals, and no human is better than another, regardless of the

> classification. As followers of Christ, we must fight against these hierarchies wherever we find them.

While heirs are children, they are no different from servants even though they own everything until parents declare otherwise. When we were spiritual children, we were under the Law until Jesus came to free us and adopt us as his heirs. God has sent the Spirit of his Son into our hearts so that we can call him Father and Daddy. You are no longer slaves, but God's children and heirs.

When you did not know God, you were enslaved to those who are not gods. But now that you know God and he knows you, how can you return to the worthless promises of the world and enslave yourselves again? I am afraid that I may have preached to you in vain; I beg you to become like me in your faith.

I first preached to you because of an illness, and although it was a burden to you, you didn't look down on me. Instead, you treated me like an angel or even Christ himself. You would have even given me your own eyes if you could have. I'm not your enemy; those trying to convince you of a different gospel are only trying to alienate us from each other. It's fine to be zealous for good, but you should act this way even if I'm not with you. My children, I wish I could be with you because I'm perplexed and worried about you.

Abraham had two sons, Ishmael, through a slave woman, and Isaac through a free woman. The slave's son was born according to the flesh, while the free woman's son was born through the promise. Hagar, the slave, represents the Law and corresponds to earthly Jerusalem because she was enslaved with her children. But Sarah, the free woman, corresponds with the Jerusalem from above; she is our mother. You are like Isaac, the children of the promise. Just as Ishmael persecuted Isaac, those under the Law want to oppress you now. But we should cast out the slave woman and her son because we are children of the freewoman.

> **Abraham and his children**
>
> Abraham was the first of the Jewish ancestors that he revealed himself to in the Old Testament. God promised him a son even though Abraham and his wife were past child-bearing age. In a lapse of faith, he had a son named Ishmael with a slave girl named Hagar. Later, God fulfilled his promise with a son named Isaac with his wife, Sarah.

Christ has set us free, so don't enslave yourselves any longer. If you accept circumcision to justify yourselves, then Christ can't help you because you must obey the whole Law. If you are trying to justify yourselves with the Law or anything else, you are alienated from Christ and have fallen from grace. Through the Spirit and faith, we eagerly wait for the hope of righteousness; neither circumcision nor uncircumcision matters, only faith working through love.

You were doing so well, don't stop now because this temptation isn't from God; beware because a little yeast leavens the whole batch. I am confident that you will agree with me because the one causing confusion will bear the penalty. If circumcision mattered, I shouldn't face persecution because the cross has been abolished. I wish these people would go all the way and not just circumcise, but emasculate themselves.

God called you to be free, but don't use your freedom to indulge the flesh. Use it to serve one another humbly in love. The entire Law is summed up in the command to love others as yourself. If you bite and devour each other, you will destroy one another.

Walk in the Spirit, and you won't gratify the flesh's desires, for the flesh is against the Spirit and vice versa. They war against each other, so don't do whatever you want; the Spirit leads you and is not under the Law. The acts of the flesh are sexual immorality, impurity, sensuality, idolatry, witchcraft, hatred, discord, jealousy, fits of rage, selfishness, dissensions, factions, envy, drunkenness, orgies, and the like. People who indulge in these acts will not inherit the kingdom of God.

The fruit of the Spirit is love, joy, peace, patience, kindness, goodness, faithfulness, gentleness, and self-control; there is no law against them. Those who belong to Jesus Christ have crucified the flesh along with its passions and desires. Since we live by the Spirit, let's walk by the Spirit and not become conceited, provoking, and envying each other.

If you see people caught in sin, those who are spiritual should restore them with a gentle spirit. Watch yourselves so you won't be tempted as well. Bear each other's burdens and fulfill the Law of Christ. If you think you are something when you are nothing, you are fooling yourself. Test your work, and then you won't take credit for someone else's work; you must bear your own load. If you are taught the Word, you must share with the one who teaches.

Do not be deceived; you cannot mock God. You will reap whatever you plant. If you plant according to the flesh, you will harvest corruption; if you plant according to the Spirit, you will harvest eternal life. Don't get tired from doing good because, in time, you will gather a harvest. Do good if you have the chance, especially for other believers.

Those who want to impress people through the flesh want you to be circumcised and are only trying to avoid persecution. But they don't even keep the Law themselves; they only want you to be like them so they can boast. I will only boast in the cross of our Lord Jesus Christ; the world is dead to me and I'm dead to it. Neither circumcision nor uncircumcision matters, only a new creation. If you live by this rule, peace and mercy are on you and the God of Israel. Don't cause me any more trouble because I bear the scars of the gospel on my body.

May the grace of our Lord Jesus Christ be with you all.

CHAPTER EIGHTEEN

PAUL'S MINISTRY AND COLLECTION FOR THE SAINTS
II Corinthians 1-9

> **Paul's second letter to Corinth**
>
> With all the issues in Corinth, Paul's first letter was not enough to fix their problems. Paul had a painful visit between his first and second letters to the Corinthians, and there is evidence of a sorrowful letter he wrote them in between the two letters. He wrote this letter from Macedonia, and it gives us the best insight into how Paul felt about himself as an apostle. He co-wrote this letter with Timothy.

Praise God, the Father of our Lord Jesus Christ, who is the source of all compassion and comfort. He comforts us in our troubles so that we can help others who go through problems. Just as we share in Christ's sufferings, we also share his comfort with others. Whether we suffer or are comforted, it is for your benefit as you patiently endure the same sufferings we do. Our hope for you is strong because we know that you will share in our comfort just as you share in our sufferings.

We were under enormous pressure when we were in Asia, far beyond what we could endure, and we despaired of life itself. We thought God had given us a death sentence, and we trusted he was using that to get us to rely on him who raises the dead. But he delivered us from danger and he will do it again; we set our hope on him to deliver us. Please pray for us that our labor might be fruitful and cause many to rejoice.

We have behaved with simplicity and godly sincerity, showing you God's grace and not earthly wisdom. Don't look for hidden meanings; we have only written simple truth. We want you to be as proud of us as we are of you when we stand before Jesus.

I intended to visit you twice, but I couldn't. I wasn't trying to make false promises, just as our message wasn't fake. I didn't make it to you to spare you pain, not to manipulate you. We work with you for your joy so that you can stand firm in your faith.

Another visit would have been painful for both of us; that's why I wrote what I did (this refers to the missing letter); I thought that was best. But it turned out that I wrote with many tears because I love you so much. It's time to forgive the one who caused both of us so much pain. His punishment has been enough; if you keep piling on, you could destroy him. It's time to love this brother and that's why I last wrote. I have already forgiven anyone that you forgive and this is for your sake so that Satan might not outwit us.

***

When I arrived in Troas, I found an open door for the gospel, but I couldn't relax without finding Titus there. So, I went to Macedonia, looking for him to reassure me about you because God causes us to give off a sweet fragrance of Christ to both believers and those who are perishing. We are not like some preachers of God's Word who water it down to make it acceptable; we preach from a sincere heart as God has commissioned us.

We aren't patting ourselves on the back or seeking your approval; your lives are all we need. You are a letter from Christ, written by the Spirit on human hearts. Only God could write this kind of letter and it authorizes us to carry out this New Covenant. The Law kills, but the Spirit gives life; the Law came on tablets of stone with such glory that the Israelites couldn't even look at Moses in the face. If the ministry of condemnation brought glory, the ministry of righteousness will far outshine it. The glory of righteousness far surpasses the Law, and it is permanent.

With this hope, we are much bolder than Moses was, who put a veil over his face. But the Israelites' minds were hardened, and even now, when they read the Law, the veil remains over their hearts because only Christ can take it away. But when people turn to the Lord, God takes away the veil, and they see that he is a living Spirit and that the old, restrictive Law is obsolete. We are free! We will behold the Lord's glory without a veil as he transforms us from one degree of glory to another as we become more like him.

Having this ministry, we do not lose heart; we have renounced disgraceful, underhanded ways. We refuse to tamper with God's Word. Our lives are a statement of our clean conscience in God's eyes. Even if our gospel is veiled, it is only veiled to those who are perishing because Satan has blinded their hearts. We don't proclaim ourselves; we proclaim Jesus and ourselves as his servants; he shines in our hearts so that people may know God's glory in the face of Jesus Christ.

We have this treasure in fragile jars to show that this power belongs to God and not us. We are afflicted in every way, but not crushed; perplexed, but not despairing; persecuted, but not forsaken; struck down, but not destroyed. We carry his death with us so that Jesus might be manifested in our lives. Our lives are always at risk for his sake, making his life even more evident in us.

While our lives are horrible, yours are extraordinary. We have the same spirit of faith and we know that the one who raised Jesus will raise us too. All of this is for your sake so that more people might believe. Even though we are wasting away, God is renewing our souls. This momentary pain does not compare to the eternal glory God will give us. The things we see are nothing, but what we cannot see will last forever.

We know that if God destroys the tent of our earthly home, he has a building for us that he made in heaven. We long for our heavenly dwelling, waiting to be fully clothed so that life would swallow up death. God has prepared this building for us and has given us the Holy Spirit as a promise. We are confident that while we are at home in this body, we are away from the Lord.

We live by faith and not sight. I would rather be with him than here in my body; so, we make it our goal to please him wherever we are. One day, we will all stand before the judgment seat of Christ so that we will receive what we deserve, whether good or bad.

Since we know what it means to fear the Lord, we try to persuade others, and I hope you know the same. We want to give you the chance to take pride in us so that you can answer those who trust in the visible rather than the heart.

If we sound insane, it's for God; if we are in our right mind, it's for you. Christ's love controls us because he died for us so that we might live for the one who died and rose again. We no longer regard anyone from a worldly point of view. We once saw Christ in this way, but not anymore because if we are in Christ, we are a new creation; the old has gone, the new has come!

This is all from God who has reconciled us to himself through Christ and given us this ministry to preach that God forgave people's sins through his death. We are Christ's ambassadors, and we implore you, on his behalf, to be reconciled to God. For our sake, God made Jesus, who knew no sin, to become sin so that we might become God's righteousness in him.

Do not receive God's grace in vain; he is calling you; now is the day of salvation.

We don't want to put obstacles in anyone's way. Instead, as God's servants, we endure trouble, hardship, persecution, beatings, imprisonments, riots, hard work, sleepless nights, and hunger. We face these hardships in purity, understanding, patience, kindness, the Holy Spirit, love, truth, and God's power. We hold the weapons of righteousness in both hands through glory and dishonor, good and bad reports, those who are genuine but believed to be dishonest, known yet unknown, dying while we live, beaten but not killed, sad but rejoicing, poor but making many rich, having nothing but possessing everything. We have opened our hearts to you and spoken freely about Christ; open your hearts to us.

***

Do not be partners with unbelievers because light has nothing to do with darkness and God's temple has nothing to do with idols. We are the temple of the living God; he lives with us and makes us his people. The Lord tells us to leave them and be separate, to leave unclean things behind. He will be a father to us and we will be his children. Therefore, let us purify ourselves from everything that defiles us.

> **Partners with unbelievers**
>
> Paul warns the Corinthians not to become partners with unbelievers, which is good advice for us as well. In situations like marriage and business, it can be difficult to have successful relationships because our motivation should be God's glory while they focus on other objectives.

Please accept us in your hearts; we have not wronged, corrupted, or exploited anyone. I have spoken frankly; I take great pride in you; in fact, we would live or die with you. We were greatly distressed in Macedonia and Titus comforted us when he came and told us how you longed for us.

I don't regret any sorrow I caused you because it only hurt for a little while. Your grief led to a repentance that leads to salvation. Your pain brought an earnest desire to justify yourselves and prove your innocence. My letter showed God how devoted you are to us and your response encouraged me.

I bragged to Titus about you and you proved me right. His affection for you grew because of your obedience and how you received him with fear and trembling.

We want you to know about what the gift the Macedonian church sent has done. During their affliction and extreme poverty, their generosity has brought them great joy. They gave beyond their means to help other believers, but first, they gave themselves to the Lord and then to us. As you excel in faith, speech, knowledge, earnestness, and love, excel in the collection for other believers. I am not commanding you to do this, but asking so that you may prove your genuine love.

You know about Christ's grace and how he became poor for your sake so that you might become rich in his poverty. You started this work a year ago, finish strong out of fairness to those who have also given. Let your prosperity supply others' needs so that everyone may have enough. Right now, you have plenty and can help those in need; later, they will share with you if you have need.

I thank God that he gave Titus the same concern that I have for you. He is coming to see you because he misses you and the churches have chosen him to administer this gift. We want to avoid criticism and do what is right. Titus is my co-worker with you; show these men the proof of your love and the reason for our pride in you.

I don't need to write about this because I know how eager you are to help and your attitude has caused others to give. I am sending these brothers to you so that you will be ready when the Macedonians arrive. So, I urge you to finish the work you started so that your generous gift won't be a grudging duty.

Whoever plants a little will harvest a little, and whoever plants a lot will harvest a lot. Each of you should give what you've decided, not reluctantly or under compulsion, because God loves a cheerful giver.

God can bless you abundantly so that you will always have enough. God, who supplies the seed and food, will also increase your harvest of righteousness. He will bless you so that you can be generous and magnify God's glory. Your service not only supplies your needs but also gives an avenue for praising God. Thank God for his indescribable gift!

CHAPTER NINETEEN

PAUL'S DEFENSE OF HIS MINISTRY
I Corinthians 10-13

I appeal to you in humility and gentleness because I know I am timid in person, but bold in my letters. I hope that I don't have to be so bold when I come. Though we live in the world, we do not wage war as the world does; we fight with divine weapons strong enough to destroy strongholds.

We destroy arguments and lofty opinions against God; we take every thought captive and make it obedient to Christ. Then we may punish the disobedient once you obey. If you are confident in your faith, remember that we are his as well. Even if I boast too much about my authority in Christ, my goal is to build you up, not tear you down.

I'm not trying to scare you with my letters because I know some of you think my writing is severe, but my speaking is unimpressive. You should know that my actions will match my letters when I arrive. I'm not speaking out of turn; I only boast about what God has given me as a ministry. My only hope is that as your faith grows, the sphere of our influence might increase and that we might preach to those who haven't heard the gospel. We won't take credit for others' work; we will only boast in what God has done.

I hope you put up with my foolishness because I have godly jealousy for you. I promised that I would present you to Christ pure, but I'm afraid that just as Satan deceived Eve, you might be led away from your devotion to Christ. You do well enough with those who preach a different gospel. I am not inferior to so-called super-apostles, and even though I'm not a very good speaker, I do have knowledge.

I wasn't wrong to take from other churches so that I could preach to you for free. When I was in need while I was with you, I didn't take anything from you because the Macedonians were generous. I have never wanted to be a burden to you and I will continue in this manner.

I will not stop boasting and I will keep doing what I do so that I can cut the legs out from under those who want to take credit for our work. These people are false workers who pose as apostles, just like Satan poses as an angel of light. In the end, they will get what they deserve. I repeat, don't think I'm a fool; I only picked up this habit of boasting from others. In your wisdom, you put up with fools who enslave you and rip you off, but I'm not strong enough to do that.

I am just as much a Jew and a servant of Christ as they are, even more so. I've done more and suffered far more imprisonments, beatings, and almost died. I received 39 lashes from Jews five times, was beaten with rods three times, I was stoned, and shipwrecked three times. I've been in danger from rivers, robbers, my own people, Gentiles, and false brothers; in the city, wilderness, and at sea; I've faced every possible hardship. On top of that, I bear the weight of all the churches; if anyone is weak or falls, I feel it. If I'm going to boast, I will only boast about my weaknesses.

God knows I'm not lying. When I was in Damascus, I escaped the governor by being lowered over the wall in a basket. Fourteen years ago, God took me to heaven, and I saw incredible things that I can't even describe. I can't boast about things like this so that no one thinks too highly of me.

To keep me from pride, God gave me a thorn in my side, harassment from Satan to keep me humble. I begged God three times to take this away, but he denied me because he perfects his power in my weakness. So, I will boast of my weaknesses, so that Christ's power may rest on me. I'm okay with my weakness, insults, hardships, persecutions, and troubles because when I'm weak, that's when I'm strong in Christ.

You have made me act like a fool because I'm not inferior to these super-apostles even though I'm nothing. I showed you the authentic marks of an apostle with signs, wonders, and miracles. I'm coming to visit you for the third time, but I won't be a burden because I'm after your hearts, not your money. Parents should save up for their children, not the other way around; so, I will gladly spend everything I have on your behalf, even my life. But in all of this, I have not taken advantage of you; everything I do is for your benefit. When I come, I'm afraid I will find arguments, jealousy, anger, hostility, gossip, conceit, and chaos. I'm worried that those who sinned through impurity, sexual immorality, and sensuality will not have truly repented.

This is the third time I'm visiting you; two or three witnesses should confirm every fact. I warned you the last time I was there and I won't go easy on anyone who keeps sinning. You are demanding proof that Christ speaks through me and he will not be weak when dealing with you. He was crucified in weakness, but he lives in God's power; in the same way, we are weak in him, yet we live in his power.

Test yourselves to see if you truly have faith; know that Jesus is in you unless you fail the test. We have not failed the test and we pray that you will not do anything wrong. Not so that we look good, but so that you do the right thing even if people think we failed. We can only act for the truth.

> **Testing our faith**
>
> The admonition to test our faith is a reference to the practice of soldiers testing their weapons before taking them into battle. Before entering a fight, soldiers wanted to ensure their equipment wouldn't fail when the stakes were highest. We can test our faith by continually checking our belief and behavior to make sure they align with the Bible.

We pray for your restoration and are glad when we are weak, but you are strong. I don't want to be severe when I visit you, but I want to use my authority to build you up rather than tear you down.

Finally, rejoice! Aim for restoration, comfort one another, and agree with each other; live in peace, and the God of love and peace will be with you. Greet each other with a holy kiss. May Jesus' grace, God's love, and the Holy Spirit's fellowship be with you all.

CHAPTER TWENTY

THE PROBLEM OF SIN
Romans 1:1-3:20

Paul's letter to Rome

We are unsure of how this church started, although it is likely a result of either people converted at Pentecost or people who heard the gospel during one of Paul's missionary journeys and then moved to Rome. It appears that the church consisted of several congregations that met in home groups. The Roman church was a mix of Jews and Gentiles, though it seems that Gentiles were the majority. Tertius probably wrote Paul's words down and Phoebe likely carried the letter to the believers.

The book of Romans is the longest letter in the New Testament. Paul wrote it from Corinth during his third missionary journey around 57 A.D. He was in his mid-40's at the time and had been a Christian for about 20 years. This letter is unique because it does not deal with a specific issue that the church had reported to Paul. It is essentially a theological treatise that Paul wrote to prepare them for his arrival (he had been unable to visit them before this). The central theme is that God saves us through his righteousness and grace. These are available to those who trust in Jesus Christ.

I thank God for all of you because news of your faith has spread around the world. God is my witness of how often I pray for you and that I might join you. I long to see you so that I can strengthen your faith and that we might encourage each other. I have wanted to come to you for quite some time to preach the gospel as I have to others. I have many obligations, that is why I am so eager to preach to those in Rome.

I am not ashamed of the gospel because it is God's power to save everyone who believes. First for the Jew, then for the Gentile. It reveals God's righteousness through our faith.

God is revealing his wrath against the ungodly and wicked who suppress the truth. God has plainly shown himself to them through his creation. He has shown us his invisible qualities, eternal power, and divinity, through nature, so we have no excuse not to believe in him. Even though they knew God, they did not worship him; instead, they chose to worship created things. Although they claimed to be wise, they chose foolishness.

> **Natural revelation**
>
> Paul tells the Romans that God has revealed himself through his creation. His fingerprints are all over creation from the number pi's infinite precision to the exclusive design of fingerprints. As we see the beauty of the universe and the intricacies of design, it shows God's existence beyond question. Current scientific interpretation of the world favors a universe without God, but that is a far greater leap of faith than accepting his existence. His existence means that we must answer to our Maker.

Therefore, God let them follow their sinful desires into sexual impurity and degrading their bodies. They traded the truth about God for a lie and worshipped creation rather than the Creator. He gave them over to shameful lusts and they exchanged natural passions for unnatural ones. Women had sex with women, and men committed shameful sexual acts with each other. God gave them over to depravity and they committed great sins. They were full of evil: envy, murder, strife, lies, malice, gossip, slander, hating God, insolence, arrogance, disobedience to parents, foolishness, faithlessness, ruthlessness; they even invented new ways of sinning. They knew God's commands, and not only did they disobey, but they also encouraged others to disobey.

Therefore, those of you who judge condemn yourselves because you do the same things. We know God judges those who do such things. Do you think you can escape God's judgment? Do you have contempt for his kindness and patience? Don't you realize his kindness is meant to lead you to repentance? Because of your stubborn and unrepentant hearts, you are saving up his wrath for Judgment Day. God will repay everyone for their deeds. He will give eternal life to those who patiently do good, seeking glory, honor, and immortality. But there will be anger and wrath for those who are self-seeking, disobedient, and unrighteous.

There will be trouble and distress for those who do evil; glory, honor, and peace for those who do good, first for the Jew, then for the Gentile. God does not show favoritism.

All who have sinned without the Law will die without it and all who have sinned under the Law will be judged by it. It is not the hearers of the Law who are righteous, but those who are obedient. When those who don't have God's commands do it by nature, they show that God wrote his Law on their hearts. Their conscience will alternately accuse and defend them on the day God judges everything through Jesus.

If you claim to be a Jew and rely on the Law and boast in God, if you approve what is right and claim to be a light to those in darkness, if you claim to teach others, don't you teach yourself? Do you preach that people shouldn't steal, commit adultery, or worship idols and then do the same? If you preach the Law and then do the same, then you dishonor God. The Gentiles blaspheme God's name because of you.

Circumcision is valuable if you obey the Law, but if you break it, you may as well not be circumcised. Those who are not physically circumcised but obey the Law will condemn you. People are truly Jews if they are Jews on the inside, because circumcision is of the heart, by the Holy Spirit, not by written Law. Their praise is from God and not people.

If this is true, then is there any advantage to being a Jew or circumcision? Of course, there is! First, God entrusted the Jews with his Word; if some were unfaithful, that doesn't nullify God's faithfulness. Even if we are all liars, God is true. If our unrighteousness causes God's righteousness to be more evident, that doesn't make him a liar or prove him unjust. If it did, he could not judge humanity. Some would argue that if my sin increases God's glory, then why am I condemned? Why not do evil if the result is good? They deserve their condemnation.

So, Jews are not better off since we are all sinners. None of us are righteous; none of us seek God. We have all turned away and become worthless; none of us do good. We lie, curse, and are swift to shed blood; we do not truly fear God. We know that the Law speaks to those under it so that every mouth may be silenced and the world would be held accountable. Therefore, the Law will not justify us; instead, it reveals our sin.

CHAPTER TWENTY-ONE

SALVATION THROUGH FAITH
Romans 3:21-5:21

God reveals his righteousness both in the Law and apart from it. This righteousness comes through faith in Jesus to all who believe. We have all sinned and fallen short of God's glory. God only justifies us by his grace through the redemption we have in Jesus Christ. God gave Christ as an atoning sacrifice that we receive by faith through the shedding of his blood. He did this to show God's righteousness and because he had not punished our sins yet. He did this so that he can justify those who have faith in Jesus.

So, we cannot boast in the Law because we follow a law of faith and not works. Our faith justifies us, not the works of the Law. He is the God of all, and he justifies us all through faith, regardless of circumcision. This does not mean we overthrow the Law by faith; on the contrary, we uphold it.

> **Faith and the Law**
>
> The change from justification through the Law to justification by faith was a massive shift in thinking for people in the First Century. The Law gave commands for the people to follow, and if they did, they were righteous. However, none of the people could obey all the rules, so God gave the sacrificial system as a temporary remedy for sin. But after Jesus' death, righteousness could now be based on faith as opposed to our actions. It is about what Jesus has done as opposed to what we do.

If works justified our ancestor Abraham, then he could boast, but not before God. Scripture tells us that Abraham believed God and it was counted as righteousness. Those who work receive their wages as an obligation, not a gift. For those who believe in God, their faith is not counted as work, but as righteousness. David says the same thing when he writes that God blesses those whom he forgives.

This blessing has nothing to do with circumcision; Abraham's had faith before he was circumcised. He was circumcised as a sign of righteousness so that he could be the father of all who believe without circumcision. Then God will count them as righteous as well if they walk in the same footsteps of the faith that Abraham walked in.

> **Circumcision**
>
> Circumcision was the sign of the covenant God made with Abraham in the Old Testament. Every Jewish male was to have the foreskin of his penis cut off at eight-days-old to show that the Israelites were set apart from the people around them. Nearly 2,000 years later, it seems foolish to argue about circumcision, but this was a big deal in the First Century. Circumcision was a requirement for Jews, and one of the things that helped them remain distinct from the nations around them. However, since Jesus brought a New Covenant, circumcision is no longer a requirement for Christians. This was a massive change in thinking for Jewish converts to Christianity.

The promise to Abraham and his offspring was that he would become the heir of the world, not through the Law but through the righteousness that comes with faith. If it is through the Law, then faith is null, and the promise is void. For the Law brings wrath, but without it, there is no sin. That is why justification is by faith so that the promise is by grace and not through the Law.

That's why he is the father of many nations. He is our father in God's eyes, the God who gives life to the dead and creates something out of nothing. Abraham believed in the hope that he would be the father of many nations even when he was 100 years old and his wife was barren. His faith did not waver; he worshipped, convinced that God would fulfill his promises. That's why Abraham's faith counted as righteousness, not just for his sake alone, but for ours as well. It will count as righteousness for all who believe in Jesus' Resurrection from the dead. He died for our sins and rose to make us right with God.

Therefore, since we are right with God by faith, we have peace with God through Jesus Christ. This faith allows us to stand in his grace and now we boast in the hope of God's glory. Beyond this, we also rejoice in our suffering because it leads to endurance, character, and then hope. Our hope does not shame us because God pours his love into our hearts through the Holy Spirit.

At the right time, while we were helpless, Jesus died for the ungodly. Rarely will anyone die for a righteous person and only occasionally for a truly good person. But God demonstrates his love for us in that Jesus died for us while we were still sinners.

Since Jesus' blood justifies us, it will also save us from God's wrath. If God reconciled us to him by his Son's death, his life will save us. Now we will rejoice in God through Jesus because he has given us reconciliation and made us his friends.

Just as sin entered the world through Adam and his sin led to death, we all face death because we have all sinned. Sin was in the world before the Law, but without the Law, no one was guilty. Yet death reigned from Adam to Moses, even over those who didn't break any commands. Adam was an example of Jesus, who was to come.

Adam's sin

In the Garden of Eden, Adam sinned on our behalf, and we all suffer from his decision. Some argue that this is unfair because God punishes us for Adam's sin, but we would make the same choices if we were in his place. Regardless of Adam's sin, we rebel against God every day whenever we sin.

But the gift is not like the sin. The punishment for one sin brought death, but the gift, even after many transgressions, makes us right with God. If death ruled because of one man's sin, even more so will the gift of righteousness rule through one man's life, Jesus Christ. As one person's sin led to everyone's death, his righteous life made us right with God. Just like Adam's sin made us all sinners, Jesus' obedience will make many righteous.

The Law came to identify sin, but where sin increased, grace increased even more. Sin reigned in death, now grace reigns through righteousness to bring eternal life through Jesus Christ our Lord.

> **Salvation by faith**
>
> In this passage, Paul tells us that we cannot justify ourselves with our actions alone because we have all sinned. The only way that we can be right with God is through our faith in Jesus' perfect life and death on the cross. Abraham's faith is an example for us to follow. Just as he believed God's promises and trusted that he would follow through, we should trust God's promises and know that he will fulfill them.

CHAPTER TWENTY-TWO

RESULTS OF SALVATION
Romans 6-8

So, should we keep sinning so that there is even more grace? Of course not! If we have died to sin, we can't live in it any longer. If we are baptized into Christ, then we are baptized into his death. We were buried with him through baptism into death, and just as he was raised from death, we too can live a new life. Just as we join with him in his death, we unite with him in his Resurrection. Our old selves were crucified with him so that our sins would die and we would no longer be slaves to sin. If anyone has died, they have been set free from sin.

> **Baptism into Christ's death**
>
> Our baptism doesn't save us, but it is symbolic of our faith. The act of immersing ourselves in water is symbolic of dying to our old selves and as Christ died on the cross.

If we died with Christ, we know we will also live with him. If Christ rose from the dead, he cannot die again; death has no power over him. He died to sin once for all and now he lives to God. So, we are also dead to sin but alive to God. Don't let sin rule in your body so that you obey its evil desires. Don't offer any part of yourselves to wickedness, but offer every part of yourselves to God as an instrument of righteousness. Sin is no longer your master because you are under grace and not the Law.

Should we sin because we are under grace and not the Law? Of course not! You serve whomever you obey, either sin, which leads to death or God, which leads to life. Thank God that though you used to be slaves to sin, now your heart obeys his teaching. You have been set free from sin and serve righteousness. When you were slaves of sin, you were free regarding righteousness. But that life only leads to death and destruction. Now that you are free from sin, you bear fruit that leads to sanctification and eternal life. The wage of sin is death, but the gift of God is eternal life in Jesus Christ.

The Law only has authority over people if they are alive. For example, a married woman is bound to her husband while he is alive, but she is free from the Law if he dies. If she sleeps with another man while her husband is alive, she commits adultery; but she can marry another man if her husband dies.

In the same way, you have died to the Law through Christ, so that you may belong to God and bear fruit for him. While we lived under the Law, our sinful desires led us towards death. But now that we are free, we serve the Holy Spirit and not the letter of the Law.

That does not mean that the Law is sinful. The Law is perfect, and I would not have known what sin was if it didn't exist. But sin took the opportunity from the commandments and produced all kinds of evil in our lives. The Law that was meant to bring life revealed our sin and brought death. The Law is holy, righteous, and good; it did not cause our sin or death, but it revealed our sin and that sin leads us to death.

We know that the Law is spiritual, but I am unspiritual, a slave to sin. I don't understand my actions, because I don't do what I want, I end up doing what I'm trying to avoid. Now, I am no longer the one doing it, but it is the sin that lives within me. Nothing good lives in my flesh because I have the desire to do the right thing, but I don't do it.

My soul delights in God's Law, but my flesh keeps waging war against my mind making me a prisoner to sin. I am wretched! Who will deliver me from this body of death? I thank God that he delivers me through our Lord Jesus Christ! Even though I serve God with my mind, my sinful nature serves sin.

Now, there is no condemnation for those who are in Christ because the Holy Spirit who gives life sets us free from the law of sin and death. The Law was powerless to free us, but God has freed us by sending his Son as a man to be a sin offering. He condemned sin in the flesh to fulfill the Law's righteous requirements for those of us who live by the Spirit. Those who live according to the flesh set their minds on the flesh and death rules over them; they are hostile to God and cannot please him. But those who live by the Spirit set their mind on the Spirit's desires and life and peace rule over them. If anyone is in Christ, even though your body is subject to sin and death, the Spirit gives life because of righteousness. If the Spirit who lives in you raised Jesus from the dead, he will give you life as well.

Therefore, we must not live according to the flesh and sin. If you live according to the flesh, you will die, but if you live by the Spirit, you will put to death the deeds of the body and live. Those who are led by the Spirit of God are his children.

You did not receive a spirit of slavery to fall back into fear. God has adopted us as sons and we can cry out, "Daddy! Father!" The Spirit witnesses with our spirit that we are children of God and fellow heirs with Christ. If we suffer with him, then we will also have glory with him.

Our current suffering is not worth comparing to the glory God will reveal. Creation did not choose to be subjected to frustration, but the Creator subjected it in the hope that it would one day be freed from bondage to decay and brought into the freedom and glory of God's children. All of creation groans as in childbirth until now. We hope for this even though we have yet to see it. If it had already happened, we would not have to hope, but we patiently wait until it happens.

Sin's impact on the earth

Sin has had a tremendous impact on the world. When God created the universe, it was perfect; there were no natural disasters, no disease, and no death. But Adam and Eve sinned and ruined everything. Since then, we see sin take its slow, gradual effect on the world around us. While we may not be able to blame a hurricane or COVID-19 on a specific sin, these were not a part of God's original design and only exist because of sin's impact on the universe.

In the same way, the Holy Spirit helps us in our weakness. When we do not know how to pray, the Spirit intercedes for us through groans deeper than words. God, who searches our hearts, also knows the Spirit's mind because the Spirit intercedes on our behalf by God's will.

We know that God works all things for good for those who love him and he has called according to his purpose. Those God foreknew, he also predestined to be conformed to the image of his Son so he could be the firstborn among many brothers and sisters. Those he predestined, he called; those he called, he justified; and those he justified, he also glorified.

> **Predestination**
>
> Predestination is a doctrine that can be difficult to understand and there is not a single interpretation of it. It is the concept that God ordains all events and chooses whom to save. Some struggle with this because it seems to remove human choice from the equation. However, the Bible makes it clear that we make choices about our actions. These two ideas create a seeming paradox about whether we choose God or he chooses us.
>
> God is far beyond our understanding and we cannot comprehend how an infinite God can manage both with our finite minds. The reality is that both are true and we may never fully get it before his return. This is a complicated doctrine and I recommend further study.

If God is for us, then who can be against us? If he sacrificed his Son for us, he will also graciously give us everything. No one can bring a charge against God's chosen people because he is the one who declared us innocent. No one can condemn us because Jesus died and rose from the dead for us and now intercedes for us at the right hand of God.

Nothing can separate us from the love of Christ, not hardship, persecution, famine, nakedness, danger, or sword. We face death all day and are like sheep to be slaughtered. But in all these things, we are more than conquerors through him who loves us. I am convinced that nothing can separate us from God's love in Jesus Christ, our Lord; not death, life, angels, demons, things present or to come, powers, height nor depth, or anything else in creation.

> **God's promise to us**
>
> Even though we have faith, we still struggle with sin. Jesus lived as a human and he understands our weakness. He has even given us the Holy Spirit to live inside us and help us overcome our sin. No matter what, God promises us that we are still his and that nothing can separate us from him.

CHAPTER TWENTY-THREE

JEWS AND GENTILES
Romans 9-11

I have great sorrow over my fellow Israelites. I wish I could trade places with them and be cut off from Christ for their sake. God adopted them as children; they received the divine glory, the covenants, Law, temple, and God's promises. They have the Patriarchs and the Messiah, who is God over all. Amen!

But that doesn't mean God's Word failed because not all Israel's descendants truly belong to Israel, and not all of them are Abraham's children just because they share his blood. It is not the children of the flesh who are God's, but the children of the Promise who are Abraham's offspring.

Isaac was evidence of the Promise as were his sons through Rebekah. But before Jacob and Esau (his sons) were born or had done anything good or bad, God chose Jacob to prove God's election. That doesn't make God unjust; just as he said to Moses, "I will have mercy and compassion on those I chose to." It doesn't depend on our effort or desire but God's mercy. Therefore, God raised Pharaoh so the Lord could display his power and that his name would be great in all the earth.

If he has mercy on who he wants and hardens who he wants, why does he still find fault because no one can resist his will? But who are we to question God? The created cannot ask the Creator why it was made this way. The potter uses the same clay to make some vessels for special purposes and some for everyday uses. What if God wants to show his wrath and power by making some vessels of wrath prepared for destruction? What if the Lord did this to reveal the riches of his glory to his objects of mercy that he prepared in advance for glory?

God has called us his people even though we were not his family, and he loves us even though we don't deserve it. Isaiah also told us that even though the Israelites will be as numerous as the sand on the shore, God will save only the remnant because the Lord will judge the earth. If he had not left us as his descendants, we would have become like Sodom and Gomorrah.

> **Sodom and Gomorrah**
>
> Sodom and Gomorrah were two wicked cities in the Old Testament. They became so evil that God destroyed them with fire and sulfur from heaven.

Those who did not pursue righteousness have obtained it by faith, but the Israelites who sought the Law have not reached their goal. Jesus has become a rock that people stumble over, but those who believe in him will not be ashamed.

I pray to God that he would save the Israelites; they are zealous for him but lack knowledge. Being ignorant of God's righteousness, they tried to do it on their own but have not submitted to him. Christ is the fulfillment of the Law for righteousness to everyone who believes.

Those who seek righteousness through the Law seek to obey the commandments. But righteousness through faith tells us that God will save you if you confess that Jesus is Lord and believe that God raised him from the dead. No one who trusts him will ever be ashamed.

There is no distinction between Jews and Gentiles because God is the Lord of both and he gives his riches to all who believe. But they cannot call upon the Lord unless they believe, they cannot believe unless they hear, they cannot hear unless someone preaches, and no one will preach unless someone sends them. Those who preach bring good news, but not all Israelites believe. Faith comes from hearing the gospel of Christ.

Moses told us that God would make Israel envious and angry by a people who don't understand; Isaiah told us that those who didn't seek him would find God, and he would reveal himself to people who did not ask for him. God has held out his hands to Israel though they were a disobedient and rebellious nation.

God has not rejected his people that he knew beforehand. Elijah protested that Israel had killed the prophets, demolished God's altars, and sought his life. But God told Elijah that there were still 7,000 who had not bowed to false gods. In the same way, there is a remnant chosen by grace and not because of works.

Israel did not find what it was seeking; God's chosen found it, but the rest were hardened. God gave them a spirit of stupor, eyes that don't see, and ears that don't hear. He gave them an obstacle; now, their backs will be bent forever.

But they did not stumble so they would fall; their transgression led to salvation for the Gentiles to make Israel jealous. If their sin leads to riches for the world, how much more their faith! If their rejection brought reconciliation to the world, then their acceptance brings life from the dead. If the root is holy, so are the branches; God broke off some of the branches and grafted you into the tree. Now you share the nourishing sap with the root, but don't consider yourself better than the other branches.

Consider this; God grafted you in because he broke off other branches due to unbelief. You stand in faith, but don't be arrogant, tremble. If God didn't spare the natural branches, he won't spare you either. Consider God's severity to those who fall, and his kindness to you if you remain in him; otherwise, he will cut you off. If they do not persist in unbelief, God will graft them back in because he can do that.

Understand that God has partially hardened Israel until the full number of Gentiles has come in. God will save all Israel because the Savior will come from Zion and turn godlessness away from Israel. That is his covenant with them when he takes away their sins. As far as the gospel is concerned, they are enemies of God for your sake, but he still loves them for the sake of Abraham, Isaac, and Jacob; his gifts and call are irrevocable. Just as you were once disobedient and have received mercy, now they are rebellious and will receive mercy so he can fulfill his plan.

Oh, the depth of the riches of the wisdom and knowledge of God! His judgments and paths are beyond understanding! We cannot possibly know his mind or give him counsel. Everything that exists is from him and through him. All glory to him forever! Amen.

CHAPTER TWENTY-FOUR

A TRANSFORMED LIFE
Romans 12-16

Present your bodies to God as a living sacrifice, which is your spiritual act of worship. Don't conform to this world, but transform your mind in Christ; then, you will know God's will and what is right, acceptable, and perfect.

> **Worship**
>
> Worship is defined as making much of something or someone. Often, we think of this as singing praises to God in private or as part of a group. Worship includes this, but it is also the way we live our lives. Serving God and loving others is an essential part of our worship. As humans, we worship whether we want to or not; it is a part of our design. As Christians, we should worship with our words and actions.

Don't think more highly of yourself than you should, but judge with sober judgment according to the faith God has given you. We have many members in the body of Christ, but not all of them have the same function; we are one body in Christ and members of each other. By grace, we have different gifts, and we should use them accordingly. Whether in prophecy, faith, service, encouragement, giving, leadership, or mercy; use them well.

Love must be sincere; hate what is evil and cling to what is right. Devote yourselves to each other in love and honor each other. Serve the Lord with zeal; rejoice in hope, be patient in trouble, and persistent in prayer. Give generously and practice hospitality. Bless those who persecute you and do not curse them. Rejoice with those who rejoice and mourn with those who mourn. Live in harmony and do not be proud, instead be willing to associate with the lowly. Do not repay evil with evil, but always do the right thing. Don't take revenge, but leave room for God's vengeance. Give your enemies food and drink, and you will heap burning coals on their heads; overcome evil with good.

Everyone should be subject to the governing authorities because God established them. If you resist authority, you are resisting God because he appointed them, and he will judge. The government wields God's power for good; they do not bear the sword for no reason. Therefore, submit to the authorities to avoid punishment and for the sake of conscience. This is also why you pay taxes.

> **Christians and authority**
>
> Paul tells his readers to be subject to their government and this is the same for us today. During the First Century, the government was not perfect. The Roman Empire persecuted Christians and put them to death. When dealing with an oppressive government, we should engage, protest, and do everything we can to make a difference. We should not go against the Bible to be at peace with them because we answer to God. But at the end of the day, we must still live in subjection to their authority.

Pay to everyone what you owe, whether it be taxes, wages, respect, or honor. The only thing you should owe others is love, that is the fulfillment of the Law. All the commandments are summed up in the command: love your neighbor as yourself. Love does not harm and thus is the fulfillment of the Law.

Understand the present time; wake up because salvation is closer now than when we first believed. Put aside the deeds of darkness and put on the armor of light. Behave decently, not in drunkenness, sexual immorality, dissension, or jealousy. But put on the Lord Jesus Christ and don't think about how to gratify the flesh's desires.

Accept those who are weak in faith without arguing over secondary matters. Some have the faith to eat anything, but some only have the faith to eat vegetables. Neither should treat the other with either contempt or judgment because God accepts them both. Regardless of the issue in question, do whatever you do for the Lord. We don't just live for ourselves; we live for him; we don't die for ourselves; we die for him. No matter what, we are his because he is the Lord of both the living and the dead.

So, don't treat other believers with contempt or judgment because we will all bow before the Lord, and each of us will give him an account for our lives. Stop judging each other; instead, make up your mind not to cause anyone to stumble.

Nothing in and of itself is unclean, but if you think something is, then it is a sin for you. If your brother or sister is offended by what you eat or drink, you are no longer acting in love. Don't destroy someone else that Christ died for and don't let what you know is good be called evil.

The kingdom of God isn't about eating or drinking; it is about righteousness, peace, and joy in the Holy Spirit. Anyone who serves Christ pleases God and gains human approval; so, do whatever leads to peace and edification. Don't destroy God's work for food or drink because it's all clean unless it causes someone else to stumble. It is much better to abstain if it keeps someone else from falling. Be fully convinced of what you believe about questionable things. If someone does something that they are not convinced is right, it is a sin.

Those who are strong should accept the weak and not just please ourselves; we should do what's best for others and build them up. Not even Jesus lived to please himself but for us. The Scriptures exist to teach and encourage us so that through endurance, we might have hope. May we have the same attitude that Jesus had so that we may be unified in worshipping the Lord.

Accept one another as Christ accepted you so that you may praise God. Christ served the Jews on behalf of God's truth to fulfill the promises to the Patriarchs and so that the Gentiles would glorify the Lord. May the God of hope fill you with all joy and peace so that you may overflow with hope through the Holy Spirit's power.

I am convinced that you are full of goodness and knowledge and able to teach each other. I have written strong words to remind you about some issues so that you may minister to the Gentiles. He gave me the duty of preaching to them so that they might be an offering acceptable to God, sanctified by the Holy Spirit. I give glory to God because of what he has accomplished through me with them. I have faithfully preached and aim to continue to preach to those who have not yet heard.

I have wanted to come to you for some time, but now I'm on my way to Jerusalem to serve God's people. Once I'm done there, I want to go to Spain and visit you on my way. Please pray that I would be safe from the Jews there and that I would receive favor with those in Jerusalem so I can come to you and be refreshed. May the God of peace be with you all. Amen.

I urge you, brothers and sisters, to watch out for those who cause divisions and put obstacles in your way, contrary to what you've learned. People like these are not serving Christ, but themselves with their smooth talk and flattery; they want to deceive whomever they can. I rejoice because of your obedience; be wise about what is good and innocent of evil. The God of peace will soon crush Satan underneath your feet.

To the only wise and powerful God who has revealed himself and can establish you in faith, be the glory forever through Jesus Christ! Amen.

CHAPTER TWENTY-FIVE

PAUL'S ARREST
Acts 21:1-23:11

> **Resumption of the historical narrative**
>
> We don't know the exact timeline of what Paul was doing while he wrote his letters, but the historical record of the church's spread picks up again with him leaving Ephesus.

Paul and his companions sailed from Ephesus on a course to Phoenicia and stopped at Tyre to load cargo and Paul decided to spend time with the church there. Through the Spirit, the church tried to convince them not to go to Jerusalem. After seven days, they prepared to leave, and the church came out to pray for Paul.

Eventually, they made their way to Caesarea, where they stayed with Philip, one of the original deacons. While staying there, a prophet named Agabus came from Judea. He took Paul's belt, bound his own hands and feet with it and said, "Thus says the Holy Spirit, 'the Jews will bind the man who owns this belt like this and turn him over to the Gentiles.'"

When the people heard this, the people tried to convince Paul not to go to Jerusalem. But Paul replied, "Why are you weeping and breaking my heart? I'm ready to not only be tied up but also die in Jerusalem for the name of Jesus." When the people saw that he wouldn't change his mind, they let it go.

Paul and his companions left for Jerusalem, and the people warmly received them. The next day, Paul met with James and the other elders to tell them everything God had been doing amongst the Gentiles. The church glorified God when they heard Paul's stories.

They told Paul, "There are thousands of Jews here who believe, and they are all zealous for the Law, but they've heard that you teach Jews to forsake Moses and our customs. They will certainly hear that you've come, so please do what we ask. We have four men under a vow; go with them to purify yourselves and pay for their expenses to shave their heads. Then they will know that the rumors they heard are false and that you do obey the Law. As for the Gentiles who have believed, we sent a letter stating that they should stay away from food sacrificed to idols, blood, meat from strangled animals, and sexual sin." The next day, Paul purified himself and the men then took them to the temple and provided the offering for them.

Near the end of the purification process, some Jews from Asia saw Paul in the temple and stirred up the crowd, crying out, "Men of Israel, help us! This is the man who preaches against Moses and the Law. He has even brought Gentiles into the temple to defile it."

The city was in an uproar, and a mob grabbed Paul and dragged him out of the temple; immediately, they shut the city gates. As the crowd was trying to kill Paul, word reached a city official that the city was in chaos. The official took troops to the temple and the mob stopped beating Paul. He took Paul into custody and bound him with two chains while trying to determine what Paul had done.

There were too many competing voices, so the official had Paul carried to the barracks to find out what was happening. As they were about to enter, Paul asked the official if he could speak to him. The man was surprised that Paul spoke Greek and answered, "Aren't you the Egyptian who started a revolt and led 4,000 terrorists into the wilderness?"

Paul replied, "I'm a Jewish citizen from Tarsus; please let me speak to the crowd." The official permitted him. Paul stood on the barracks' steps and motioned for the crowd to be quiet.

Once they were calm, Paul spoke to them in Hebrew, "I am a Jew, born in Tarsus, raised in Jerusalem, and educated by Gamaliel according to our laws' strictest interpretation. I have zealously lived my life for God, just like you. As the high priest and council can testify, I persecuted Christians, arresting them, and even putting some to death. I took some of them to Damascus in chains for punishment when suddenly a great light shone from heaven and I fell to the ground. Then Jesus told me that I had been persecuting him and that I should go into the city where he would tell me what to do. The people with me saw the light but did not understand the voice.

"They led me by the hand into Damascus, where Ananias came to me and restored my sight. He told me that the God of our fathers had appointed me to know his will, to see and hear from Jesus, and then tell the world his message. Then, I was baptized in the name of Jesus.

"When I returned to Jerusalem, I was praying in the temple when the Lord told me to leave the city because the people would not believe me. I tried to argue that my changed life would convince them of his power, but the Lord told me that he would send me to the Gentiles."

Once Paul mentioned Gentiles, the crowd cried out that Paul should die and threw off their cloaks and tossed dust in the air. The official pulled Paul into the barracks and commanded the soldiers to question him by flogging to determine why the mob was so angry.

Once the soldiers had stretched Paul out to whip him, Paul protested that he was a natural-born Roman citizen and that they had not convicted him of a crime. The official was afraid because he had put a citizen in chains, so they released him.

The next day, the official brought Paul back before the chief priests and court to figure out why the Jews were so angry. Paul looked at the council and said, "Brothers, I have always lived my life with a good conscience."

But Ananias, the high priest, cut him off and commanded that someone hit him in the mouth. Paul was furious and retorted, "God is going to strike you, you whitewashed wall! How will you judge me when you break the Law by ordering me to be hit?"

Who was this Ananias?

This was a fairly common name during the First Century. There were three different men named Ananias in the New Testament. The first was a man who deceived the church along with his wife, Sapphira. The second was a believer that helped Saul after the Lord met the

> apostle on the road to Damascus. The third Ananias was the high priest, who also presided over Jesus' trial.

Those nearby said, "Are you going to stand there and insult God's high priest?"

Paul apologized, "I'm sorry, I didn't know he was the high priest because we are commanded not to speak evil of our rulers." Paul looked around the room and realized that half the room was Pharisees, and the other half were Sadducees. So, he cried out, "Brothers! I am a Pharisee and I am on trial for the hope of the resurrection of the dead!"

When Paul said this, the crowd began to argue because the Pharisees believe in angels, the spirit, and resurrection, while the Sadducees deny them all. The two groups stopped listening to Paul and began arguing with each other. It became so heated that the official was afraid the two sides would rip Paul apart, so the man ordered the soldiers to take him back to the barracks. That night the Lord came to him and said, "Take courage, because you must testify about me in Rome after you are done here."

CHAPTER TWENTY-SIX

PAUL TRANSFERRED TO CAESAREA
Acts 23:12-26:32

The next day, more than 40 Jews planned to kill Paul, and they swore to neither eat nor drink until he was dead. They went to the chief priests and elders and told them of their plan and asked them to notify the conspirators when they were moving Paul so they could attack.

Paul's nephew heard of the plot, so he went to the barracks and told his uncle. Paul called for one of the soldiers to take his nephew to the official and he shared the plot with him. After hearing the conspiracy, the official dismissed the boy and told him not to tell anyone else about the situation.

The official called for two commanders of a hundred soldiers and told them to take Paul with a squad of nearly 500 men in the middle of the night to Felix, the governor. He also sent a letter: "The Jews seized this man and were about to kill him when I learned he was a Roman citizen. I wanted to find out why they wanted to kill him, and I found out that there was a disagreement over their Law, but nothing requiring death or imprisonment. When I discovered a secret plot to kill him, I sent him to you so that we could find out what they have against him."

The soldiers brought Paul to Caesarea and delivered the letter. Felix received Paul and decided to keep him there until his accusers arrived.

***

After five days, Ananias and Tertullus came to Caesarea with some of the elders to make their case against Paul. When everyone had assembled, Tertullus began, "Felix, we have prospered so much under your rule, and we are so grateful for this audience, so I will get to the point. This man is a plague; he stirs up Jews around the world and is a ringleader of the Christians. He was trying to profane our temple when we stopped him. When you examine him, you will see everything we are accusing him of is true." The other Jews there joined in the accusations against Paul.

Felix nodded to Paul and he began his defense, "I am happy to make my case to you because you have judged our nation for many years. You can verify that it was only twelve days ago that I went to worship in Jerusalem and didn't argue with anyone or start a riot. Neither can you prove their accusations. But I confess this to you, this Christianity that they call a sect, I worship the God of our fathers and everything written in the Scriptures. We hope in God that there will be a resurrection of both the just and the unjust. I have always tried to live my life with a clear conscience towards both God and men.

"After several years, I went to Jerusalem to present my alms and offerings. They found me purified in the temple without any riot or disturbance. But then some Jews from Asia, who should be here to accuse me, came and stirred up a mob. Let them, or these men, present evidence against me for anything except that I cried out that I was on trial for the resurrection of the dead."

Felix knew a bit about Christianity, so he dismissed the case until Lysias, an official from Jerusalem, arrived. He gave orders to keep Paul in custody but not restrict his movement and allow him to have visitors.

Felix was married to a Jew named Drusilla, and they sent for Paul because they wanted to hear about faith in Jesus. As Paul reasoned with them about righteousness, self-control, and the coming judgment, Felix became alarmed and sent Paul away. Felix secretly hoped that Paul would bribe him for his freedom, so he sent for him often. After two years, Porcius Festus succeeded Felix, and he wanted to do the Jews a favor and left Paul in prison.

***

Three days after taking power, Festus went to Jerusalem, and the Jews asked him to transfer Paul to Jerusalem because they wanted to ambush him along the way and kill him. Festus replied that he was heading back to Caesarea and that Paul's accusers should come with him. He stayed for a little while longer and then headed back to Caesarea.

When he arrived, he took his seat and summoned Paul. Many Jews came before him and accused Paul of many heinous crimes, but they could not prove any of them. Paul stood to make his defense and appealed that he had not committed any crime against Rome or Jewish Law. Festus asked if Paul was willing to go to Jerusalem to stand trial.

Paul answered, "I'm standing before Caesar's court, where I ought to be tried. You know very well that I haven't committed any crime. If I committed some capital crime, I'm not afraid to die, but if they can't prove anything, I appeal to Caesar." Festus conferred with his counselors and then ruled that Paul would go to Caesar.

***

Many days later, Agrippa (the ruler over the Syrian region) came to Caesarea with his sister, Bernice, on an unrelated matter. Festus laid Paul's case before the king, and Agrippa was intrigued, so he asked to see Paul the next day.

The next day, Agrippa and Bernice made a very showy entrance, and they brought Paul before them. Festus said, "King Agrippa and everyone present, you see this man before you that the Jews wish to kill, but I can't find any reason he should die. Now that he's petitioned to go before the emperor, I intend to send him. But I have no idea what to write, so I was hoping that all of you could help me figure out what to say. It seems foolish to send a prisoner with no charges."

Agrippa permitted Paul to speak and he said, "King Agrippa, I am fortunate to have this opportunity to make my case before you because you know a lot about Jewish customs. Everyone knows how I have lived from birth and how I have lived my life according to our religion's strictest party. Now I stand here on trial because of the hope I have in the promises made to our ancestors, the same promises that they hope for as they worship both day and night. It is for this hope that I am on trial! Why is it so unbelievable that God can raise the dead?!

"I used to be convinced that I should oppose Jesus of Nazareth; I locked up believers in prison and even agreed to put them to death. I punished them in the synagogues, tried to make them blaspheme, and even chased them to foreign nations.

"In my fury, I was on my way to Damascus when I saw a light brighter than the sun surrounding me and my companions. I fell to my knees and I heard Jesus' voice tell me that I was persecuting him. He told me to stand because he had appointed me to testify about everything that had happened and everything he was going to tell me. He told me that he would deliver me from the Jews and send me to the Gentiles to open their eyes and that they would turn from darkness to light and from the power of Satan. All of this so he could forgive their sins and save them.

"King Agrippa, I obeyed Jesus, and I preached everywhere that people should repent, turn to God, and live holy lives. Therefore, the Jews seized me in the temple and tried to kill me. Even to this day, God has helped me so that I can stand here before you to testify that God has fulfilled the promises. That the Messiah must suffer and that by being the first to resurrect, he would proclaim light to both Jews and Gentiles."

Festus cut Paul off and said, "Paul, you are out of your mind; all your learning is driving you crazy!"

Paul replied, "I am not crazy; I am speaking truthfully and rationally. I know King Agrippa knows all these things because none of this happened in secret. King Agrippa, I know you believe the Prophets."

Agrippa answered, "Paul, are you trying to make me a Christian?"

Paul said, "I wish that everyone would become like me other than these chains."

Agrippa, Bernice, and Festus stood up and left. As they conferred with each other, they agreed that he wasn't guilty of any crime. Then Agrippa said, "We could set him free except he appealed to Caesar.

CHAPTER TWENTY-SEVEN

PAUL'S JOURNEY TO ROME
Acts 27-28

Festus delivered Paul to an Augustinian centurion named Julius and they began the journey to Rome. They changed ships and continued their journey along the coast. Summer was over, so they began to face rough weather. Paul warned them that if they continued, they could lose the cargo and people's lives. But Julius listened to the captain rather than Paul, and they kept going.

Not wanting to spend the winter where they were, they thought they had good enough weather to proceed, so they launched again. But a vicious storm overtook them and they were adrift at sea. They did everything they could to save the ship, throwing anything they could overboard.

After several days, Paul stood before them and said, "You should have listened to me. But God appeared to me last night and told me that I must stand before Caesar and that we would all survive, but we will lose the ship. Take heart, because I believe that God will keep his promise to me. But we must run aground on an island."

After two weeks adrift, it seemed like they were finally approaching land. They feared hitting rocks, so they set anchor and prayed for morning to come. The sailors tried to escape, but Paul warned Julius that they would die if they left the ship. The centurion cut the ropes to the lifeboat and let it go.

Paul encouraged everyone on board to eat something because it had been two weeks, and they would need their strength. Paul took bread in the sight of all of them, thanked God, and ate. The 276 people on board ate their fill and threw the rest of the food overboard to lighten the load.

When morning came, the sailors did not recognize the land, but they saw a bay with a beach, and they made their way to run the ship aground. But they hit a reef and the boat began to break apart. The soldiers planned to kill the prisoners, but Julius believed Paul and told everyone to jump overboard and make their way to land. Those who could swim, did, and the others made their way to shore on planks from the ship; everyone made it to land safely.

Once safely on shore, they found out that they were on the island of Malta. The people on the island were very kind and they built a fire for the survivors. Paul gathered a bundle of sticks and threw it on the fire. As he did, a poisonous snake came out of the blaze and bit his hand. When the local people saw this, they assumed that Paul was getting his just reward; since the sea didn't kill him, the snake would. But when nothing happened to him, they believed that he was a god.

Publius was the head of the island and he welcomed them for three days. His father was very sick with fever and dysentery, and Paul prayed for him and healed the man. When word of this miracle spread, all those who were sick on the island came to Paul, and he healed them. The grateful islanders allowed the survivors to stay with them for three months.

When it was finally time to depart, the local people provided everything that they needed. Eventually, the group made it to Rome, and they allowed Paul to stay on his own with the guard assigned to him.

Once Paul had been in Rome for three days, Paul called together the local leaders so he could lay out his case before them. He described his arrest and appealed to Caesar when the Jews could not prove any charges against him. The Roman Jews told him that they had not heard anything about him or the charges against him. But they set up an appointment for him to speak to them because they wanted to learn more about Christianity.

On the appointed day, many of the Jews came to Paul, and he spent all day reasoning with them from the Scriptures, explaining the kingdom of God and trying to convince them about Jesus. Some believed, and others did not, but they decided to leave when Paul said, "Isaiah was right when he said, 'these people would see and hear, but never understand. These people have closed their eyes, shut their ears, and let their hearts become dull.' Now, God is sending his salvation to the Gentiles because they will listen."

I have heard of your faith in the Lord Jesus and your love for other Christians, so I have not stopped thanking God for you. I continuously pray that God would give you a spirit of wisdom and revelation so that you will know him better. I also pray that he will open the eyes of your heart so that you may know the hope of his calling, the riches and glory of his inheritance for the saints, and the exceedingly great power for those who trust him. This is the same power and strength that God used to raise Christ from the dead and seated him at his right hand in heaven. He is far above all other rulers, authority, power, and everything else that ever has been or will be. God has put all things under Christ's authority and has made him the head of the Church, which is his body.

You were dead in the sin you lived in when you followed the ways of the world and Satan, the spirit that is at work in the hearts of the disobedient. We all lived that way and gratified the desires of our sinful flesh and minds; we were children of wrath by nature, just like everyone else. But God loves us and showed us great mercy by making us alive even when we were dead in our sins.

God saved us by grace, and he has raised us up with Jesus and seated us with him in heaven so that he could show the incredible riches of his grace through Christ. God saves us by grace through faith, and this is not from ourselves; it is the gift of God. It is not the result of works, so that no one can boast about their salvation. We are God's masterpiece, created in Christ to do the good works that God prepared for us to do.

Salvation by grace

Salvation through grace is one of Christianity's fundamental teachings and it separates us from every other religion. Grace is favor that we have not done anything to earn. That is a perfect definition of our salvation because it has nothing to do with our actions. God saves us based on Jesus' death and Resurrection and not what we do. We cannot do anything to make us good enough for God, so he did it for us. This is grace. All other major religions require adherents to do certain things to earn salvation, but Christianity focuses on what God has done for us instead of our actions.

Therefore, remember that you Gentiles used to be called "uncircumcised" by those who are physically circumcised. Remember that you were separate from Christ, excluded from citizenship in Israel. You were unfamiliar with the covenants of promise and lived a hopeless and godless life. But now you belong to Jesus, and although you used to be far away, his blood has brought you near.

Jesus is our peace and he united Jews and Gentiles into one people by breaking down the wall of hostility. He has abolished the Law with its commandments and regulations to make the two groups into one. Christ has established peace through his death on the cross and reconciled the two into one body to God by putting their hostility to death. So, he preached peace to those who were far off and those who were near; now, we both have access to the Father through Christ in one Spirit.

Therefore, you are no longer strangers and aliens, but citizens and members of God's household. Our faith builds upon the foundation of the apostles and prophets, with Jesus as the chief cornerstone. Christ joins the whole building together and raises it to become a holy temple for the Lord. He is also building you into a spiritual dwelling place for God.

This is why I am a prisoner for Christ, for the sake of you Gentiles. Surely you have already heard about God's grace that he gave me; this is what I wrote about before.

I am a prisoner of Christ for the sake of the Gentiles and I know that you've heard about my ministry. So, you should understand my insight into God's revelation that we are all a part of Christ's body and share in his inheritance. I am a servant of God's grace, even though I'm the least deserving of all believers. He gave me this ministry to make the gospel clear to everyone, even though it was once hidden. God intended that the church would teach all God's wisdom and eternal purpose that he accomplished in Jesus Christ, our Lord. He gives us our faith so that we can approach God with freedom and confidence. Therefore, don't let my suffering discourage you because it's for your glory.

I bow my knees before the Father, who gives every family its name. I pray that from his glorious riches, he might strengthen you with the power of his Spirit so that Christ can live in your hearts through faith. I pray that as he grounds you in his love that you would have the power with all believers to understand the boundless depths of Christ's love. I pray that you would know this love that goes beyond knowledge and that God would fill you with his fullness. To him, who can do more than we can ask or imagine through his power within us, be glory in the church and in Jesus Christ forever! Amen.

***

I urge you to live a life worthy of your calling; be gentle and humble, patiently bearing with one another in love. Keep the Spirit's unity through peace because there is one body, one Spirit, one hope, one Lord, one faith, one baptism, and one God and Father who rules over everything.

He has given us all his grace as he desired; that's why it says, "When he ascended on high, he led forth many captives and gave his people gifts." When it says that he ascended, that means Jesus descended to the earth and that he has ascended to the highest heavens, to fill the whole universe.

He gave his people the gifts of apostleship, prophecy, evangelism, pastoral care, and teaching to equip his people for ministry and building up the church until we reach the full unity of the faith, the knowledge of Christ, and maturity. Then we will not be tossed about by every new teaching, human cunning, craftiness, and deceit. Instead, we should speak the truth in love so that we might grow in every respect to the maturity of Christ. From him, the whole body is joined together, and every part works together so that it grows and builds itself up in love.

You should no longer live like the Gentiles, in the futility of their thinking. They don't understand God, and they are separated from God's life through their ignorance and hard hearts. They have lost sensitivity and given themselves to sensuality, impurity, and greed. But that's not the life you learned when you heard the truth of the gospel in Christ. You were taught to put away your old self and its deceitful desires; to have a new attitude and put on the new self, created to be like God in true righteousness and holiness. Put off falsehood and speak the truth to each other because we are all members of one body.

If you are angry, don't sin; don't let the sun go down on your anger because you will give the Devil a foothold. Stop stealing and do something useful with your life so that you can help the needy. Don't speak unwholesome words, but only what can build others up and benefit them. Don't grieve the Holy Spirit, who sealed you for the day of redemption. Get rid of bitterness, rage, brawling, slander, and every form of malice. Be kind and compassionate to each other, forgiving each other, just as Christ forgave you.

Therefore, imitate God like children imitate their parents. Walk in love like Jesus loved us and gave himself as a sacrifice to God. There should not be even a hint of sexual immorality, impurity, or greed in you because people like that are idolaters and will not inherit the kingdom of God. Don't even let there be obscenity, foolish talk, or coarse joking in your speech; instead, give thanks.

Don't be deceived by empty words, because these things bring God's wrath on the sons of disobedience. Do not become partners with them because you are children of light and no longer in the dark. Walk as children of light because the fruit of light brings all that is good, right, and true. Find out what is pleasing to God and avoid the unfruitful works of darkness. Their actions are shameful and will be exposed when the light comes and illuminates everything. Watch how you live, be wise, and make the most of every opportunity because the days are evil. Don't be foolish, but understand what the Lord's will is.

Don't get drunk because that leads to debauchery; instead, be filled with the Spirit speaking to one another with psalms, hymns, and songs. Make music for the Lord, giving thanks to God the Father for everything, in the name of our Lord Jesus Christ.

Submit to one another out of reverence for Christ. Wives, submit to your husbands as you do the Lord, for the husband is the head of the wife as Christ is the head of his body, the church. As the church submits to Christ, wives should submit to their husbands in everything. Husbands, love your wives like Christ loved the church and gave up his life to make her holy, cleansing her with the Word so he could present her as a perfect bride. Husbands should love their wives as they love their own bodies; loving your wife is the same as loving yourself. We all take care of our bodies, just like Christ does the church; we are all members of his body. This is why a man will leave his parents and be united with his wife, and the two shall become one flesh. This is just like

Christ and the church; husbands must love their wives, and wives must respect their husbands.

> **Mutual submission**
>
> Many have used this passage to demand that women submit to men, but this command is in the context of mutual submission. As believers, we are to submit to each other and look out for other believers' best interests. Christianity is not about gender; it is about following Christ and putting others before ourselves.

Children, obey your parents in the Lord. Honor your father and mother is the first command with a promise so that life will go well and you will live a long time. Fathers, don't provoke your children to anger; instead, teach them the Lord's discipline and instruction. Servants, obey your earthly masters with sincerity like you serve Christ, not so that you gain their favor but because you are also serving the Lord, and he will repay you. Masters, treat your servants the same way because you both have the same Master, and he does not show favoritism.

Finally, be strong in the Lord's power and put on the full armor of God so that you might stand against the Devil's schemes. We do not wrestle with flesh and blood, but against the rulers, authorities, and spiritual forces of this present world and the heavenly realms. Therefore, put on the full armor of God so that you can resist evil and stand strong. Put on the belt of truth, the breastplate of righteousness, the shoes of the preparation of the gospel, the shield of faith, the helmet of salvation, and the sword of the Spirit, which is God's Word. Always pray in the Spirit for the other believers and me so that we might boldly proclaim the gospel.

> **Spiritual armor and warfare**
>
> This passage advises us to arm ourselves with spiritual armor for battle. The reality is that the most important battles we fight are

> spiritual ones. While it is wise to prepare ourselves for what we face in life, our spiritual preparation is far more critical. Satan wants to destroy us and God's work and will use any means possible to drag us down with him. He will throw difficulties at us at every turn and the best way to fight them is through our spiritual armor.

So that you can know how I'm doing, I'm sending Tychicus to you, and he will fill you in. May the God and Father of our Lord Jesus Christ grant you grace, peace, and undying love.

CHAPTER TWENTY-NINE

REJOICE IN THE LORD
Philippians 1-4

Paul's letter to Philippi

The Philippian church was the first congregation in Europe and one that Paul planted himself. He had planted the church about ten years before he wrote to them and they continued to have a positive relationship. The church had collected a gift for Paul and sent it with Epaphroditus to bless Paul. While in Rome with Paul, Epaphroditus became deathly ill. Paul sent him back with this letter to thank the church for their generosity, to warn them against divisions, and prepare them for Timothy's visit. This letter was written around 62 A.D. when Paul was in his late 40's. He wrote this letter from prison in Rome.

I thank my God for everything we have been through, and I always pray for you with joy because you have helped me spread the gospel from the first day you heard it until now. I am confident that God will perfect the good work he started in you until the day Jesus returns. It's only natural that I should feel this way about you because you love me and you have shared in God's grace with me whether I was in prison or out defending and confirming the gospel. God is my witness how I long for all of you with Christ's affection.

I pray that you would love each other more and keep growing in real knowledge and discernment. Then you can determine what is excellent so that you can be pure and blameless until Jesus returns. He will fill you with the fruit of righteousness through Jesus Christ, to God's glory and praise.

I want you to know, brothers, that my situation has helped spread the gospel. Now everyone here, including the palace guard, knows that I'm in prison because I'm a Christian. Because of my imprisonment, many believers trust in the Lord and are boldly sharing the gospel. It is true that some of them have impure motives and preach the gospel out of selfish ambition, envy, and strife so they can make my imprisonment even more painful. However, some of them preach Christ out of love and goodwill because they know that I am here to defend the gospel. It doesn't matter to me if their motives are pure, just that they proclaim Christ; therefore, I will rejoice.

I will continue to rejoice because I know that your prayers and the Spirit of Jesus Christ's help will deliver me. I eagerly expect and hope that I will never be ashamed, but will continue to be bold and exalt Christ in my body, whether I live or die. In my opinion, to live is Christ and to die is gain. Living means fruitful labor for me, and I don't know which I prefer. I want to depart and be with Christ because that is much better for me, but it is better for you that I live. Therefore, I know that I will remain with you to share in your growth and joy in the faith so that after I arrive, your boasting in Christ can increase because of my presence.

Live a life worthy of the gospel, so that whether I see you or not, I will hear that you are united in spirit and mind as you walk together in faith. Don't be alarmed by opponents of the gospel, because God will save you and destroy them. God has given you the honor of believing in Christ and suffering for his glory as you experience the same problems I have.

If being in Christ encourages you, if his love comforts you, if we share the Holy Spirit, or if you have affection and compassion, then make me happy by being united in mind, love, and spirit. Don't act out of selfishness or pride, but be humble and think of others as more important than yourselves; don't just look out for yourselves, but look out for others as well.

You should have the same attitude that Jesus had: even though he was God, he didn't demand his rights, but made himself nothing, and came to earth as a servant. As a man, he humbled himself by being obedient to the point of death, even death on a cross. Therefore, God exalted him to the highest place and gave him the name above all names, so that at the name of Jesus, every person who ever lived will bow down and confess that Jesus Christ is Lord, to the glory of God the Father.

> **God's sacrifice**
>
> When Jesus came to earth, he did not stop being God. In his earthly body, he did not access all his power as God. He loves us so much that he was willing to suffer in our place so that we can have a relationship with him.

Therefore, my dear friends, work out your salvation with fear and trembling by continuing to obey, just like you did when I was there. God is the one that gives you the desire and power to please him. Do everything without complaining or arguing so that you may become pure, innocent children of God that shine like lights in a crooked and perverse generation. Hold onto the Word of Life, so that I will be able to rejoice when Christ returns because I did not run or work for nothing. But even if I die in service to your faith, I still rejoice and share my joy with you. In the same way, I urge you to rejoice and share your joy with me.

Lord willing, I want to send Timothy so that his report about you might encourage me. He's the only one I know that shares my mentality and will be genuinely concerned about your welfare. All the others focus on their interests rather than Jesus, but he has proven himself and has helped me spread the gospel like a child serving his father. Therefore, I want to send him to you as soon as I find out how things turn out for me. I trust in the Lord that I will be coming shortly after him.

I sent this letter with my brother and fellow worker Epaphroditus, whom you sent to minister to my needs. He missed you and was distressed because you had heard that he was sick. He was so sick that he almost died, but God showed him (and me) mercy because I would have been despondent if he had passed away. Therefore, I am eagerly sending him back to you so that you can see him again and so that I won't be as worried. Welcome him back in the Lord, with joy, and honor men like him, because he almost died for Christ by helping me with what you could not.

Finally, rejoice in the Lord. It's not a problem for me to write the same things again, and it helps protect you. Beware of the dogs, evil workers, and the false circumcision. We are the true circumcision, and we worship in the Holy Spirit, boast in Jesus Christ, and put no confidence in the flesh.

If anyone could have confidence in the flesh, it's me. I was circumcised on the eighth day, a pureblooded Jew from the tribe of Benjamin. I was a Pharisee, I zealously persecuted the church, and was blameless according to the righteousness found in the Law.

But I have counted those things as nothing compared to Christ. In fact, everything is worthless compared to knowing my Lord Jesus, and I have given up everything for him and count it as rubbish. Now I can gain Christ and be found in him, having a righteousness that comes from God through faith in Christ rather than the works of the Law. Now I can know him, the power of his Resurrection, and share in his sufferings as he conforms me to his death so that I might be raised from the dead. I haven't obtained it yet, and I'm not perfect, but I keep going so that I may become what Jesus wants me to be. I am not there yet; but I forget the past and reach for what lies ahead, as I press on towards the prize of God's heavenward calling in Jesus.

Those of us that are mature should have this attitude, and if you disagree, then God will make that clear to you as well. However, let us keep living by the same standard that we have been. Imitate my life and learn from those that follow our example. As I have told you before, I tell you now with tears, that many are enemies of the cross. Their end is destruction, their god is their appetite, they take pride in what should cause them shame, and they set their minds on earthly things. But we are citizens of heaven and we eagerly await the Lord Jesus Christ's return as our Savior. He will transform our humble bodies and make them like his glorious body by his power that brings everything under his control.

Brothers and sisters, stay true to the Lord. I love you and want to see you because you bring me joy, and you are the reward for my labor; therefore, stay faithful to the Lord. I urge Euodia and Syntyche to agree in the Lord. My true companions, I ask that you help these women get along because they have struggled with me to spread the gospel along with Clement and the others who have their names in the Book of Life.

Always rejoice in the Lord, and at the risk of repeating myself, rejoice! Let everyone see that you are gentle and kind; the Lord is near. Don't be anxious about anything; instead, take everything to God in prayer. Thank him for what he has done as you make your requests and God's unfathomable peace will guard your hearts and minds in Jesus.

Finally, let your mind dwell on things that are true, honorable, right, pure, lovely, and of good repute. Spend your time thinking about things that are excellent and worthy of praise. Practice the things that I taught you and that you saw in my life, and the God of peace will be with you.

I'm happy, and I thank God that you are concerned about me again; I know you were worried before, but you couldn't do anything about it. I'm not saying this because I'm in need; I've learned to be content in whatever circumstances I'm in. I know how to live in prosperity and poverty because I have learned how to be happy, whether I have food or go hungry. I can do all things through Christ who strengthens me. But it was good of you to share with me in my current affliction.

When I first preached the gospel after leaving Macedonia, you were the only church that gave financially; you even sent multiple gifts to me when I was in Thessalonica. I'm not just looking for the gift itself, but I'm excited that God will reward you for your generosity. I've received your gift from Epaphroditus and I'm doing well; I have plenty because you sent a gift that greatly pleases God. My God will supply all your needs according to his glorious riches in Christ.

May our God and Father receive glory forever! Amen. Greet all the Christians there in my name, and all the believers that are with me greet you. All the Christians send their greetings, especially those in Caesar's household. May the grace of the Lord Jesus Christ be with you.

CHAPTER THIRTY

CHRIST'S SUPREMACY
Colossians 1-4

Paul's letter to Colossae

Paul wrote the letter to the Colossian church during his Roman imprisonment around 62 A.D. in conjunction with Timothy He wrote it at the same time as he wrote the letter to Philemon and it is to a primarily Gentile audience. Paul had never been to Colossae, and the church there was likely founded by Epaphras, one of the men Paul had introduced to Christ. The book's central message is that Christ is sufficient and we do not need to add anything to his gospel.

We thank God for you when we pray because we have heard of your faith in Christ and the love you have for his people because of the hope laid up for you in heaven. You heard of this in the gospel, which has spread everywhere and is now bearing fruit and growing worldwide. Our brother Epaphras preached to you and he has told us of your love in the Spirit.

Since the day we heard of you, we have not stopped praying that you would know God's will with all spiritual wisdom and understanding so that you would live a life that pleases him and bears fruit in every good work. Then you will grow in the knowledge of God, strengthened with his power and might so that you might patiently endure and give thanks to the Father. He rescued you from darkness and made you qualified to inherit the kingdom of light through his Son, who gives us redemption and the forgiveness of sins.

Jesus is the image of the invisible God, the firstborn of all creation. He created all things on heaven and earth, whether visible or invisible, for his glory; he is before everything, and he holds everything together. He is the head of the church, the beginning, and firstborn from the dead so that he might be supreme. God was pleased to have his fullness dwell in

Christ so that he can reconcile everything to himself, making peace by shedding his blood on the cross.

> ### The Trinity
>
> In this passage, Paul tells us that the fullness of God's deity dwells in Jesus. This is an explicit declaration that Jesus is God and the second person of the Trinity. For more information on the Trinity read the box in Chapter 8 of The Life of Jesus.

Your evil behavior alienated you from God, but now he has reconciled you through Christ's physical death, so you could be blameless if you continue in your faith. This is the same message that I've been preaching since day one.

I rejoice in my suffering and finish whatever is lacking in Christ's afflictions for the church's sake. God has commissioned me to preach the full Word of God to you that he hid for many generations. But now, he has chosen to reveal his glorious riches to you in Christ. He gives me energy and power to proclaim him, warning and teaching everyone with all wisdom so we can be mature in Christ.

I want you to know how hard I'm working for you and those I have not yet met in Laodicea. I want to encourage their hearts to be united in love and to know the riches of understanding, knowledge, and wisdom of God in Christ. Don't let anyone deceive you with fancy arguments because although I'm not there with you, my spirit is with you, and I rejoice to see your faith in Christ.

Keep living your lives in Christ, grounded, and built up in the faith we taught you. Don't let anyone capture your minds with philosophy and lies according to the world rather than Christ. All of God's deity lives in Jesus and gives him authority; now, he fills you.

He metaphorically circumcised your hearts; now, you have been buried with him in baptism and raised with him through faith by God's power. You were dead in your sin and uncircumcision, but God has brought you to life and forgiven all our sins. He has canceled our debts and taken away our condemnation by nailing it to the cross. He has disarmed this world's powers and authorities and made a spectacle of them in his triumph through the cross.

Therefore, don't let anyone judge you regarding food, drink, Sabbath, or festivals because these are only the shadow of what is to come, but the reality is in Christ. Don't let anyone who insists on severe discipline, angel worship, or who goes on and on about visions lead you astray. They are proud for no reason, and they have separated themselves from Christ, who is the head of the church.

If you died with Christ to this world's spiritual forces, why do you still behave as if you are subject to its legalism and rules about eating and drinking? While these seem like wisdom, they are only self-made religion and asceticism, neither of which help you truly control the flesh.

Since you have been raised with Christ, set your hearts on heavenly rather than earthly things. You died, and now your life is in Christ, who sits at God's right hand. When Jesus appears in glory, you will appear with him as well. Therefore, put your earthly nature to death: sexual immorality, impurity, lust, evil desires, greed, and idolatry. Put away anger, wrath, malice, slander, obscene talk, and lies because you used to practice these things, and God's wrath is coming for those who do them. Take off your old self along with its practices and put on the new self, which is being renewed in knowledge after the image of its Creator.

There is no more hierarchy or division because Christ is all and is in all. As his holy, chosen people, clothe yourselves with compassion, kindness, humility, gentleness, and patience. Put up with each other and forgive each other if you have any grievances just as the Lord forgave you. Above all, love one another because this will bind you together in perfect unity. Let Christ's peace rule in your hearts and be thankful. Let the gospel live in you as you teach and admonish each other with wisdom, psalms, and songs from the Spirit. Sing to God with gratitude, and no matter what you say or do, do it all in the name of the Lord Jesus.

Wives, submit to your husbands, as is fitting in the Lord; husbands, love your wives and do not be harsh with them. Children, obey your parents in everything because this pleases the Lord. Fathers, do not antagonize your children so you won't discourage them. Servants, do what your earthly masters tell you to do; give your best and not just the bare minimum because you are working for Jesus. One day, he will repay your labor with either his inheritance or punishment. God does not show favorites. Masters, treat your servants justly and fairly because your Master lives in heaven.

Devote yourselves to prayer, being watchful and thankful. Pray for us as well that God may give us opportunities to preach the gospel wherever possible and that I would know how to proclaim his name. Walk wisely with outsiders, making the most out of your opportunities. Let your conversation always be full of grace so that you may know how you should answer everyone.

I am sending Tychicus and Onesimus to you to fill you in about what's been happening with me. My companions send you greetings, share them with everyone who is there in Colossae.

CHAPTER THIRTY-ONE

RECONCILIATION WITH ONESIMUS
Philemon 1

> **Paul's letter to Philemon**
>
> Paul wrote this letter to Philemon, urging his reconciliation with Onesimus. Paul likely wrote it at the same time as Colossians. Onesimus had been a servant to Philemon, and he escaped, possibly even stealing from his master at the same time. He made his way to Rome, where Paul led him to faith. Now, Paul was sending him back, seeking reconciliation between the two.

When I pray for you, I always thank God for what I hear about your faith in Jesus and love for all the other believers. I pray that you would be effective in sharing your faith so you may share our knowledge of every good thing for Christ's sake. The ministry and love that you provide to others brings me so much joy and comfort.

Even though I have the authority in Christ to command you to obey, I would rather appeal to you in love as an older man who is a prisoner for Jesus. I am sending Onesimus back to you even though previously, he was worthless to you. During my imprisonment, I led him to faith, and now he is useful to both of us. I am sending him back to you as if sending my heart.

I would have been happy to keep him serving me on your behalf while I'm in prison. But I didn't want to do anything without your consent so that your goodness would be voluntary, not compelled. Maybe he was away from you for a time that he could be back with you as more than a servant, but now as a brother to both of us in flesh and the Lord.

So, if you consider me your partner, receive him as you would me. If he has wronged you or owes you anything, charge it to my account; I will repay it (even though you owe me yourself). Brother, please redeem this situation, refresh my heart in Christ.

I know you will take him back and do even more than what I ask. Please prepare a guest room for me because I hope that God will answer your prayers, and I will be able to join you soon. Finally, all my fellow workers send their greetings. May the Lord Jesus' grace be with you.

CHAPTER THIRTY-TWO

TRUE AND PRACTICAL RELIGION
James 1-5

> **James' letter**
>
> This is a general letter without a specific audience that Jesus' half-brother James wrote to Jewish believers. At first, he did not believe Jesus was the Messiah, but he converted after the Resurrection. He wrote this letter as the leader of the church in Jerusalem. These believers were likely poor and oppressed and looked down on by Jews and Gentiles alike. James likely wrote this letter around 62 A.D.

Brothers, consider it pure joy when you experience various trials because tests of your faith produce patient endurance. Let endurance finish its work so that you may be mature and complete, not lacking anything.

> **Trials**
>
> Trials in life are inevitable; we will face difficult times regardless of our status. We can use these as an opportunity to draw closer to God or harden our hearts. God intends our trials to bring us to maturity and produce greater faith. He also uses them so we can share the comfort God gives us with others in similar circumstances.

If you need wisdom, ask God because he will generously give it to you without reproach. But if you ask, believe that he will answer and don't doubt because the one who doubts is like a wave of the sea, driven and tossed by the wind. People like that are double-minded and unstable; they should not expect to receive anything from the Lord.

Let the poor brother glory in his exaltation and the rich glory in their humiliation because they will disappear like a flower of the field. The sun rises with its scorching heat and withers the flowers and grass and destroys their beauty; in the same way, the rich man will fade away amid his pursuits.

Blessed are those who endure trials; after they have proved their faith, God will give them the crown of life that he promised to those who love him. During temptation, no one should say, "God is tempting me," because evil cannot tempt God, and he does not tempt anyone. Our evil desires tempt us, entice us, and then drag us away. These evil desires lead to sin, and sin leads to death. Don't be deceived.

Every good and perfect gift comes from the Father of Lights above; he does not change like shifting shadows. He chose to give us new birth through the Word of Truth so that we might be the first fruits of creation.

Be quick to listen, slow to speak, and slow to get angry because your anger does not produce God's righteousness. Therefore, get rid of all moral filth and evil and humbly accept the Word planted in your hearts that can save your souls.

Don't deceive yourselves by merely listening to God's Word; do what it says. Those who hear God's teaching and don't do anything about it are like people who look in a mirror and then forget what they look like as soon as they walk away. But God will bless those who look intently at the perfect Law of freedom and stick with it and obey rather than forgetting what it says.

If you think you are religious yet fail to control your tongue, you have deceived yourself, and your religion is worthless. True religion that God accepts is to look after widows and orphans in their troubles and to keep yourself unstained by the world.

My brothers, as believers in our glorious Lord Jesus Christ, don't show favoritism. If you save the best seats in church for rich people who come in with beautiful clothes and jewelry and the worst seats for the poor people wearing dirty rags, you have discriminated and become judges with evil thoughts.

Listen, my beloved brethren, hasn't God chosen the poor of this world to be rich in faith and receive the kingdom that he promised to those that love him? You dishonor the poor even though it is the rich that oppress you, drag you into court, and slander the good name of Christ by which he called you. You will be doing the right thing if you obey the royal Law found in Scripture: "Love your neighbor as yourself." But if you show favoritism, then you are sinning and breaking the Law.

Whoever obeys the entire Law, but stumbles in one area, is guilty of breaking it all. The same God who commanded not to commit adultery also commanded not to commit murder; if you don't commit adultery, but do commit murder, then you are a Law-breaker. Speak and act as those about to be judged by the Law of freedom because those who do not show mercy will be judged without mercy; however, mercy triumphs over judgment.

What good is it if a man claims to have faith and does not have works? Can that kind of faith save him? If someone lacks clothing and food, what's the use of saying, "Be warm and well fed," if you don't do anything about the physical needs? In the same way, faith without works is dead. Some will argue that they have faith and others have works. Show me your faith without works and I will show you my faith by what I do. Do you believe in God? Good! Even demons believe that and tremble in fear.

You fool, don't you see that faith without works is dead? Our father Abraham's works justified him when he offered his son Isaac on the altar. His faith and actions were working together and his actions completed his faith. That's why Scripture says, "Abraham believed God and it was credited to him as righteousness," and he is God's friend. Our actions justify us, not just our faith. Similarly, Rahab's works justified her when she welcomed the spies and sent them out a different way. Just as the body without the spirit is dead, faith without works is dead.

Faith and works

Some people have struggled with this passage in conjunction with the many passages on salvation by faith alone. Our faith alone saves us and we do not need any additional action for salvation. But our works are evidence that we have a faith that has saved us. If we claim to have faith, but it doesn't motivate any change in our behavior, our faith

> may not be real. If we have authentic faith, then our actions will change as well.

Few of you should become teachers because they will face stricter judgment. We all stumble in many ways, and if anyone can keep from sinning with his mouth, then he is a perfect man and can control his whole body as well. We put a bit into a horse's mouth so that they will obey us and go wherever we want. Or look at ships: even though strong winds drive them, the pilot controls where he wants to go with a tiny rudder. In the same way, the tongue is a small body part, but it makes great boasts.

Small sparks set great fires! The tongue is set on fire by hell and is a world of evil that corrupts the whole person and sets his life course on fire. Humanity has tamed all kinds of animals, birds, reptiles, and sea creatures, but no one can tame the tongue because it is a restless evil that is full of deadly poison. We use our mouths to praise our Lord and Father and the same mouths to curse men that he made in his likeness. Out of the same mouth come both blessing and cursing; my brothers, this should not be! Can saltwater and freshwater flow in the same spring? Fig trees cannot grow olives, grapevines cannot grow figs, and salty water cannot produce fresh water.

If you are wise and understand God's ways, then live a good life and do deeds that come from the humility of wisdom. But if you have bitter envy and selfishness in your heart, then do not boast and lie about the truth. That kind of wisdom is not from heaven but is earthly, natural, and demonic. Wherever you have envy and selfishness, you also have disorder and everything evil. But God's wisdom is pure; then it is peaceful, gentle, reasonable, full of mercy and good fruits, impartial, and free from hypocrisy. Peacemakers who sow in peace reap a harvest of righteousness.

What causes fights and quarrels among you? Isn't it the desire for pleasures that war within you? You want and don't have; you kill and you covet, but you cannot have what you want, so you bicker and fight. You don't have because you don't ask. Even when you ask, you don't receive because you ask with wrong motives so that you can please yourselves.

You adulterous people, don't you know that friendship with the world is hostility towards God? Whoever wants to befriend the world becomes an enemy of God. Or do you think that Scripture says, "God longs jealously for the spirit that he has caused to live in us" for no reason? But God gives more grace, that's why Scripture says, "God opposes the proud, but he gives grace to the humble."

Therefore, submit yourselves to God; resist the Devil and he will run from you. Draw close to God and he will draw near to you. Wash your hands, you sinners, and purify your hearts, you double-minded. Be miserable, mourn, and cry; let your laughter turn into mourning and joy into gloom. Humble yourselves before the Lord and he will lift you up.

Brothers, do not slander one another because he who speaks against and judges a brother speaks against and judges the Law. When you judge the Law, you are no longer obedient but are now a judge. There is only one Lawgiver and Judge, the One who can give life and destroy it. So, who are you to judge your neighbor?

Some of you say, "Someday we will go to this place or that, spend a year there, do business, and make money." But you don't even know what will happen tomorrow; your life is just a vapor that is here and then gone. Instead, you should say, "If the Lord wills, we will live and do this or that." But now you arrogantly boast, and all such boasting is evil. Therefore, whoever knows what to do and doesn't do it is sinning.

Our plans and God's plans

As humans, we love to plan the future; it is one of the things that sets us apart from the other animals. It is wise to prepare for what's to come, but we must remember that God's plan is more important in the overall scheme of the universe. There are times when he will establish our plans, but others when he has something else in mind. We should make plans, but make sure that we submit them to the Lord.

Pay attention rich people, weep and wail because of the misery that is coming. Your wealth has rotted, and moths have eaten your clothes. The gold and silver that you hoarded for the last days has rusted and their rust will testify against you and eat your flesh like fire. Listen, the wages you didn't pay the workers who worked your fields are crying out against you, and the Lord Almighty has heard their cries. You have lived in luxury and self-indulgence and fattened your hearts in a day of slaughter. You have condemned and murdered righteous men, and they did not resist you.

Be patient until the Lord returns. See how the farmer waits for the earth to yield its valuable crop and how he is patient for the spring and autumn rains. In the same way, be patient and strengthen your hearts because he will return soon. Don't grumble against each other, or else you will be judged; behold, the Judge is standing at the door. As an example of suffering and patience, look at the prophets who spoke in the name of the Lord. We consider those that have suffered blessed. You have heard of Job's endurance and have seen God's compassion and mercy through what he has brought about.

Above all, don't swear by heaven, earth, or anything else; let your yes be yes, and your no be no; otherwise, you will be condemned. Are some of you suffering? Pray. Are any of you rejoicing? Sing songs of praise. Are any of you sick? Call the elders of the church and have them pray over him and anoint him with oil in the name of the Lord. The prayer of faith will heal the sick, and the Lord will raise them up and forgive the sins they have committed. Therefore, confess your sins to each other and pray for each other so that you may have healing; the prayer of the righteous is powerful and effective.

The prophet Elijah was a man just like us; he prayed that it would not rain, and it was dry for three-and-a-half years. Then he prayed again, and the heavens produced rain, and the earth produced its crops. You should know that if one of you wanders away from the truth and someone brings him back, the one that turns a sinner away from his error will save him from death and cover many sins.

CHAPTER THIRTY-THREE

PROPER LIVING DURING SUFFERING
I Peter 1-5

> **Peter's first letter**
>
> The church began to face persecution as it spread because those in power didn't like Christians acknowledging a different king. Christians were killed and blamed for many of the problems during the First Century. As a result, many of them scattered from where they had first known Jesus and took the gospel with them.
>
> Peter wrote this letter to Christians who were scattered during Nero's persecution of the early church. Nero was an emperor of Rome who had allowed much of the capital to burn and then blamed Christians for the inferno. He wrote this letter during the mid-60's A.D. The message went to both Jewish and Gentile believers and talked about how they were to live during their suffering.

Praise be to the God and Father of our Lord Jesus Christ! In his great mercy, he has given us new birth into a living hope through Jesus' Resurrection from the dead. He is giving us an inheritance that can never die, spoil, or fade, and it is waiting for us in heaven. He will reveal it to us at the last time and he is guarding us until then. We rejoice in this, even though we currently suffer various trials so that our faith may prove to be more genuine than gold and jewels refined by fire. This results in praise, glory, and honor at Jesus Christ's revelation.

Even though we don't see him, we love and believe in him with an inexpressible joy, filled with glory and faith that saves our souls. The prophets, who spoke of the grace to come, carefully searched for this salvation, trying to figure out how and when it would happen. They were serving you and not just themselves when they spoke of the gospel that you have heard through the Holy Spirit. Even angels wish they could understand these things.

Therefore, prepare your minds for action, be sober-minded, and set your hope on the grace that Jesus will bring when he is revealed. Don't conform to the passions of your former ignorance, but be holy as God is holy. You call on a Father who will judge everyone's work impartially. Therefore, live in fear during your exile, knowing that Christ's perfect blood has ransomed you from the ways of your ancestors, rather than perishable things like silver or gold. God chose Christ before creation but has revealed him in these last times for your sake. God raised him from the dead and glorified him, so your faith and hope are in God.

Now that you have purified yourselves by obeying the truth, love one another from a pure heart because you have been born again through God's living and abiding Word. All flesh will wither and fall, just like the glory of grass and flowers, but the Lord's Word remains forever. This is the good news that we preached to you.

Get rid of all malice, deceit, hypocrisy, envy, and slander and crave spiritual milk like newborn babies so that you may grow up in your salvation now that you have tasted that the Lord is good.

You are living stones that God is building into a spiritual house to be a holy priesthood that offers spiritual sacrifices acceptable to God through Jesus Christ. He is the living Stone that humans rejected. God has made him the chosen cornerstone and whoever trusts in him will never be ashamed. To those who believe, the stone is precious, but to those who do not believe, it is an obstacle that makes them fall. Their disobedience causes them to stumble, which is their destiny. But you are a chosen people, a royal priesthood, a holy nation, God's special possession, so that you may praise the one who called you out of darkness into his wonderful light.

Once you were not a people and had not received mercy, but you are now God's people who have received his mercy. I urge you as foreigners and exiles to abstain from sinful desires which wage war against your soul. Keep your behavior among the Gentiles honorable, so that when they slander you, they may see your good deeds and glorify God.

For the Lord's sake, submit yourselves to every human authority because God sent them to punish wrongdoers and commend those who do what is right. God wants you to silence the ignorant talk of foolish people by doing good.

Live as free people, but don't use your freedom as a cover-up for evil; live as God's servants. Honor everyone, love the brotherhood, fear God, honor the emperor. Servants, be subject to your masters with all respect, regardless if they are righteous or not. It is commendable if someone endures sorrow because they are suffering unjustly for God. But if you are punished for sinning, your endurance doesn't matter.

Christ set an example for you and you should suffer as he did. Jesus was sinless, and when they insulted him, he did not retaliate; when he suffered, he did not threaten in return. Instead, he entrusted himself to God, who judges justly. Jesus bore our sins in his body on the cross so that we might die to our sins and live for righteousness because his wounds heal us. We were like sheep going astray, but now we have returned to the Shepherd and Overseer of our souls.

Wives should submit to their husbands so that if they are unbelievers, their wives' behavior might win them over. Your beauty should not only come from outward adornment but should come from the inner self, the unfading beauty of a gentle and quiet spirit, which is valuable in God's sight.

The holy women of the past adorned themselves this way by submitting to their husbands. For example, Sarah obeyed Abraham, and you are her children if you do good and do not fear. Also, husbands should live with their wives, showing understanding and treating them as a more delicate vessel, since they are fellow heirs of the gracious gift of life. Then nothing will hinder your prayers.

> ### More delicate vessels
>
> Peter describes women as more delicate vessels, but this does not mean they are weak. This is a generalization that means they are different than men and we should treat them as such. God created men and women differently to help fulfill his plan. Neither is better than the other and we should not expect them to be the same.

Finally, you should all be like-minded, sympathetic, love one another, be compassionate and humble. Do not repay evil with evil or insult with insult. On the contrary, repay evil with blessing because this is your calling. Those who want to love life and see good days should keep their tongues from evil and lips from lies; they should turn away from sin and do good, always seeking peace. The Lord watches over the righteous and listens to their prayers, but his face is against those who do evil.

No one will harm you if you are zealous for good, but God will bless you even if you suffer. Don't be afraid of threats, but revere Christ as Lord in your hearts. Always be ready to make a defense to anyone who asks you about why you have the hope that is in you. Answer with gentleness, respect, and a clear conscience so that those who slander your good behavior would be ashamed.

If it is God's will to suffer, it should be for good rather than evil. For Christ also suffered for sins, the righteous suffering for the unrighteous to bring you to God. He died in the body but is alive in the Spirit. Then he proclaimed the gospel to the spirits in prison who had not obeyed. God waited patiently in the days of Noah and he only saved eight people. Baptism corresponds to this; it saves you, not because it cleans you from dirt, but because it presents you to God through Jesus' Resurrection with a clear conscience. He is now at the right hand of God and everything is in submission to him.

Therefore, since Christ suffered in the body, arm yourselves with this same attitude. Whoever suffers in the body is finished with sin. Now, they live their earthly lives for the will of God rather than evil human desires. You have spent enough time acting like pagans, living in sensuality, passions, drunkenness, orgies, drinking parties, and lawless idolatry. Some of your former companions are surprised that you don't still partake, and they make fun of you, but they will give account to God, who judges the living and the dead. Therefore, the gospel was preached even to those who are now dead, so that they might be judged according to human standards regarding the body but alive according to God regarding the Spirit.

The end of all things is near; therefore, be self-controlled and sober-minded so that you may pray. Above all, love each other deeply because love covers many sins. Be hospitable without grumbling and each of you should use your gifts to serve others as faithful stewards of God's grace.

Whatever you do, do it as if you are doing it for God so that he may be praised. To him be the glory and the power forever! Amen.

***

Dear friends, do not be surprised at the fiery ordeal you face as if something strange were happening to you. But rejoice when you participate in the sufferings of Christ so that you may be overjoyed when he returns. God blesses you if others insult you for Christ's name because the Spirit of glory and God rests on you. Don't suffer as a murderer, thief, criminal, or meddler, but if you suffer as a Christian, praise God that you bear that name.

It is time for judgment to begin with God's household, and if it starts with us, it will be much worse for those who do not obey the gospel. If it is hard for the righteous to find salvation, what will become of the ungodly and the sinner? Those who suffer according to God's will should commit themselves to their faithful Creator and continue to do good.

I urge the elders to be shepherds of God's flock that is under your care. Watch over them willingly; not pursuing dishonest gain, but eager to serve; not domineering but as an example. When the Chief Shepherd appears, you will receive the crown of glory that will never fade away.

In the same way, young people should be subject to their elders. Clothe yourselves with humility because God opposes the proud and gives grace to the humble. Humble yourselves under the mighty hand of God so that he may exalt you at the proper time. Cast all your anxieties on him, because he cares for you.

Be alert and sober-minded because your enemy, the Devil, prowls around like a roaring lion looking for someone to devour. Resist him and stand firm in your faith because you know that the family of believers worldwide is undergoing the same kind of suffering. After you have suffered for a little while, the God of all grace, who has called you to his eternal glory in Christ, will restore, confirm, strengthen, and establish you. To him, be the power forever! Amen.

Peace to all of you who are in Christ.

CHAPTER THIRTY-FOUR

SUPERIORITY OF CHRIST
Hebrews 1:1-8:6

> **The letter to the Hebrews**
>
> This is a unique letter in the New Testament because we do not know the author or the original audience. There is evidence that Paul wrote this letter just before his death, but we cannot be sure. The author wrote this letter to people who knew about Judaism. They may have faced the temptation to return to their previous belief system or been lazy Christians who had faced resistance. Regardless, this was a letter showing that Jesus is superior to all else.

In the past, God spoke through the prophets at different times in various ways, but now he has spoken to us by his Son, who created the universe and will inherit everything. The Son is the radiance of God's glory, the exact representation of his being. He holds the universe together with the power of his Word. After making purification for sin, he sat down at God's right hand, becoming superior to the angels because his name is more excellent than theirs.

To which of the angels did God ever call his Son or command us to worship? The angels are Jesus' servants, and God says about him, "Oh God, your throne will last forever and you shall rule with a scepter of justice. You love righteousness and hate wickedness; therefore, I have set you above your companions by anointing you with the oil of joy."

In the beginning, he laid the foundations of the earth, and the heavens are the work of his hands. They will all wear out and perish, but he will remain forever. He will roll them up like a robe and change them like a shirt. But he remains the same forever. He sits at God's right hand until God makes his enemies a footstool for his feet. Angels are only ministering spirits sent to serve those who will inherit salvation.

We must pay close attention to what we've heard, so we don't drift away. If we ignore the message of salvation that angels sent us, we will not escape punishment. God announced this salvation to us and testified to it with signs, wonders, miracles, and gifts of the Holy Spirit.

But God did not subject the coming world through angels. He has made humanity a little lower than the angels, crowned us with glory, and given us rule over everything. In subjecting everything to Christ, there is nothing outside his control.

Angels

The Bible tells us about non-human, created beings, known as angels. We don't know how God created them, but we can assume he did it before making humans. Popular culture has given us the picture of angels wearing white robes, having halos, flying around, and playing harps. The truth is that angels are eternal, spirit beings without physical bodies. Although the Bible records instances of them taking visible forms as human beings or unusual winged creatures, they are usually unseen. Scripture names the rankings and different types of angels, although it does not say much about their differences. The types of angels found in Scripture are archangel, angel, seraphim, cherubim, principalities, authorities, powers, thrones, might, and dominion.

We do not know much about angels, and God likely left angels a relatively unknown area for a reason. We do know that we should not place undue focus on angels or their role; all these beings are lower than God, and we should never worship them or listen to them if they contradict the Bible. The Bible tells us that they worship God, war with demons, and minister to those who believe in God. This can happen through giving a message, protecting, providing care, etc.

Right now, we don't see everything subjected to him, but one day we will. Jesus was made a little lower than the angels for a time, but now he is crowned with glory because he suffered and died for everyone.

It's only right that the one who created everything should be the source of salvation for us, the sons of glory, through his suffering. The one who makes people holy and the holy people are of the same family, so he calls us brothers and sisters. Jesus shared our humanity with us to break Satan's power of death and free those enslaved by their fear of death. But he helps Abraham's descendants and not the angels. Therefore, Jesus became fully human to serve God as a merciful and faithful high priest and atone for people's sins. Since he suffered when tempted, he can help us when we face temptation.

Therefore, fix your thoughts on Jesus, our apostle and high priest. Jesus was faithful to the one who appointed him, just like Moses was faithful to God. But he is worthy of greater honor than Moses just as the builder of the house is greater than the building. Moses bore witness to what would come, but Jesus is the faithful Son over God's house; we are his house if we continue to hold our confidence and the hope in which we glory.

Therefore, the Holy Spirit tells us not to harden our hearts as our ancestors did when they tested him in the wilderness. God was angry with them and he swore that they would not enter his rest. Make sure that none of you have a sinful, unbelieving heart that turns away from the living God. Instead, encourage each other while it is still 'today' so that sin's deceitfulness won't harden any of you. Otherwise, you will be like our ancestors who came out of Egypt and died in the wilderness because of their unbelief.

Since the promise of entering his rest still stands, be careful that none of you fall short of it. They heard good news just like we have, but it didn't help them because they did not have faith. Those of us who believe shall enter his rest.

On the seventh day of creation, God rested from his works. Our ancestors did not enter his rest because of their disobedience. The promise is still true today if we listen and do not harden our hearts. If Joshua had given them rest, God would not have spoken of another day later on.

There is a Sabbath rest for God's people because those who enter it also rest from their works, just as God did from his. Let us do everything we can to enter that rest so that no one will die from following their disobedience.

The Word of God is alive and active, sharper than any two-edged sword. It penetrates the division of soul and spirit, joints, and marrow, and it judges the thoughts and attitudes of the heart. God sees every creature; nothing can hide from his eyes.

Therefore, since Jesus is our great high priest, and he ascended into heaven, let us hold firmly to our faith. We have a high priest who understands our weaknesses because he was tempted in every way like we are, but he did not sin. So, let us approach God's throne of grace with confidence so that we may receive grace and mercy in our time of need.

Every high priest selected from among the people is appointed to represent the people in everything relating to God. He can deal gently with them because he also knows weakness. Therefore, he must offer sacrifices for his sins as well as the people's sins. No one chooses this position; God calls him to it just as he called Aaron. In the same way, God exalted Jesus to the position of high priest forever, in the order of Melchizedek.

During Jesus' life on earth, he prayed with loud cries and tears to the one who could save him from death, and God heard him. Although he was the Son, he learned obedience through his suffering. Being perfect, he became the source of salvation to all who obey him as a high priest like Melchizedek.

> **Melchizedek**
>
> Melchizedek is a mysterious character from the Old Testament and we don't know much about him. When Abraham rescued his nephew, Lot, from kidnappers, Abraham blessed him and paid him a tenth of everything. This passage goes on to tell us much more about this man.

We have much to teach you, but it is hard because you aren't trying to understand. By now, some of you should be teachers, but you still haven't grasped the basic teachings of God's Word. You need milk, not solid food! Those who live on milk are infants and they don't understand true righteousness. But solid food is for the mature who have trained themselves to discern good from evil.

Therefore, let's move beyond the basic teachings of Christ about repentance from sin, faith in God, ceremonial rituals, the Resurrection, and judgment. God willing, we will move past this to maturity.

It is impossible for those who have been enlightened, tasted the heavenly gift, shared in the Holy Spirit, and known God's goodness to fall away and then return to faith. They crucify the Son of God all over again and hold him in contempt.

Land that drinks in the rain and produces a useful crop receives God's blessing. But the land that produces thorns and thistles is in danger of being cursed and burned. We are convinced of better things about you and your salvation.

God is just; he will remember your work and love as you continue to help his people. We want you to show the same diligence to the end so that you may realize your hope. We don't want you to become lazy, but to imitate those who inherit the promise through patience and faith.

When God made his promise to bless and multiply Abraham, he swore by himself because there was no one greater to swear by. God wanted to make the unchanging nature of his purpose very clear to the heirs and he confirmed it with an oath. Since God cannot lie, we can hold onto his promise and the hope that he will come through. Abraham waited patiently and obtained the promise because Jesus is a forerunner on our behalf, a high priest forever after the order of Melchizedek.

Melchizedek was the king of Salem and God's high priest when he met Abraham returning from rescuing Lot. Melchizedek blessed Abraham, and in return, Abraham gave him a tenth of everything. He was a king of righteousness and peace, without mother or father, having neither beginning nor end. But like the Son of God, he continues as a priest forever. He was so great that even our father Abraham gave him a tenth of everything. The Law requires the Levites to collect a tenth from the people even though they are Abraham's descendants. However, this man wasn't Abraham's descendant, yet he collected a tenth from him and blessed the one with the promises.

Typically, the lesser is blessed by the greater. For Israelites, the tenth is collected by those who die, but in Abraham's case, it was collected by one declared to be living. We can even go so far as to say that Levi paid a tenth through Abraham because when Abraham met Melchizedek, Levi was still in his loins.

If the Levitical priesthood could have brought perfection, why would there need to be a priest in the order of Melchizedek and not Aaron? When the priesthood changes, the Law changes as well. We cannot make sense of this in the framework of the Levitical priesthood because Jesus descended from Judah and the Law doesn't speak of priests in that family line.

This becomes clearer when another priest arises like Melchizedek, who is a priest through an indestructible life and not through his bloodline. The previous commandment was set aside because it was weak and useless. A better hope was introduced that allows us to draw near to God.

Priests assume their position with an oath and our perfect priest took that role when God swore that he would be a priest forever. God's promise makes Jesus the guarantee of a better covenant. There have been many Levitical priests because they die, but since Jesus is eternal, he is a permanent priest. Therefore, he can truly save those who draw near to God through him since he is always there to intercede for them. We need a priest like this, holy, innocent, unstained, separated from sinners, and exalted above the heavens.

He does not need to offer daily sacrifices for his sin and the people's sin like the Levitical priests because he gave a perfect sacrifice when he died on the cross. The Law appoints weak men as high priests, but the word of the oath, which came after the Law, appoints Jesus, who is perfect forever.

We have a high priest who sat down at the right hand of God in heaven and serves in the sanctuary, the tent of worship built by God and not man. Every high priest offers gifts and sacrifices, so Jesus had to have something to offer as well. These men are only a shadow of the heavenly things because God told Moses to set up everything as a pattern of what God established.

CHAPTER THIRTY-FIVE

SUPERIORITY OF THE NEW COVENANT
Hebrews 8:7-10:18

The ministry Jesus has received is better than the old one, since the New Covenant is based on better promises. If there were nothing wrong with the first covenant, then a new one wouldn't have been necessary. But God found fault with the people, and he promised a New Covenant that would be better than the old one because the people were unfaithful. He promised to put the New Covenant in their minds, write it on their hearts, be their God, and they would be his people. Then they will all know the Lord and he will forgive their sins by making the Old Covenant obsolete.

The first covenant had regulations for worship and an earthly sanctuary. When everything was properly set up, the priests regularly entered the outer rooms to perform ministry. But only the high priest could enter the innermost room, the holy of holies, and this was only once a year when he brought a blood offering for sin. The Holy Spirit was showing up there even though he had not yet been revealed. The gifts and sacrifices offered could not clear the worshipper's conscience because they were only external food and drink.

When Jesus came as the high priest, he brought the greater and more perfect tabernacle that is not made with human hands. He did not enter through the blood of goats and calves; he entered the holy of holies by his blood, bringing eternal redemption. Our offerings made us clean externally, but Christ's blood made us clean internally from our sin so that we may serve the living God. So, Christ is the mediator of a New Covenant. Those who are called may receive the promised eternal inheritance through his death that redeems the sins committed under the first covenant.

> ### The sacrificial system
>
> God established the Old Testament's sacrificial system to delay punishment for the people's sins until Christ came to be the ultimate sacrifice. There were different sacrifices for various transgressions and all of them foreshadowed Jesus' eventual death for the people.

A will only is in effect if there is a death since it is not valid for the living. Therefore, not even the first covenant was inaugurated without blood. Moses instituted the Law by sprinkling the people with the blood of goats and calves. In the same way, he sprinkled the tabernacle and all the utensils of worship. In fact, the Law requires nearly everything to be cleansed with blood, and there is no forgiveness without the shedding of blood. If the copies of the heavenly things needed purification with blood, then the true sanctuary is purified with Jesus' blood.

> ### Why is blood necessary for forgiveness?
>
> God requires blood for forgiveness to show the seriousness of sin. In the Garden of Eden, God promised Adam and Eve that their sin would lead to death, and Paul repeats this in his letter to the Romans. God cannot accept us with our sin because he would no longer be holy (a central aspect of his character). To forgive our sins, God required blood because it is the source of our life. Animal sacrifices were a temporary solution, but Jesus' perfect sacrifice was enough to forgive all our sins.

Jesus does not need to enter the holy of holies each year to offer animal sacrifices. He has offered his own blood once for all people because he is the culmination of the sacrificial system. Just as people die once and then face judgment, Christ was sacrificed once to take away the sins of many. He will appear a second time, not to bear sin, but to bring salvation to those waiting for him.

The Law is not the reality, but a shadow of the good things coming because it can never make people perfect through repeated sacrifices. But now we do not need to keep offering sacrifices because Christ's death cleansed us, and we don't need to feel guilt for our sin. The sacrifices were a reminder of our sins, even though they cannot take them away.

Therefore, when Christ came into the world, he did not desire our sacrifices, nor did they please him. The Scriptures were about him and he came to do God's will so that he could make us holy through his death for the last time.

Every day, priests serve by repeatedly offering sacrifices that cannot take away sins. But after Jesus died for our sins, he sat down at God's right hand, waiting for his enemies to be made a footstool for his feet. In a single offering, he perfected us for all time. The Holy Spirit gives further testimony that he will write his Law in our hearts and minds and no longer remember our sins. Where sin has been forgiven, there is no need for a sacrifice.

CHAPTER THIRTY-SIX

EXHORTATIONS
Hebrews 10:19-13:25

Therefore, we can enter the holiest place through Christ's blood because he has made a way for us through his death. Since we have a great high priest over God's house, we should draw near to God with a sincere heart and the full assurance that faith brings because he has washed us with his blood and pure water. Let us hold to the hope we profess without wavering because he is faithful.

Let us consider how we can stir each other up to love and good works, not neglecting to meet together as some do, but encouraging each other more and more as we see his return drawing near. If we keep deliberately sinning after learning the truth, the sacrifice is no longer valid. We can expect the fiery fury of judgment that will consume God's enemies.

Those who broke Moses' Law died based on the testimony of a handful of witnesses. The punishment will be much worse for those who have rejected the Son of God, profaned his blood, and outraged the Holy Spirit. We know that God will judge his people and have vengeance; it is a fearful thing to fall into the hands of the living God.

Remember how you suffered after you first believed, sometimes being publicly insulted and persecuted and sometimes being with those who suffered. You joyfully suffered with those in prison, and when your property was confiscated, you knew that you had better and lasting possessions. Don't throw away your confidence now because God will reward you. Persevere so that after doing God's will, you will receive his promise. He will come again soon and he wants you to live by faith. We do not wither and die; we have been saved by faith.

Faith is the confidence in what we hope for and the assurance of what we don't see. By faith, the people of old were commended, and by faith, we understand that God spoke the universe into existence, making the visible out of the invisible. By faith, Abel offered a more acceptable sacrifice than Cain, and God commended him as righteous. Even though he has died, he still speaks through his faith. By faith, Enoch did not die but was taken up into heaven because he pleased God. Without faith, it is impossible to please God because to draw near him, we must believe that he exists and that he rewards those who seek him.

By faith, Noah built an ark to save his household because God warned him of what was to come. By faith, Abraham obeyed when God called him to leave his homeland even though he didn't know where he was going. He went to a foreign land that God promised to him and lived in tents with Isaac and Jacob. He was looking forward to the city with foundations that God laid. By faith, Sarah had children even though she had gone through menopause because she believed God's promise. God gave descendants as numerous as the stars in the sky and grains of sand on the seashore to a man who was as good as dead.

All these people died in faith before receiving the promise, only seeing it far off because they were strangers and exiles on the earth. They sought a better homeland than the one they left, a heavenly one and not one where they could return. The Lord is not ashamed to be their God because he has prepared a city for them.

By faith, Abraham offered up his only son, Isaac, even though God had promised that his descendants would come through him. He believed that God would raise him from the dead if necessary. By faith, Isaac blessed Jacob and Esau. By faith, Jacob blessed his sons from his deathbed. By faith, Joseph spoke of the exodus and gave instructions concerning his bones before he died.

By faith, Moses' parents hid the child for three months after his birth because they were not afraid of the king's command. By faith, Moses refused to be the son of Pharaoh's daughter, instead, choosing mistreatment with God's people rather than enjoying sin. He believed the insult of Christ was better than Egypt's wealth and he waited for the reward.

By faith, Moses left Egypt without fearing the king because he was looking to God. By faith, he kept the Passover and put blood on the doorposts so that the firstborn of Israel would not die. By faith, the people crossed the Red Sea on dry land, but when the Egyptians followed, they drowned. By faith, the walls of Jericho fell after the army had marched around them for seven days. By faith, Rahab did not die because she welcomed the spies.

I don't have time to write about Gideon, Barak, Samson, Jephthah, David, Samuel, and the prophets who conquered kingdoms, administered justice, and gained the promise through faith. Through their faith, they shut the mouths of lions, quenched the fury of flames, and escaped the sword. Through their faith, weakness became strength, and they powerfully routed their enemies in battle. Women had their dead raised, and some were tortured, refusing release so that they might have a better resurrection. Some have faced insults, flogging, imprisonment, stoning, being sawed in two, and death by the sword. They were poorly clothed, broke, persecuted, and mistreated even though the world was not worthy. They lived on the fringes of society, and all of them were commended for their faith. However, none of them received the promise because God planned something better so that we might become perfect with them.

Therefore, since such a great cloud of witnesses surrounds us, let us throw off everything that hinders and the sin that entangles us. Run with endurance the race set before us, keeping our eyes on Jesus, the founder and perfecter of our faith. He endured the cross, despising its shame because he knew the joy that was to come, and now he is sitting at the right hand of God's throne. Think about his example so that you don't lose heart; in your struggle against sin, you have not resisted to the point of shedding blood.

You are enduring the Lord's discipline because he loves you like a father loves a son; if he didn't discipline you, you are not truly his children. Our earthly fathers disciplined us, and we respected them; we should submit to God even more so! They disciplined us for a little while as they thought best; but God disciplines us for our good, so that we may share in his holiness.

At the time, discipline seems painful, but later, it produces a harvest of righteousness and peace for those trained by it. Therefore, strengthen your feeble arms and weak knees, making level paths for your feet so that the lame may not be disabled, but rather healed.

Strive to live at peace with everyone and be holy so that you can see God. Make sure that no one falls short of God's grace and that no bitter root grows up to cause trouble and defile many. Make sure that people are not sexually immoral or godless like Esau, who sold his birthright for a single meal. Later, when he wanted to inherit his blessing, he was rejected even though he sought it with tears.

You have not come to a mountain burning with fire, shrouded in darkness, gloom, and storm, to a mountain that cannot be touched and inspires terror and trembling. You have come to Mount Zion, the city of the living God, the heavenly Jerusalem. You have come to the church of the firstborn, whose names are written in heaven with countless angels in joyful assembly. You are in God's presence, the judge of all; the spirits of the righteous; Jesus, the mediator of a New Covenant; and the sprinkled blood that speaks a better word than the blood of Abel.

Don't refuse God, because if they didn't escape when they refused, we will not survive if we reject him either. He has promised that his voice will one day shake both the earth and the heavens. The shaken things will not remain, for they are created; the things that cannot be shaken will stand. Therefore, let us gratefully receive a kingdom that cannot be shaken and offer God acceptable worship with reverence and awe because he is a consuming fire.

Keep loving each other as brothers and sisters and do not forget to show hospitality to strangers, because some have entertained angels without knowing it. Remember the prisoners and mistreated as if you suffered with them. Everyone should honor marriage, and the marriage bed should be pure, for God will judge the sexually immoral and adulterous. Stay away from the love of money and be content with what you have because God will never leave or forsake you.

We can confidently claim that the Lord is our helper and we have no need to fear mere mortals. Remember your leaders who preached God's Word to you, consider their lives, and imitate their faith. Jesus Christ is the same yesterday, today, and forever. Don't be carried away by various strange teachings, but let your hearts be strengthened with grace.

Don't worry about ceremonial foods, because they don't benefit us; we have access to a better altar and tabernacle than the Israelite priests. The high priest brings animals' blood into the holy of holies as a sin offering and burns their bodies outside the camp. Jesus also suffered outside the city gate to make his people holy through his blood; let us go outside the camp with him and bear the disgrace he bore. We do not currently live in an enduring city; we are looking for a city to come.

Therefore, let us continually offer a sacrifice of praise to God, the fruit of lips that openly profess his name. Don't forget to do good and be generous, because such sacrifices please God. Obey your leaders and submit to them because they watch over your souls and they will have to give an account for you. Make their work joyful and not painful because it doesn't benefit you to be a burden. Pray for us because we have a clear conscience and want to live honorable lives. Also, pray that I can come to see you soon.

May the God of peace equip you with what you need to do his will so that he may accomplish what is pleasing in his sight through Jesus. He raised Jesus from the dead and is our great Shepherd. May Christ receive all glory forever and ever! Amen. Grace be with you.

CHAPTER THIRTY-SEVEN

LEADING A CHURCH
I Timothy 1-6

> **Paul's first letter to Timothy**
>
> This letter was in a group that Paul wrote not long before his death, known as the Pastoral Epistles. They are grouped like this because they were written to young men leading churches instead of the members of a congregation. He wrote this letter to a developed church in Ephesus led by Timothy. Paul's ministry partner had a Jewish mother and a Greek father and had worked extensively with Paul throughout his journeys. Paul gives his young friend instructions for leading a church.

I urge you to stay in Ephesus to instruct people not to teach false doctrine or devote themselves to myths and conspiracies. These things promote controversy rather than advancing God's work. Our goal is love from a pure heart, good conscience, and a sincere faith. Some have left these and turned to meaningless talk; they want to be teachers, but they are clueless.

We know that the Law is good if one uses it correctly. We know that the Law did not come for the just, but for the lawless, disobedient, ungodly, sinners, unholy, profane, killers of parents, murderers, sexually immoral, homosexuals, enslavers, liars, perjurers, and those who do whatever is contrary to sound doctrine.

I thank our Lord Jesus Christ, who gives me strength that he has appointed me to preach the gospel of his glory. Even though I was once a blasphemer, persecutor, and violent, he showed me mercy because I was ignorant in my unbelief. He poured out his grace and love upon me. Jesus came into the world to save sinners, among whom I am the worst.

> **Paul's growing humility**
>
> As Paul continued in his Christian journey, he grew in his humility. In his first letter to the Corinthians, he calls himself the least of the apostles. In his later letter to the Ephesians, he calls himself the least of all believers. Finally, in this letter (written near the end of his life), he calls himself the worst of all sinners. The closer he got to God, the more in touch he was with his need for grace and God's salvation.

But he showed me mercy so that Jesus might display his perfect patience as an example to those who trust in him for eternal life. To the King eternal, immortal, invisible, the only God, be honor and glory forever! Amen.

My son, I am giving you this command so that you remember the prophecies about you, so that you would stand firm in faith and fight the battle well. Some have rejected this and have shipwrecked their faith; I have turned them over to Satan so they can learn not to blaspheme.

I urge people to pray and thank God for everyone, especially for people in high positions, so that we may lead a peaceful, quiet life that is godly and dignified. This pleases God, our Savior, who wants everyone to be saved and come to know the truth. Jesus Christ is the one God and mediator who gave himself as a ransom for all.

He has appointed me as a preacher and apostle of this truth to the Gentiles. I desire that men everywhere should lift holy hands in prayer without quarreling; women should likewise dress modestly with self-control and not in flashy clothing. They should clothe themselves with godliness and good works, focusing more on the spiritual than the physical.

Women should learn quietly without contention; they should not exercise authority over men but should remain quiet. God made Adam first and then Eve and she was deceived before Adam. Yet, women are saved through childbearing if they continue in faith, love, holiness, and self-control.

> **Women in the church**
>
> This is one of the most controversial passages in the New Testament and we must take it in the context of all Scripture. In other places, Paul argues for the equality of all believers and mutual submission. There is also evidence that points to this teaching being for the church in Ephesus and not for all believers. This is too large of a topic for this book and I recommend further study.
>
> The statement that women will be saved through childbearing references the curse in Genesis 3 and does not mean that women must have children to be saved. As sin has continued to wreak havoc on the world around us, not all women can or want to have children. The only thing that saves or condemns us is what we do with the person of Jesus.

Those who want to be elders desire a noble task. An elder should be above reproach, faithful to their wife, sober-minded, self-controlled, respectable, hospitable, able to teach, gentle, not drunkards, not quarrelsome, and not in love with money. They must manage their households well and have obedient children because if they can't manage their own families, they can't take care of God's church. They should not be recent converts, so that they don't become conceited and fall under the same judgment as the Devil. They must also have a good reputation with outsiders so that they don't fall into disgrace.

Deacons must also be dignified, not double-tongued, drunkards, or greedy for dishonest gain; they must have faith with a clear conscience. Test them and let them serve as deacons if they prove to be blameless. Their wives must also be dignified, not slanderers, but sober-minded and faithful in all things. They must be the husbands of one wife, and manage their children and households well. Those who serve well as deacons gain good standing and great confidence in their faith in Jesus Christ.

I hope to come to you soon, but if I can't make it, I want you to know how the church of the living God should operate. The mystery of godliness is great: he came in the flesh, vindicated by the Spirit, seen by angels, preached to the world, believed in, and taken up in glory.

The Spirit tells us that some will abandon the faith and follow deceiving spirits and demons in later times. This comes through hypocritical liars with burned consciences who forbid marriage and require abstinence from foods that God created for us to enjoy with thanksgiving and faith. God created everything good and makes it holy through his Word and prayer, so we should not reject it if we receive it with thanksgiving.

You serve Christ well if you teach these things to the church. Have nothing to do with irreverent, silly myths, but train yourself for godliness. Training the body has some value, but godliness is valuable in every way as it has promises for this life and the life to come. We work for these things because we set our hope on the living God who saves all people who believe.

Don't let anyone look down on your youth. Set an example for all believers in your speech, actions, love, faith, and purity. Devote yourself to the public reading of Scripture, exhortation, and teaching. Don't neglect your gift that was confirmed through prophecy and the elders' laying on of hands. Immerse yourself in these things so that everyone might see your growth; watch yourself and your teaching, and you will save yourself and your hearers.

Don't rebuke older men, but treat them like you would your father; treat older women as mothers, young men as brothers, and young women as sisters with absolute purity. Honor women who are truly widows, but if they have family who can take care of them, they should because this pleases God. Women are truly widows if they are alone and have set their hope on the Lord with constant prayers, but if they are self-indulgent, they are already dead while they live.

If people do not provide for their own families, they have denied their faith and are worse than unbelievers. Women should only be on the list of widows if they are older and have a reputation for good works, having raised children, shown hospitality, served the church, and cared for the afflicted. But don't enroll younger widows because they eventually will want to remarry. Besides, they get in the habit of idleness, gossip, and speaking out of turn. These women should remarry and manage their new households, so they don't allow the enemy to slander us. Some have already turned away to follow Satan. If anyone is already taking care of widows, they should continue so that they don't burden the church.

Elders who lead the church well are worthy of extra honor, especially if they preach or teach; they are worthy of their wages. Don't listen to accusations brought against them unless there are multiple witnesses. But you should rebuke those elders who persist in sin in front of the congregation so that the others might take warning. Listen to this teaching without partiality and don't play favorites. Don't commission others by laying hands on them in haste so that you don't share in their sin.

Drink a little wine and not just water because of your frequent stomach problems. Some sins are obvious, while others take longer to become known. In the same way, some good deeds are obvious, but even hidden ones eventually become known.

> **Drink a little wine**
>
> The instruction to drink a little wine is an example of teaching for the original recipient, Timothy, and not for us today (see the box in chapter 2). It is okay for us to consume wine, but this is not something that everyone must do.

Servants should respect their masters so that they won't slander God's name and our teaching. Those with believing masters should not disrespect them just because they are fellow believers, but they should serve them all the more. If anyone teaches anything different, they are conceited and don't understand anything. They have an unhealthy fascination with controversies and teachings that lead to envy, strife, malicious talk, evil suspicions, and constant friction.

They believe that godliness is a means to financial gain, but godliness with contentment brings great profit. We came into the world with nothing, and we will leave with nothing, so we should be content with enough food and clothing. Those who want to be rich fall into temptation and the many senseless and harmful desires that lead to destruction. The love of money is the root of all kinds of evil, and it has led many away from the faith and into great pain.

> **Money**
>
> In our world, money has become one of the most common things for people to worship. People kill for money and prestige, and this is what Paul writes about when he says that "the love of money is the root of all kinds of evil." Money is neither evil nor good, but it becomes problematic when we elevate its purpose.
>
> Some have pitted the rich against the poor, but this is the wrong battle. God is not interested in the wealth we have, but how we obtained it and how we use it. God wants us to love people and use money, not the other way around.

Flee these things and pursue righteousness, godliness, faith, love, endurance, and gentleness. Fight the good fight of the faith and take hold of the eternal life that God called to when you confessed your faith in the presence of many witnesses. I charge you in God's presence, who gives life, to keep the commandment free from reproach until Jesus comes back at the proper time.

Command those who are rich not to be arrogant or put their hope in their wealth; instead, they should put their hope in God who gives us everything for our enjoyment. Command them to do good, be rich in good deeds, and generous, willing to share. Then they will lay up treasure for themselves in the coming age and take hold of true life.

Guard what God entrusted to you and turn away from godless chatter and the opposing ideas of what is falsely called knowledge. Some have professed this and, in doing so, have left the faith. Grace be with you all.

He is the blessed and only Ruler, King of kings, and Lord of lords; he is the only Immortal who lives in unapproachable light that no one has seen or can see. To him be honor and might forever. Amen.

CHAPTER THIRTY-EIGHT

STAY STRONG
Titus 1-3

> **Paul's letter to Titus**
>
> Paul wrote this letter to Titus, who led the church in Crete. Titus was a Greek convert and had a difficult job of leading an immature church. Paul had worked with Titus in Macedonia and he sent Timothy to Crete to help bring them to maturity.

I left you in Crete so you could finish our work of appointing elders in every church. Elders must be blameless, faithful to their wives, and have obedient children. Since they will manage God's household, they should not be overbearing, quick-tempered, drunkards, violent, or after dishonest gain. Instead, they should be hospitable, lovers of good, self-controlled, upright, holy, and disciplined. They must hold on to the gospel so they may encourage others with sound doctrine and rebuke those who contradict it.

Many rebellious people are full of empty talk and lies, especially the circumcision group. Silence them because they are disrupting entire households with their false teaching for dishonest gain. They are evil brutes and lazy gluttons, so rebuke them sharply so they might have a solid faith and ignore myths and false commands. Everything is pure to the pure, but nothing is pure to the unbelieving and defiled because their minds and consciences are corrupted. They claim to know God, but they deny him with their lives; they are detestable, disobedient, and unfit for any good work.

But you must teach sound doctrine. Teach the older men to be sober-minded, dignified, self-controlled, strong in faith, love, and endurance. Likewise, teach older women to live reverent lives and teach what is good and not to be slanderers or drunkards. Then they can teach younger women to love their families, be self-controlled and pure, busy at home, kind, and submit to their husbands so that no one would speak ill of the gospel. Teach young men to be self-controlled.

In everything, set an example by doing good, showing integrity, dignity, and sound speech so that our opponents are ashamed. Teach servants to be subject to their masters, please them, not talk back, and show that they are trustworthy so that the teaching about God, our Savior, is attractive.

For God's grace has appeared and offers salvation to all people. It teaches us to reject ungodliness and worldly passions and live self-controlled, upright, and godly lives while waiting for Jesus to come again. He gave himself to redeem us from wickedness and purify a people of his own who are eager to do good. Teach these things, encourage, rebuke with all authority, and do not let anyone despise you.

Remind people to be subject to authority, obedient, ready to do good, to not slander, to be peaceful, considerate, and gentle towards everyone. At one time, we were also foolish, disobedient, deceived, and enslaved by passions and pleasures. We were full of malice, envy, and hate. But when God's kindness and love appeared, he saved us, not because of our righteousness, but his mercy. He saved us through baptism and renewal by the Holy Spirit, whom he generously poured out on us through Jesus. We have been justified by grace so that we might inherit eternal life.

Those who believe in God must be careful to do good because this is excellent and profitable for everyone. Avoid foolish controversies, genealogies, and arguments about the Law because they are unprofitable. Warn divisive people twice and then have nothing to do with them because they are sinful and self-condemned.

Do your best to meet me at Nicopolis this winter. Our people must devote themselves to doing good, provide for urgent needs, and live productive lives. Greet those who love us in the faith; grace be with you all.

CHAPTER THIRTY-NINE

FINISH YOUR MINISTRY
II Timothy 1-4

> **Paul's second letter to Timothy**
>
> This is the last letter that Paul wrote and he penned it a year before his death in 67 A.D. He wrote to encourage his disciple to finish his ministry in leading the church in Ephesus.

I have a clear conscience as I thank God in my daily prayers for you. I long to see you so that I might be filled with joy. Your grandmother Lois and your mother Eunice had a sincere faith, and I'm convinced that you have it as well.

Fan the flame of God's gift that you received when I laid hands on you for God did not give us a spirit of fear, but of power, love, and self-control. Therefore, don't be ashamed of the gospel or me, his prisoner, instead share in suffering for the gospel. He saved us and called us to a holy life, not because of anything we did, but because of his purpose and grace.

Christ gave us this gift before the beginning of time and now he has given it to us by appearing on earth. He abolished death and brought life and immortality to light through the gospel that God appointed me to preach and is the reason I suffer. But I am not ashamed because I know whom I believed and I am convinced that he can guard what I entrusted to him until he returns. Follow my pattern of sound teaching with faith and love in Christ. Guard the gift that God gave to you with the help of the Holy Spirit, who lives in us.

You know that everyone in Asia has left me, including Phygelus and Hermogenes. May God show the household of Onesiphorus mercy because he often refreshed me and was not ashamed of my chains. When he came to Rome, he searched for me, and you know how much he helped me in Ephesus.

Be strong in Christ's grace and teach what I've taught you to reliable people who will also be able to teach others. Suffer with me like a good soldier of Christ because soldiers do not entangle themselves in civilian affairs; instead, they try to please their commanding officer. Similarly, athletes don't win unless they follow the rules, and hardworking farmers should have the first share of the crops. Reflect on my words because the Lord will give you insight into all of this.

> **Discipleship**
>
> God is the ultimate author of his glory and he works all things together for his plan. However, he allows us to be a part of it and share in his splendor. The most effective way that he allows us to do this is through discipleship. God wants us to share the gospel with others and train them to do the same so that others may also share in his work. Jesus himself showed us this model by teaching his disciples to train others who would then train others.

Remember Jesus, who descended from David and rose from the dead. This is the gospel that has imprisoned me, but God's Word is not chained. Therefore, I endure everything for the sake of the chosen so that they might have faith and eternal glory in Jesus Christ. If we died with him, we will live with him; if we endure, we will reign with him; if we disown him, he will disown us; but if we are faithless, he remains faithful because he cannot disown himself.

Remind God's people of these things and warn them about arguments because they only ruin those who listen to them. Present yourself to God as an approved worker who handles God's Word well and does not need to be ashamed. Avoid godless chatter because it only leads to further ungodliness and it spreads like gangrene. Hymenaeus and Philetus are like this and have departed from the truth. They say that the resurrection has already happened and they have destroyed some people's faith. But God's foundation stands firm because he knows his people and they should turn away from sin.

In a big house, there are items with special purposes and some for everyday use. Those who cleanse themselves from dishonorable things will be vessels for honorable use, set apart as holy, useful, and ready for every good work. Flee the evil desires of youth and pursue righteousness, faith, love, and peace along with those who call on the Lord from a pure heart. Don't have anything to do with foolish arguments because they only produce trouble.

The Lord's servants must not be quarrelsome but kind to everyone, able to teach, and not resentful. Gently instruct your opponents in the hope that God will lead them into repentance and a knowledge of the truth. Then they will come to their senses and escape the Devil's snares, who has captured them to do his will.

In the last days, there will be much trouble; people will be lovers of self and money, proud, arrogant, abusive, disobedient, ungrateful, unholy, heartless, unforgiving, slanderous, uncontrolled, brutal, haters of good, treacherous, rash, conceited, lovers of pleasure rather than God. These people have a form of godliness but deny its power. Avoid these people because they worm their way into homes and gain control of gullible people weighed down by evil desires, always learning but never finding the truth. These teachers oppose the truth, just like Jannes and Jambres opposed Moses; they have depraved minds and have rejected the faith. They will not get very far because their folly will become evident to everyone.

> **Faith will not be easy**
>
> We like God's promises for our lives. It is comforting to know that he will always be with us, that he loves us, and that he came to offer the perfect sacrifice to reunite us with him. One of the uncomfortable promises that he gives is that we will face persecution and suffering. The world that is perishing doesn't want to hear God's good news and will battle against us to drag us down. But we can take heart because we know that he wins in the end.

But you have followed my teaching, actions, way of life, faith, patience, love, endurance, persecutions, and sufferings. Everyone who wants to live a godly life will face persecution. Simultaneously, evil people will go from bad to worse, deceiving others, and being deceived. But you should continue in what you've learned and believed. You have learned these things from the Scriptures since childhood and how they can lead to salvation in Jesus. All Scripture is from God and is profitable for teaching, reproof, correction, and training in righteousness so that his servants may be competent, equipped for every good work.

I charge you in the presence of God and Christ, who will judge the living and the dead, to preach the Word, to always be ready to reprove, rebuke, and exhort with patience. For a time will come when people will not listen to sound teaching but will look for instruction that satisfies their own passions; they will turn away from the truth and wander off into myths.

But you should be sober-minded, endure suffering, share the gospel, and fulfill your ministry. I am being poured out as a drink offering and my death is at hand. I have fought the good fight, finished the race, and kept the faith. A crown of righteousness is waiting for me that God will give to everyone who believes when he returns.

Try to come to me with Mark as soon as possible because only Luke is with me and everyone else has deserted me. But the Lord has stood by me and strengthened me so that I might fully preach the gospel to all the Gentiles. The Lord will rescue me from every evil deed and bring me safely into his heavenly kingdom. May the Lord's grace be with your spirit. To him, be the glory forever! Amen.

CHAPTER FORTY

STEADFAST IN CHRIST
II Peter 1-3

> **Peter's second letter**
>
> Peter wrote his second letter to the believers scattered across Asia Minor around 66 A.D. before Nero's suicide. Peter wrote just before his death and wanted to make sure that his readers remained strong in their faith.

God's divine power has given us everything we need for a godly life through our knowledge of him who called us by his glory and goodness. Through these, he has given us his precious and very great promises so that we may participate in the divine nature, having escaped the corruption of evil desires.

Therefore, make every effort to build upon your faith with goodness, knowledge, self-control, endurance, godliness, brotherly affection, and love. If you keep increasing in these qualities, they will keep you from being ineffective or unfruitful in the knowledge of our Lord Jesus Christ. Those who lack these qualities are so nearsighted that they are blind, having forgotten their cleansing from sin. Be diligent to make sure of your calling and election, for if you practice these qualities, you will never fall. You will receive a rich welcome into the eternal kingdom of our Lord and Savior, Jesus Christ.

Even though you already know this, I will keep reminding you of these truths. It's good to have reminders while we live in this body because we will put it aside before long. I will try to see you soon so that after my death you will always remember these things.

We did not follow clever stories when we told you about the power and coming of our Lord Jesus Christ; we were eyewitnesses of his majesty. He received honor and glory from God the Father when he called him his beloved son who pleased him. We heard this same voice from heaven when we saw Jesus transfigured. We also have the prophetic message that you should obey. It will shine like a lamp in a dark place until a new dawn rises in your hearts. Prophecy has never been the matter of one's own interpretation; it comes from people who spoke God's Word as the Holy Spirit carried them along.

But false prophets arose among the people just like there will be false teachers among you. They will secretly introduce destructive heresies and even deny the Lord, bringing swift destruction on themselves. Many will follow their depravity and bring the faith into disrepute. In their greed, they will exploit you with made-up stories; their condemnation hangs over their heads.

God did not spare angels when they sinned, but sent them to hell in chains of darkness for judgment. He did not spare the ancient world when he flooded it, but only saved Noah, a preacher of righteousness and his family. He condemned the cities of Sodom and Gomorrah by burning them to ashes as an example of what will happen to the ungodly. But he rescued righteous Lot, who was tortured by the lawless deeds he saw and heard.

If these things are true, then the Lord knows how to rescue the godly from trials and hold the unrighteous for punishment on Judgment Day. Especially those who indulge in the lust of defiling passion and despise authority. They are bold and arrogant and not afraid to heap abuse on angels and beings who are greater than themselves.

These people blaspheme in matters they don't understand; they are unreasoning animals born to be caught and destroyed. The Lord will repay them for the harm they've done; they are blemishes who carouse in broad daylight. They are full of adultery and sin; they seduce the unstable and are experts in greed. They have left the straight path and follow the way of Balaam, looking for wicked wages. But his donkey rebuked him for his sin to restrain his madness.

These people are springs without water and God reserves the blackest darkness for them. They speak empty, boastful words and appeal to the lustful desires of the flesh; they entice people who are barely escaping error. They promise freedom, but they are slaves of corruption because whatever enslaves us overcomes us.

After they have escaped the world's defilements through knowledge of our Lord and Savior Jesus Christ, they are entangled in it again and worse off at the end than at the beginning. It would have been better for them not to be ignorant of righteousness than to have known it and then turned their backs on it. They are like dogs that return to their vomit or washed pigs that return to wallowing in the mud.

This is the second time I'm writing to you to remind you of the holy prophets and the Lord and Savior's commands through the apostles. In the last days, scoffers will come following their evil desires. They will claim that Jesus is not coming since everything continues as it always has. But they overlook the fact that it was the same way when God destroyed the world with the flood. Now, God reserves the present heavens and earth for fire on Judgment Day. Don't forget that a day is like 1,000 years and 1,000 years like a day with the Lord. He is not slow in keeping his promises; instead, he is patient with you, wanting everyone to repent.

The Day of the Lord will come like a thief, the heavens will pass away with a roar, the stars and heavens will burn, and God will expose the earth and its works. Since all of this will pass away, you should live holy and godly lives, waiting for the Day of the Lord. But according to his promise, we are waiting for new heavens and earth where righteousness will dwell.

Since we are waiting for these things, be diligent to live at peace without spot or blemish. Count the Lord's patience as salvation, just as Paul has written to you. His letters can be challenging to understand and the ignorant and unstable try to twist them just as they do other Scriptures. Therefore, be careful that lawless people's error doesn't carry you away, and you lose your stability, but grow in the grace and knowledge of our Lord and Savior Jesus Christ. To him, be the glory now and forever! Amen.

Paul's death

Paul never made it out of his Roman imprisonment. Around the time of Peter's martyrdom, Nero also had Paul beheaded. Paul's death likely happened sometime around 67 A.D.

CHAPTER FORTY-ONE

WARNING AGAINST FALSE TEACHING
Jude 1

> **Jude's letter**
>
> Jude, Jesus' half-brother, wrote this letter around the same time as Peter's two letters as a warning to Jewish Christians. This is a general letter and Jude warns his audience against false teaching.

Beloved, I had been preparing to write to you about our salvation, but I found it necessary to urge you to fight for the faith given to the saints. Some people have slipped in among you, saying that God's grace provides us with a license to sin. These godless people were condemned long ago, and they have turned their backs on our only Master and Lord, Jesus Christ.

Even though you already know, I want to remind you that the Lord delivered his people out of Egypt and destroyed those who did not believe. God has even kept the angels that did not keep their positions in eternal chains for judgment when he returns. Similarly, Sodom, Gomorrah, and the surrounding cities became sexually depraved and serve as an example of those that suffer the punishment of eternal fire.

These dreamers pollute their flesh, reject authority, and slander angelic majesties. Even when the archangel Michael was disputing with Satan about Moses' body, he did not dare slander him, but said, "The Lord rebuke you!" But these men speak evil about things that they do not understand. What they do know, they know by instinct, just like unreasoning animals; destroy them. Woe to them! They have followed the way of Cain, rushed into Balaam's error, and destroyed themselves in Korah's rebellion. These men are blemishes at your love feasts; they fearlessly eat with you, serving only themselves. They are clouds without rain, carried along by the wind, autumn trees without fruit, uprooted, and doubly dead. They are like the wild waves of the sea, foaming up their own shame; they are like wandering stars, reserved for blackest darkness.

> **What are these errors Jude warns against?**
>
> Jude writes about three errors here, and without context, this passage can be confusing. Cain was Adam and Eve's second child, and he tried to pass off inferior sacrifices to God and then killed his brother out of jealousy. He attempted to worship God with impure motives. Balaam's error was to be an unfaithful prophet. God gave him a message, but he wanted to use his position to profit rather than proclaim what God had told him. Korah's rebellion was false teaching. While the Israelites were in the wilderness, he revolted against Moses and Aaron and tried to get the people to follow him. All these errors may look good on the surface, but amount to nothing.

Enoch, the seventh from Adam, prophesied about these men, saying: "See, the Lord is coming with innumerable of his holy ones to judge everyone and convict the ungodly of their evil deeds and all the harsh things that ungodly sinners have said against him. These men are grumblers and complainers that follow their lusts, speak arrogantly, and flatter others for their own advantage.

Beloved, remember that the apostles of our Lord Jesus Christ told you beforehand that, "In the last time there will be mockers that follow after their own desires." It is these worldly people that do not have the Spirit that divide you. But you, beloved, build yourselves up on your most holy faith and pray in the Holy Spirit. Keep yourselves in God's love as you wait for our Lord Jesus Christ's mercy to bring you to eternal life. Have mercy on those that doubt; save others by snatching them out of the fire. Show mercy to others, mixed with fear, hating even the clothing that has been stained by the flesh. God can keep you from falling and make you stand in the presence of his glory without fault and with great joy.

To the only God our Savior, through the Lord Jesus Christ, be glory, majesty, power, and authority in the past, present, and forever! Amen.

CHAPTER FORTY-TWO

JESUS CAME IN THE FLESH AND GIVES ETERNAL LIFE
I John 1-5

> **John's first letter**
>
> The apostle John wrote this letter around the end of the First Century. He was likely writing to the churches in Ephesus and the surrounding area. His purpose is to assure Christians of their salvation and to counter teaching that denied Jesus had come in the flesh.

We proclaim to you what we have seen and heard concerning the Word of Life and how it appeared to give us eternal life. Now you may have fellowship with us, the Father, and his Son, Jesus Christ, to make our joy complete.

God is light and there is not even a shadow of darkness in him. If we claim to have fellowship with him while we walk in darkness, we lie and do not practice the truth. But if we walk in the light, we have fellowship with one another, and Jesus' blood cleanses us from our sin.

If we say we have no sin, we lie to ourselves, and the truth is not in us. But if we confess our sins, he is faithful and just to forgive and cleanse us from all unrighteousness. If we claim to have not sinned, we make him a liar, and his Word is not in us.

My dear children, I write so that you will not sin, but if anybody does, Jesus is our advocate with the Father. He is the atoning sacrifice for our sins and the sins of the whole world. We know him if we keep his commands, those who claim to know him but disobey, lie; the truth is not in them. But God's love is perfected in those who obey. We know that we are in him if we walk in the same way he walked.

Dear friends, I am not writing a new command, but an old one that you already know. However, it is also a new commandment because the darkness is passing away, and the true light already shines. Those who claim to be in the light but still hate their brothers and sisters are in the dark and do not know where they are going. Those who love their brothers and sisters walk in the light and there is no cause for suffering.

Dear children, I write to you because Jesus has forgiven your sin, and you know the Father. Fathers, I am writing to you because you know him, who is from the beginning. Young men, I write to you because you are strong, the Word of God lives in you, and you have overcome the evil one.

Do not love the world or worldly things because those who love the world do not have the Father's love. All the desires of the flesh and pride in possessions are from the world and not the Father. The world is passing away along with its desires, but those who do God's will abide forever.

Dear children, it is the last hour, and the Antichrist is coming, and many antichrists have already come. They went out from us because they do not belong to us; if they had been, they would have stayed. But you have been anointed by the Holy One and you all know the truth. I write to you because you know the truth and there is no lie in it. Those who deny that Jesus is the Christ are antichrist; no one who denies the Son has the Father, and those who acknowledge the Son have the Father.

> **Who is the Antichrist?**
>
> The Bible talks about the antichrist in two ways. The first is the Antichrist, the one John writes about in the book of Revelation. He is the one who revolts against Jesus at the end of history. It also talks about those who are antichrist, who is anyone who claims that Jesus is not God. Many people in the world are antichrist, but not all who deny him are the Antichrist.

Make sure that what you've heard from the beginning remains in you, and then you will remain in the Son and the Father. He has promised us eternal life. Some want to lead you astray, but the anointing you received remains in you. We know it is real because it teaches us about all things, so stay in him.

Dear children, continue in him so that when he appears, we may be confident and unashamed when he comes. If he is righteous, then all who do right are born of him.

How great is the Father's love for us that he should call us his children? The reason the world does not know us is that it did not know him. We are God's children now, and what we will be has not yet appeared; but when he appears, we will be like him. Those who hope in him purify themselves as he is pure. Everyone who makes a habit of sinning practices lawlessness because sin is lawlessness. He appeared to take away sin and he is sinless. Those who live in him don't keep on sinning; those who keep sinning have neither seen nor known him.

Dear children, don't let anyone lead you astray; those who do right are righteous just as God is righteous. Those who do what is sinful are from the Devil, who has sinned from the beginning. The Son of God appeared to destroy the Devil's work. None of those born of God continue to sin because God's seed lives in them, and they cannot keep sinning. They are born of God. It is evident who are children of God and who are children of the Devil: those who don't practice righteousness are not from God, nor are those who don't love their brothers or sisters.

The message you have heard from the beginning is to love each other. We should not be like Cain, who was from the Devil and murdered his brother. He murdered his brother because his deeds were evil and his brother's were righteous. Don't be surprised that the world hates you; we have passed out of death into life because we love, but those who don't love remain in death. Those who hate their brother are as guilty as murderers and no murderer has eternal life.

We know love because Jesus laid down his life for us, and we should lay down our lives for our brothers and sisters. If we have the world's goods and see someone in need and close our hearts, God's love is not in us. We should not love in words alone, but with our actions. This proves we are of the truth and reassures our hearts before him. Whenever our hearts condemn us, God is greater than our hearts, and he knows everything. If our hearts don't condemn us, we have confidence before God, and he will give us what we ask for because we do what pleases him.

His commandment is that we believe in the name of his Son, Jesus Christ, and love each other just as he commanded us. Those who obey his commandments remain in God and God in them; we know we are in him because of his Spirit.

Dear friends, don't believe every spirit but test them to see if they are from God because there are many false prophets in the world. You will recognize the Spirit of God because every spirit that acknowledges that Jesus Christ has come in the flesh is from God. Every spirit that does not acknowledge Jesus is not from God. This is the antichrist spirit, which you have heard is coming and is already in the world.

Dear children, you are from God and have overcome them because the Spirit in you is greater than the one in the world. They are worldly and speak from the world's point of view, so the world listens to them. We are from God and whoever knows God listens to us; that is how we know the Spirit of truth from the spirit of lies.

Dear friends, let us love one another because love comes from God, and those who love have been born from and know God. Those who do not love do not know God because God is love. God showed us his love by sending his only Son into the world so we might live. We know love because God sent his Son as an atoning sacrifice for our sins. Since God loved us, we should love one another. No one has ever seen God, but if we love one another, God lives in us, and his love is made complete in us.

We know that we are in God, and he is in us because he has given us his Spirit. We have seen and testified that the Father has sent his Son to save the world, and God is in those who confess Jesus is the Son of God, and he is in them. We know and believe the Lord loves us; God is love, and those who love stay connected to him.

Love is perfected in us so that we may have confidence for Judgment Day because we are as he is in this world. There is no fear in love because perfect love casts out fear; fear has to do with punishment, and those who fear have not been perfected in love. We can only love because he first loved us. If people claim to love God but hate their brothers or sisters, they are liars because those who do not love those whom they have seen cannot love God whom they have not seen. Anyone who loves God must love their brothers and sisters.

Those who believe that Jesus is the Christ are born of God and those who love the Father love his Son as well. We love the children of God when we love God and obey his commandments. Loving God is obedience and his commands are not a burden. Those who are born of God overcome the world because of our faith that Jesus is the Son of God.

The Spirit testifies that Jesus Christ has come in both the flesh and the spirit. God's testimony is greater than human testimony and he testifies about his Son. Those who believe in the Son of God have the testimony; those who do not believe call God a liar. God has given us eternal life and this life is in his Son. Those who have the Son have life; those who do not have the Son of God do not have life.

These things are for you who believe in the Son of God so that you can know you have eternal life. The confidence we have is that he listens to and will give us anything that we ask for according to his will.

If you see a brother committing a sin that does not lead to death, you should pray for him; some sins lead to eternal death, don't pray for those. All wrongdoing is sin, but some sins don't lead to death. Those who are born of God do not keep sinning, Jesus protects them, and the Devil cannot harm them. We are children of God and the whole world is under the Devil's control. We also know that the Son of God has come and gives us understanding so that we may know the truth. We are in God by being in his Son, Jesus Christ, the true God and eternal life.

Levels of sin

On a forensic level, all sins are the same. All sin separates us from God, from white lies to murder, and even if we only sin once, we are guilty and worthy of death. But there also levels to the impacts of our sin. Some sins are minor in comparison to others. A lifestyle of denying Christ and his work is far more destructive and leads to eternal damnation.

Dear children, keep yourselves from idols.

Idols

An idol is anything that we put in a higher position than God. Our world is full of them and many tempt us to place them above Jesus. If we find anything competing with our devotion to Christ, then we need to avoid it.

CHAPTER FORTY-THREE

JOHN'S SECOND AND THIRD LETTERS
II John - III John

> **John's second and third letters**
>
> The apostle John wrote these letters around 90 A.D. to believers who were living as they should. A common practice in the First Century was for believers to welcome traveling missionaries into their homes. John writes his letters to two such believers. John's purpose was to remind his readers that they should love others and support those who spread the gospel, a common theme in the New Testament.

II JOHN

It gives me great joy to find some of your children walking in the truth, just as the Father commanded us. I am giving you the same commandment we have always known, to love one another. Love is to obey his commands. Many deceivers who deny that Jesus Christ came in the flesh are in the world; they are antichrist.

Do not lose what you've worked for; keep your reward. Those who run ahead and do not remain in Christ's teaching do not have God, but those who stay in his teachings remain in the Father and the Son. Reject anyone who brings you a different teaching and do not share in their wicked work.

I hope to visit you soon so that our joy may be complete.

III JOHN

Dear friend, I pray that you might have good health and that everything goes well with you. I greatly rejoiced when the brothers told me that you were walking in the truth because that is my greatest joy.

Beloved, you are faithful in what you do for the brothers and sisters, even though you don't know them. Please send them on their way in a manner that honors God. It was for Jesus' name that they went out, receiving no help from the pagans. Therefore, we should support them so that we may be fellow workers for the truth.

I already wrote to the church, but Diotrephes does not acknowledge our authority. If I can come, I will expose his wickedness because he refuses to welcome the brothers and stops those who want to help. Do not imitate evil but imitate good. Those who do good are from God; those who do evil have not seen him.

I have much more to say but prefer to do it face to face. I hope to see you soon.

CHAPTER FORTY-FOUR

JOHN'S VISION AND LETTERS TO THE CHURCHES
Revelation 1-3

> **John's Revelation**
>
> The apostle John wrote this letter from exile on Patmos during the Domitian persecution near the end of the First Century. Jesus gave him a vision one Sunday showing him what was to happen during the End Times. This is an apocalyptic letter, a writing style we are unfamiliar with, and this has made it the source of much confusion in the modern church. It is full of symbolism and we must understand it to interpret this letter. This was a popular writing style at the time and the early church likely had no problem understanding what John meant.

The revelation of Jesus Christ that God, through his angel, gave to John to show his servants the things that must happen. John bears witness to the Word of God and the testimony of Jesus Christ that he saw. Blessed are those who read these words as are those who obey them for the time is near.

Grace and peace to the seven churches from God, the one who was, is, and is to come, the seven spirits who are before his throne, and Jesus Christ, the faithful witness, the firstborn of the dead, and the ruler of the earth. May all glory and power be to him who has made us a kingdom and priests forever! Amen.

> **What does "was, is, and is to come" mean?**
>
> The title "who was, is, and is to come" means is a reference to God's eternal nature. He sees everything in an eternal instant because he was at creation, is now, and will be for all eternity.

He is coming with the clouds, everyone will see him, and the world will wail on his account. Even so, let it be. The Lord God is the Beginning and the End, the one who was, is, and is to come, the Almighty.

***

I was exiled on the island of Patmos because I kept preaching the gospel. One Sunday, I was praying, and I heard a loud voice behind me like a trumpet telling me to write what I saw in a book to the seven churches in Ephesus, Smyrna, Pergamum, Thyatira, Sardis, Philadelphia, and Laodicea.

I turned to see the voice, and I saw seven golden lampstands. Amid them, I saw Jesus, clothed in a long robe with a golden sash across his chest. His hair was white like wool or snow, his eyes like a flame, his feet like bronze glowing in a furnace, and his voice was like the roar of rushing waters. He held seven stars in his right hand, and from his mouth came a sharp, double-edged sword, and his face shone like the noonday sun.

> **John's use of "like."**
>
> John's vision was far beyond what he could understand. If we look through this book, John uses the word "like" frequently. He had to do this because his vision was so far beyond his comprehension. The things he wrote about may not be exactly what he saw, but that's because we lack the human language to describe God and his works.

When I saw him, I fell at his feet like a dead man. But he laid his right hand on me and said, "Don't be afraid, I am the First and Last, the Living One. I died, and now I live forevermore, and I hold the keys of Death and Hades. Write what you see, things that are, and those that will take place. The seven stars you saw in my right hand are the angels of the seven churches and the seven golden lampstands are the seven churches.

> **Letters to the churches**
>
> John wrote these letters to real churches that existed in the First Century. But we can also find ourselves in his messages.

To the angel of the church in Ephesus, these are Jesus' words:

I know your deeds, hard work, endurance, and how you cannot tolerate the wicked and false apostles. I know that you have not grown weary and patiently endure for my name's sake, but you have abandoned your early love. Remember where you were before you fell; repent, and do the deeds you did at first, or I will remove your lampstand from its place. But you hate the evil of the Nicolaitans, which I also hate. They forget me and try to fit in with the world around them. Listen to what the Spirit says to the churches; I will give the victorious the right to eat from the tree of life in God's paradise.

To the angel of the church in Smyrna, these are Jesus' words:

I know your afflictions and your poverty, though you are rich. I know how the false Jews who are of Satan's synagogue slander you. Don't be afraid of what you are about to suffer; the Devil is about to test you by throwing some of you into prison and persecute you for a time. Be faithful, even to the point of death, and I will give you the crown of life. Listen to what the Spirit says to the churches; the second death will not hurt those who conquer.

To the angel of the church in Pergamum, these are Jesus' words:

I know that you live near Satan's throne, yet you remain true to my name. You did not even renounce your faith when your enemies killed Antipas. Nevertheless, I have a few things against you. Some of you follow Balaam's teaching, who taught Balak to put obstacles before the Israelites so that they would eat food sacrificed to idols and practice sexual immorality. Also, some of you follow the teaching of the Nicolaitans and practice their debauchery. Repent, or I will come to you and wage war against you with the sword of my mouth. Listen to what the Spirit says to the churches; to those who conquer I will give some of the hidden manna and a white stone with a name written on it that no one knows except those who receive it.

To the angel of the church in Thyatira, these are Jesus' words:

I know your deeds, service, and perseverance, and that you are now doing more than you did at first. Nevertheless, you tolerate the woman Jezebel who calls herself a prophet and misleads my servants into sexual immorality and eating food sacrificed to idols. I gave her time to repent of her sin, but she has not. So, I will cast her on a bed of suffering along with those who commit adultery with her unless they repent. I will kill her children, then all the churches will know that I search hearts and minds, and I will repay you according to your deeds.

To the rest of you in Thyatira who do not follow her teachings and have not learned Satan's so-called deep secrets, I give you no other burden except to hold onto what you have until I come. To those who conquer and do my will to the end, I will give authority over the nations to rule with a rod of iron that shatters pottery; I will give them the morning star. Listen to what the Spirit says to the churches.

To the angel of the church in Sardis, these are Jesus' words:

I know your deeds and your reputation for being alive even though you're dead. Wake up and strengthen what is about to die because your work is not finished yet. Remember what you have learned and repent! If you do not wake up, I will come like a thief when you aren't ready. However, you have a few people who have not soiled their clothes; they will walk with me wearing white because they are worthy. God will also clothe the ones who conquer in white, their names will be in the Book of Life, and I will confess them before my Father and his angels. Listen to what the Spirit says to the churches.

To the angel of the church in Philadelphia, these are Jesus' words:

I know your deeds and I have set an open door before you that no one can shut. You don't have much power, but you have kept my word and not denied my name. I will make the fake Jews of Satan's synagogue come to bow down at your feet and learn that I love you. I will protect you from the trial coming to the earth because you have patiently endured. I am coming soon; hold on to what you have so that no one can take your crown. I will make those who conquer pillars in my God's temple and they will not leave it. I will write God's name, the name of the new Jerusalem, and my name on them. Listen to what the Spirit says to the churches.

To the angel of the church in Laodicea, these are Jesus' words:

I know your deeds, and that you are neither hot nor cold, I wish you were one or the other! Since you are lukewarm, I'm going to spit you out of my mouth. You think that you don't need anything because you're rich, but you don't realize that you are wretched, pitiful, poor, blind, and naked. You should buy gold refined in fire from me so that you can become rich, white clothes to cover your nakedness, and salve to put on your eyes so you can see. I rebuke and discipline those whom I love, so be earnest and repent. I stand at the door and knock; if you hear my voice and open the door, I will come in and eat with you. I will give those who conquer the right to sit with me on my throne, just as I sat with my Father when I was victorious. Listen to what the Spirit says to the churches.

CHAPTER FORTY-FIVE

THE SEVEN SEALS AND FIRST FIVE TRUMPETS
Revelation 4:1-9:12

> **Numbers in apocalyptic literature**
>
> One of the key features in apocalyptic writing is the use of numbers. Sometimes, the numbers represent actual quantities, but they often hold a deeper meaning. In the book of Revelation, most of the numbers that John uses have meaning beyond just amounts. Some of the primary meanings are:
>
> Three: God's number, fulfillment, or unity.
> Four: The world or all of creation.
> Six: The number of man or imperfection.
> Seven: The number of God or perfection.
> Ten: Earthly government.
> Twelve: Divine government, the tribes of Israel, or the apostles.
> 24: A witness to God's divine government represented by the twelve tribes of Israel and the twelve apostles.
> One-third or one-quarter: Not an exact calculation, but a significant portion.
> Three-and-a-half: Half of seven, a relatively short time that is precarious and dangerous.
> One thousand: A vast amount, often paired with other numbers.

After this, I saw a door in front of me open in heaven, and the voice said to me, "Come here and I will show you what must take place. Immediately, I was in the Spirit, and I saw someone seated on a throne in heaven. The one on the throne looked like jasper and ruby, and a rainbow shone around the throne like an emerald. Surrounding the throne were 24 other thrones with 24 elders seated on them, dressed in white with golden crowns.

There were flashes of lightning and peals of thunder coming from the throne and seven torches of fire before it, representing the perfection of God's Spirit. Before the throne was a sea of glass like crystal, and there were four living creatures around the throne, full of eyes all around them. The first was like a lion, the second like an ox, the third had a man's face, and the fourth looked like an eagle in flight. All four of them had six wings and were covered with eyes. They never stopped saying, "Holy, holy, holy, is the Lord God Almighty, who was, is, and is to come!"

Whenever the living creatures gave glory, honor, and thanks to the Eternal One on the throne, the 24 elders fell down before him to worship. They cast their crowns before the throne, saying, "Worthy are you, our Lord and God, to receive glory, honor, and power, for you created everything, and it exists because of your will."

Then I saw a scroll with writing on front and back, with seven seals, in the right hand of the one seated on the throne. I saw a strong angel cry out, "Who is worthy to break the seals and open the scroll?" There was no one in heaven, on earth, or under the earth who was worthy to open the scroll or read it, so I began to weep.

Then one of the elders said to me, "Do not weep, the Lion of the tribe of Judah, the Root of David, has conquered, he is worthy to break the seals and open the scroll." Between the throne and the four living creatures, I saw a Lamb standing amid the elders, looking as though it had been killed. The Lamb had seven horns with seven eyes, which are the seven spirits of God, and it took the scroll from the one sitting on the throne.

When he took the scroll, the four living creatures and the 24 elders fell down before the Lamb, each holding a harp and golden bowls of incense with the believers' prayers. They sang a new song, "Worthy are you to break the seals and open the scroll because you died and your blood ransomed people for God from everywhere on earth. You have made them a kingdom of priests to our God; they shall rule on earth."

Then I looked, and I heard around the throne, the living creatures, and the elders, the voices of countless angels declaring, "Worthy is the Lamb who was slain, to receive power, wealth, wisdom, might, honor, glory, and blessing!"

Every creature in heaven, on earth, and under the earth and sea cried out, "To God the Father and the Lamb be blessing, honor, glory, and might forever!"

The four living creatures said, "Amen!" and the elders fell down and worshipped.

I watched as the Lamb opened the first four of the seven seals, and as he opened each, one of the four living creatures said in a voice like thunder, "Come!" After the first seal, a rider came out on a white horse holding a bow; he was given a crown, and he rode out to conquer. After the second seal, a rider came out on a fiery red horse, and he was given a sword and the power to remove peace and cause people to kill each other. After the third seal, a rider came out on a black horse, and a voice told him a day's wages for a handful of grain, but not to hurt the oil and wine. After the fourth seal, a rider came out on a pale horse, and its name was Death, and Hades followed him. These four were given authority over a fourth of the earth to kill with sword, famine, pestilence, and the earth's wild beasts.

Color in Revelation

Much like numbers have symbolic meaning in this letter, colors have meanings as well. Some of the primary meanings are:

White: Purity or victory.
Red: Blood or violence.
Black: Death.
Purple: Royalty.
Gold: God's splendor.

When he opened the fifth seal, I saw the souls of those martyred for God's Word underneath the altar. They cried out with a loud voice, "O Sovereign Lord, holy and true, how long before you judge and avenge our blood on those who dwell on the earth?" They were each given a white robe and told to rest a little longer until the number of other martyrs was complete.

When he opened the sixth seal, there was a great earthquake; the sun became black as sackcloth, and the moon like blood. The sky's stars fell to the earth like a fig tree sheds its winter fruit in a strong wind. The heavens vanished like a scroll rolled up and every mountain and island moved from its place. Then everyone on earth hid in caves and among the rocks of the hills. They called to the rocks, "Fall on us to hide us from the face of the one on the throne and the wrath of the Lamb because no one can stand before him."

After this, I saw four angels standing at the ends of the earth, holding back the wind so that there would be no wind on earth, sea, or against any tree. Another angel came from the east, holding the seal of the living God, and he called out, "Do not harm the earth, sea, or trees until we have sealed the servants of our God on their foreheads." The angel sealed 12,000 from every tribe of Israel for a total of 144,000 (not an exact number, but representing a vast number of God's people).

Then I saw an innumerable multitude from every nation, tribe, people group, and language standing before the Lamb's throne. They wore white robes and waved palm branches, crying out, "Salvation belongs to our God who sits on the throne and to the Lamb!"

All the angels standing around the throne, the elders, and the four living creatures fell on their faces before the throne and worshipped God, saying, "Amen! Blessing, glory, wisdom, thanksgiving, honor, power, and might be to our God forever! Amen!"

One of the elders came to me and said, "These in the white robes are the ones who have come out of the Great Tribulation; they have washed their robes and made them white in the Lamb's blood. Now, they serve before God's throne day and night in his temple, and he shelters them with his presence. They will never hunger or thirst again and the sun will not scorch them anymore. The Lamb will be their shepherd, and he will guide them to springs of living water, then God will wipe away every tear from their eyes."

When the Lamb opened the seventh seal, there was silence in heaven for about half an hour; then the seven angels who stand before God were each given trumpets. Another angel who held a golden container for burning incense came and stood at the altar. He was given incense to offer along with the believers' prayers on the golden altar before the throne. The smoke from his offering rose before God. Then, the angel filled the golden container with fire and threw it on the earth; then, there was lightning, thunder, and another earthquake.

The seven angels with the trumpets prepared to blow them. When the first angel blew his trumpet, hail and fire mixed with blood were thrown on the earth, and a third of the trees and all the green grass burned up.

The second angel blew his trumpet, and something like a vast mountain, burning with fire, was thrown into the sea, and a third of the sea became blood. A third of the sea creatures died and a third of all ships were destroyed.

The third angel blew his trumpet, and a great star fell from heaven like a blazing torch, and it fell on a third of the rivers and springs of water. The star made the water bitter and many people died who drank from those rivers and springs.

The fourth angel blew his trumpet, and a third of the sun, moon, and stars were struck so that their light might be darkened. Then I saw an eagle flying directly overhead; it cried out with a loud voice, "Woe to those who live on the earth because of the other trumpets that the three angels are about to blow!"

The fifth angel blew his trumpet, and I saw a star fall from heaven to earth, and he was given the key to the shaft of a bottomless pit. His name is Destroyer, and when he opened the shaft, smoke rose from it as if from a great furnace, and the sun and air were darkened. Then, locusts came from the smoke, and they were given power like scorpions. God told them not to harm any plant, but only those who did not have God's seal on their foreheads.

The locusts looked like horses prepared for battle; it seemed like they wore golden crowns, with long hair, human faces, and lions' teeth. They seemed to have iron breastplates and they sounded like horses and chariots rushing into battle. They had stinging tails and they tormented the people for five months. They could not kill, but people were so miserable that they wanted to die.

The first woe is past, but there are two more to come.

Signs of the Times

As we read about these signs in the book of Revelation, it is difficult to know what exactly John describes. Our job is not to figure out where we are in history and the End Times. When we see things that may be God's judgment, we should repent from our sin and make sure we are ready for his return. We should look for ways we can spread the gospel and tell people about Jesus.

CHAPTER FORTY-SIX

THE SIXTH AND SEVENTH TRUMPETS
Revelation 9:13-11:19

The sixth angel blew his trumpet, and I heard a voice coming from the four horns of the golden altar before God saying, "Release the four angels bound at the Euphrates." The angels, who had been prepared for this time, were released, and they led a seemingly infinite number of troops to kill a third of humanity. They wore fiery red, dark blue, and yellow breastplates, the heads of their horses resembled lions, and their tails were like serpents that wound. They breathed out fire, smoke, and sulfur, and they killed a third of the earth's population. Yet, the rest of humanity did not repent of their murders, sorcery, sexual immorality, or theft. They did not stop worshipping demons or blind, lame, and mute idols.

Then another mighty angel came down from heaven, wrapped in a cloud, with a rainbow over his head; his face was like the sun, and his legs like pillars of fire. He held a little scroll in his hand, and he set his right foot on the sea and his left on the land and then cried out like a roaring lion, and the seven thunders sounded. The angel forbade me to write what the thunder said. Then, the angel raised his right hand to heaven and swore by God that when the seventh trumpet sounded, God's mystery would be fulfilled as the prophets had promised.

The voice from heaven told me to take the scroll from the angel standing on the sea and the land. When I took the scroll from the angel, he said, "Eat this scroll; it will be sweet in your mouth, but bitter in your stomach. Then you must prophesy about many peoples, nations, languages, and kings." I obeyed, and the scroll made my stomach bitter.

I was given a measuring rod and told, "Measure God's temple and the altar with its worshippers but exclude the outer courts because they have been given to the Gentiles. They will trample the holy city for three-and-a-half years; during this time, I will appoint my two witnesses who will prophesy while mourning." They are the two olive trees and the two lampstands that stand before the Lord; if anyone tries to harm them, fire comes from their mouths to consume their foes.

These two witnesses will have the power to shut the sky so that it will not rain while they are prophesying. They will also have the ability to turn water into blood and strike the earth with every plague.

When they have finished their testimony, the beast that comes from the Abyss will attack and kill them. Their bodies will lie in Jerusalem's public square (figuratively Sodom and Egypt) for three-and-a-half days while they are denied a burial. The people of the earth will rejoice over their deaths and give each other gifts because these prophets had been a torment to the whole world. But then God will breathe life into them, and they will stand up, causing those who see to be afraid. Then they will be called into heaven in a cloud while their enemies look on. At that time, an earthquake will destroy a tenth of the city and kill thousands. The people will be terrified and glorify God.

The second woe has passed; the third is coming soon.

Then the seventh angel blew his trumpet and loud voices in heaven said, "The kingdom of the world has become the kingdom of our Lord and his Christ; he shall rule forever!"

The 24 elders on the thrones before God fell on their faces and worshipped, "We give thanks to you, Lord God Almighty, who was and is because you have used your great power and began to rule. The nations were angry, but your wrath came, and now it's time to judge the dead, reward your servants, and destroy those who destroy the earth." Then God's temple in heaven opened, the ark of the covenant became visible, and there were flashes of lightning, thunder, an earthquake, and heavy hail.

CHAPTER FORTY-SEVEN

THE GREAT DRAGON AND THE BOWLS OF WRATH
Revelation 12-17

A great sign appeared in heaven: a woman clothed with the sun, the moon under her feet, and a crown of twelve stars on her head. She was crying out in pain as she gave birth. Suddenly, there was another sign: a great, red dragon with seven heads and ten horns wearing a crown on each head. It swept a third of the stars from the sky with its tail and flung them to the earth.

The dragon stood before the woman, waiting for her to give birth so that it could eat the child. She gave birth to a son who would rule the nations with an iron scepter, and God snatched the child up to his throne. The woman fled into the wilderness to a place God had prepared and he took care of her for three-and-a-half years.

Then war broke out in heaven, and Michael and his angels fought against the dragon and his angels. The great dragon, Satan, was not strong enough, and he and his angels were thrown to the earth.

Then I heard a loud voice in heaven say, "The salvation, the power, the kingdom of our God, and Christ's authority have come. For the one who accuses our brothers and sisters day and night has been thrown down. They have defeated him by the Lamb's blood and by the word of their testimony because they did not love their lives even to death. Therefore, heavens and you who dwell in them, rejoice! But woe to you earth and sea, for the Devil is angry because he knows his time is short!"

When the dragon saw his defeat, he chased the woman who gave birth to the child. But God gave the woman an eagle's wings so that she could fly to the wilderness where she would be out of the serpent's reach for three-and-a-half years. Then the serpent spewed water from its mouth like a river to overtake the woman and sweep her away. But the earth helped the woman by swallowing the dragon's river. The dragon was angry at the woman and went out to wage war against the rest of her offspring, those who obey God's commands and keep their testimony about Jesus.

The dragon stood on the seashore, and I saw a beast come out of the sea with seven heads, ten horns, and a crown on each horn; each head had a blasphemous name on it. The beast looked like a leopard, with feet like a bear, and a mouth like a lion. The dragon gave the beast his power, throne, and great authority. One of the beast's heads seemed to have a fatal wound that had been healed and the world marveled at the beast and followed him.

People worshipped the dragon. He had given the beast authority and they worshipped him because he was mighty. The beast was given a mouth to speak proud and blasphemous words, and it was given power for three-and-a-half years. It blasphemed God, slandered his name, his dwelling place, and those who live in heaven. It was allowed to make war on the believers and defeat them; it was given authority over all people on earth whose names were not written in the Lamb who was slain's Book of Life before the world's foundation.

Those marked for capture must be captured, and those who marked for death must be killed. This is a call for the endurance and faith of the believers.

Then another beast rose from the earth, it had two horns like a lamb, and it spoke like a dragon. It had the first beast's authority and it made the world worship the first beast with the healed mortal wound. It performed great signs and even made fire fall from heaven, commanding the world to create an image of the first beast. It was allowed to bring the image to life and it killed everyone who would not worship the image of the beast. It also caused everyone on earth to be marked on the right hand or forehead so that no one can buy or sell unless they have the mark of the beast. The number of the beast is the number of a man, 666.

> ### Mark of the beast
>
> There are many theories on what the mark of the beast is, but we don't know what the beast's mark will be. It will be something that will make it difficult to participate in the world if you don't have it. The fact that

> it is the number six three times means that it will represent humanity's power. As believers, we need to make sure we are more worried about what God thinks rather than what makes our lives on earth more comfortable.

I looked and saw the Lamb standing on Mount Zion with the 144,000 who had his name and his Father's name written on their foreheads. I heard a voice from heaven like rushing water, thunder, and harpists playing. The four living creatures and the 24 elders sang a new song before the throne, and no one could learn the song except the people the Lord redeemed from the earth. These are virgins who follow the Lamb wherever he goes; they have been redeemed from humanity, are the first fruits of God and the Lamb, and there was no lie in their mouths for they are blameless.

Then I saw another angel flying directly overhead with an eternal gospel to proclaim to everyone who lives on earth. He said with a loud voice, "Fear God and give him glory because the hour of his judgment has come; worship him because he created all things."

A second angel followed him, saying, "Babylon the Great has fallen who made the nations drink the wine of her sexual immorality."

> **Babylon the Great**
>
> Babylon the Great is a symbol of the wicked people of earth. It is Satan's kingdom that God will overthrow when he returns. The wine of her sexual immorality is a symbol of the sin she leads her followers to commit.

A third angel followed them, saying, "Those who worship the beast or receive its mark will drink the wine of God's wrath, the full strength of his anger, and be tormented with fire and sulfur in the presence of the holy angels and the Lamb. The smoke of their torment goes up forever and they have no rest." This is a call for the believers' endurance, who obey God's commands and keep their faith in Jesus.

Then a voice from heaven said, "Blessed are those who die in the Lord from now on because they will have rest from their labor."

Then I saw Jesus seated on a cloud with a golden crown on his head and a sharp sickle in his hand. Another angel came out of the temple and cried out to Jesus, "Use the sickle and reap, for the earth's harvest is fully ripe, and it's time to reap." The one sitting on the cloud swung his sickle across the earth and it was reaped.

Then another angel came out of the temple with a sharp sickle. The angel with authority over the fire followed and told him, "Use your sickle and gather the grapes from the earth's vine because they are ripe." The angel swung its sickle and gathered the earth's grape harvest and threw it into the winepress of God's wrath. The winepress was trampled outside the city and blood flowed from it four feet deep for about 180 miles.

Then I saw seven angels with the seven last plagues, which complete God's wrath. I saw those who had conquered the beast, its image, and number standing next to what looked like a sea of glass and fire. They held harps and sang the song of Moses and the Lamb, "Your deeds are great and marvelous, Lord God Almighty. King of the nations, your ways are just and true. All will fear you and glorify your name because you alone are holy. Every nation will worship you for you have revealed your righteous acts."

Then I saw that the sanctuary of the tent of witness in heaven was open, and seven angels with the seven plagues came out wearing pure, bright linen with golden sashes across their chests. One of the four living creatures gave each of the seven angels golden bowls full of the eternal God's wrath and the sanctuary filled with the smoke of God's glory and power. No one could enter the sanctuary until the seven plagues of the seven angels were over.

Then I heard a loud voice from the temple tell the seven angels to pour out their bowls of God's wrath on the earth. The first angel poured out his bowl on the land, and painful, festering sores broke out on the people who had the mark of the beast and worshipped his image.

The second angel poured out his bowl on the sea, it became like a dead person's blood, and every living thing in the sea died.

The third angel poured out his bowl on the rivers and springs of water and they became like blood. Then the angel in charge of the waters said, "Holy One, who was and is, your judgments are just because they have killed your saints and prophets, and now you have given them blood to drink." The altar called in return, "Yes, Lord God Almighty, your judgments are true and just!"

The fourth angel poured out his bowl on the sun, and it began to scorch the people with fierce heat and fire. The people did not repent and give God glory but instead cursed his name.

The fifth angel poured out his bowl on the beast's throne and its kingdom was plunged into darkness. People gnawed their tongues in anguish and cursed God for their pain and sores, yet they did not repent.

The sixth angel poured out his bowl on the river Euphrates and the water dried up to prepare the way for the kings from the East. Then I saw three impure spirits that looked like frogs coming out of the dragon's mouths, the beast, and the false prophet. They are demonic spirits that perform signs and gather the earth together for the battle on the Great Day of God Almighty at Armageddon. He is coming like a thief! Blessed are those who stay awake and dressed so that they aren't naked and ashamed.

The seventh angel poured out his bowl into the air, and a loud voice came from the throne, saying, "It is done!" There was lightning, thunder, and the biggest earthquake to happen since creation. Jerusalem split into three parts, the cities of the nations fell, and God remembered Babylon the Great to make her drink the cup of his furious wrath. Every island fled away and the mountains were leveled. Hundred-pound hailstones fell from heaven and the people cursed God for the severity of the plague.

Then one of the angels who had the seven bowls said to me, "I will show you the judgment of the great prostitute seated on many waters and the kings of the earth who committed sexual immorality with her."

He carried me away in the Spirit into the wilderness. I saw a woman sitting on a scarlet beast with seven heads and ten horns covered with blasphemous names. The woman was wearing purple, scarlet, golden jewelry, and pearls. She held a golden cup full of the abominations and impurities of her sexual immorality. On her forehead was written, "Babylon the Great, mother of prostitutes and earth's abominations." She was drunk with the blood of the believers who had died for the name of Christ.

I marveled at her, but the angel asked me, "Why do you marvel? The beast you saw was, is not, and is about to rise from the bottomless pit and be destroyed. The earth's people whose names are not written in the Book of Life from the foundation of the world will marvel at the beast because it was, is not, and is to come.

> **Was, is not, and is to come**
>
> This is a reference to the mortal wound that the beast suffers. It refers to the beast's political rise, fall, and return to life.

"The beast's seven heads are seven mountains that the woman sits upon, they represent seven kings, five have fallen, one is, and the last is yet to come; his rule will only last a little while. The beast that was and is not is an eighth ruler, but it belongs to the seven, and will be destroyed.

"The ten horns are ten rulers who have not come to power yet; they will rule for a short time with the beast. These kings share one mind, and they give their power and authority to the beast. They will make war with the Lamb, but the Lamb will defeat them because he is Lord of lords and King of kings, those who are with him are the chosen and faithful.

"The waters you saw are the people of the world. The ten horns you saw, they and the beast will hate the prostitute. They will bring her to ruin, leave her naked, eat her flesh, and burn her with fire. God has put it in their hearts to accomplish his purpose by agreeing to give the beast their royal authority until God's Word is fulfilled. The woman you saw is the great city that rules over the kings of the earth."

CHAPTER FORTY-EIGHT

JUDGMENT OF BABYLON
Revelation 18:1-19:10

After this, I saw another angel coming down from heaven with great authority, and the earth was bright with his glory. With a mighty voice, he shouted, "Babylon the Great is fallen! She has become a dwelling place for demons, every unclean spirit, and every unclean bird and detestable beast. All the nations have drunk the maddening wine of her sexual immorality and the earth's powerful have made themselves rich from her luxurious living."

Then I heard another voice from heaven, "My people, come out of her so that you will not share in her sins or suffer her plagues because her sins are piled up to heaven, and God knows her crimes. Pay her back double for what she has done. Give her as much torment and grief as the glory and luxury she gave herself. She boasts that she is a queen, not a widow, and that she will never mourn. But her plagues will overtake her in a single day, death, mourning, and famine. She will be consumed by fire because the Lord God, who judges her, is mighty.

"When the rulers of earth who committed adultery with her and shared her luxury see the smoke of her burning, they will weep and mourn. They will be terrified of her torment and stand far away, crying out because they see that her doom has come. Then everyone she made rich will weep and mourn because no one buys the costly goods that she sold. Her delicacies and splendor are lost and will never be found. But heaven and God's people will rejoice because of God's judgment against her."

Then a mighty angel picked up a giant stone and threw it into the sea, saying, "Babylon will be thrown down with violence and never be found again, just like this stone. No one will make music in the city and no one will produce goods in her any longer. It will have no light and no one will rejoice because its sorcery deceived the whole earth. She is full of the blood of the prophets, believers, and everyone killed on the earth."

Then I heard the roar of a great multitude in heaven, "Hallelujah! Salvation, glory, and power belong to our God because his judgments are true and just. He has condemned the great prostitute who corrupted the earth and he has avenged his servants' blood on her. Hallelujah, her smoke goes up forever and ever!"

The 24 elders and the four living creatures fell down and worshiped God, who was seated on the throne. Then a voice came from the throne, "All God's servants give him praise, both small and great."

Then I heard the multitude shouting, "Hallelujah, the Lord God Almighty reigns! Let us rejoice, be glad, and give him glory! The Lamb's wedding is here, and his bride has made herself ready with fine linen that is bright and clean.

Then an angel told me to write, "Blessed are those invited to the Lamb's marriage supper! These are the true Words of God."

I fell at his feet to worship him, but he said, "Don't do that; I am a servant like you and your brothers who believe the testimony about Jesus. You should only worship God. It is the Spirit of prophecy who testifies about Jesus."

CHAPTER FORTY-NINE

THE FINAL BATTLE
Revelation 19:11-21:8

I saw heaven standing open, and a rider called Faithful and True (Jesus) seated on a white horse; he judges and wages war with justice. His eyes are like a blazing fire, wore many crowns, and has a name that only he knows. His robe is dipped in blood and his name is the Word of God. He led the armies of heaven on white horses, dressed in clean, white linen. There was a sharp sword coming out of his mouth to strike down the nations that he will rule with an iron scepter. He treads the winepress of God's furious wrath, and he had his name written on his robe and thigh, King of kings and Lord of lords.

> **Jesus the Conquering King**
>
> When Jesus came the first time, he was a suffering servant. Finally, we see him come as a conquering king. This is the fulfillment of the Jews' messianic expectations at Jesus' first coming. He shows up to fight in white, something unheard of in battle. He knows he will defeat his enemies and has no fear of them even coming close enough to get his clothes dirty. He has a sword coming out of his mouth, ready to strike, and tattoos on his legs. This is a true warrior.

Then I saw an angel standing in the sun who cried out with a loud voice to all the birds of the air, "Come, gather for God's great supper to eat the mighty of earth's flesh."

The beast, the rulers of the earth, and their armies gathered to wage war against Jesus and his army. The beast and the false prophet were captured, and they were thrown alive into the lake of fire that burns with sulfur. Jesus killed the rest with the sword from his mouth and the birds gorged themselves on their flesh.

I saw an angel come down from heaven with the key to the bottomless pit in his hand on a great chain. He seized Satan, the great dragon, and locked him up in the pit for 1,000 years so that he could not deceive the earth until the time was up, and he would be released for a short time.

Then I saw those with authority to judge seated on thrones, the martyrs' souls, and those who had not worshipped the beast or taken its mark. They came to life and ruled with Christ for 1,000 years, but the rest of the dead did not rise until the end of the 1,000 years; this is the first resurrection. Those who share in this resurrection are blessed and holy, the second death has no power over them, and they will be priests of God and Christ.

When the 1,000 years are over, Satan will be released from his prison and will go out to deceive the world and gather them for battle. Their number will be like the sand of the seashore, and they will march up over the broad plain of the earth and surround the believers and the beloved city. But fire will come down from heaven and consume them and the Devil who leads them. Then they will be thrown into the lake of fire and sulfur where the beast and false prophet are, and they will be tormented day and night forever.

Hell

For more information on hell, read the box in Chapter 33 of The Life of Jesus.

Then I saw Jesus on a great white throne, and the earth and sky fled from his presence, and there was no place for them. Then the dead stood before the throne, and the books, including the Book of Life, were opened. Everyone who had died was judged by everything recorded in the books, and then Death and Hades were thrown into the lake of fire, which is the second death. Anyone whose name was not found in the Book of Life was thrown into the lake of fire.

Then I saw a new heaven and earth because the first had passed away, and there was no longer any sea. I saw the new Jerusalem coming down from heaven, a beautiful bride dressed for her husband. I heard a loud voice from the throne say, "Behold the dwelling place of God is with man; he will live with them, they will be his people, and he will be their God. He will wipe away every tear from their eyes; there will be no more death, mourning, crying, or pain, for the former things have passed away. I am making all things new. Write these words down for this is trustworthy and true."

Then he said, "It is finished! I am the Alpha and the Omega, the Beginning and the End. I will give free water from the spring of life to the thirsty. Those who conquer will inherit all this, I will be their God, and they will be my children. But the cowardly, unbelieving, vile, murderers, sexually immoral, sorcerers, idolaters, and liars will burn in the fiery lake of sulfur; this is the second death."

What do we do with the book of Revelation?

The book of Revelation can be very confusing, and it has led to much debate about how we should interpret it. The purpose of this book is not to tell us when we get to leave this world but is to reassure us that God wins in the end. Even when we see the world falling apart around us, we should take comfort and use the signs of the times as motivation to draw closer to God and tell people about him.

CHAPTER FIFTY

THE NEW JERUSALEM
Revelation 21:9-22:21

One of the angels who had one of the seven bowls of God's plagues came to me and said, "Come, I will show you the Bride of the Lamb."

He carried me away in the Spirit to a great mountain. He showed me the holy city, Jerusalem, coming down from heaven. It shone with God's glory, and it was as brilliant as the rarest jewel, like a jasper, clear as crystal. It had a great, high wall, with twelve gates; there were angels at each of the gates, and they had the names of the twelve tribes of the sons of Israel written on them, three in each direction. The wall had twelve foundations, each with one of the apostles' names.

The angel had a gold measuring rod to measure the city. It was nearly 1,200 miles long, wide, and high, and the walls were more than 200 feet tall. The wall was of jasper and the city of gold as pure as glass. The foundation of the city walls was decorated with every kind of precious stone: jasper, sapphire, agate, emerald, onyx, ruby, chrysolite, beryl, topaz, turquoise, jacinth, and amethyst. Each gate was a single pearl, and the streets were made of gold, as clear as glass. There was no temple in the city because the Lord God Almighty and the Lamb were its temple.

> **Heaven**
>
> For more information on heaven, read the box in Chapter 39 of The Life of Jesus.

There is no need for the sun or moon because God and the Lamb give the city light, and all the nations will walk in its glory. The rulers of the earth will bring their glory into it and the city gates will never shut because there will be no night there. Nothing unclean will ever enter, but only those written in the Lamb's Book of Life.

Then the angel showed me the river of the water of life, clear as crystal flowing from the throne of God and the Lamb. It flowed through the middle of the city's street on either side of the river was the tree of life, bearing twelve kinds of fruit, one each month. The leaves of the tree were for healing the nations. There was no longer anything flawed, the throne of God and the Lamb was in it, and his servants would worship him. They will see his face and his name will be on their foreheads. They will rule forever.

The angel said to me, "These words are trustworthy and true; the Lord God of the spirits of the prophets has sent his angel to show his servants what will happen. I am coming soon; blessed are those who keep the words of the prophecy of this book. Then John was back in Patmos and the vision ended.

***

I am John, the one who heard and saw these things. When I did, I fell down at the angel's feet to worship him, but he said to me, "Don't do that; I am a servant like you and the other believers who obey this book's words. Worship God alone. Don't seal up the words of this prophecy because the time is near. Those who do wrong should keep doing wrong, the vile should keep being vile, those who do right should keep doing what's right, and the holy should keep being holy."

Jesus is coming soon and he will reward everyone for what they've done. He is the Alpha and the Omega, the First and the Last, the Beginning and the End. Blessed are those who wash their robes so that they may have the right to the tree of life so they may enter the city through the gates. The dogs, sorcerers, sexually immoral, murderers, idolaters, and everyone who loves and practices falsehood are left outside.

Jesus has sent his angel to testify to us about these things for the churches. He is the Root and Descendant of David, the bright Morning Star. The Spirit and the Bride beckon us to come, and whoever is thirsty should drink from the free water of life. Whoever adds to this book of prophecy, God will give him all the plagues in this book. Anyone who takes away from the words of this book of prophecy, God will take away his share in the tree of life and the holy city described in this book.

Jesus is coming soon. Amen. Come, Lord Jesus! May the grace of the Lord Jesus be with us all. Amen.

EPILOGUE

WHAT'S THE POINT?

In the beginning, God created the heavens and the earth. He made it for his glory and gave it to people as a perfect gift. There were no flaws, no bad things, and nothing ever went wrong. God put Adam and Eve in the Garden of Eden and gave them the task of tending the garden. He intended them to stay there and gave them one rule to protect them, not to eat from the Tree of the Knowledge of Good and Evil. God promised that if they disobeyed, they would die.

But this perfection didn't last long. Before long, Satan tempted our ancestors, and they failed. But God was gracious and didn't kill them immediately. Instead, he cursed them, Satan, and the earth. Since then, we have all sinned as our ancestors did. Sin is anytime we fall short of God's perfect standard, disobey his commands, or do what we know we should not do.

Sin is the cause of every bad thing in this world (creation was perfect before sin). Sometimes, bad things happen because of our sin; sometimes, they happen because of someone else's sin; sometimes, they happen just because earth is suffering the consequences of sin (things like disease and natural disasters).

It is easy to dismiss this because we all sin and we don't see God's immediate judgment. But our sin separates us from God; since he is perfect, he cannot accept us in our fallen state. But he does not kill us the moment we sin, even though we deserve it.

We all have this problem and we try different methods to deal with it. Some ignore it, but that doesn't fix anything. Others believe that trying to do more good than bad will solve the problem, but it doesn't. We cannot argue our way out of a speeding ticket because of all the times we didn't speed. Another option is to earn our way into God's favor, but that falls short as well. God tells us that our best deeds are like filthy rags in his sight. It seems like we have no hope.

But once again, God is gracious. Even though he didn't have to, God laid aside his glory and came to the earth in the person of Jesus. He was born in poverty, grew up, lived the perfect life we could not, and died in our place. He took our place on the cross and died. But he didn't stay dead; he rose again on the third day, defeating Satan, sin, and death.

After reading about Jesus' life, the astonishing things he did, his death, and resurrection, it can be tempting to walk away thinking that he was an amazing teacher and not much else. But he fits into the larger story of what God is doing in history.

We must deal with the same question that Pilate faced at Jesus' trial, what do we do with Jesus? C.S. Lewis put it best when he summed up the choice we have with this statement:

"You must make your choice. Either this man was, and is, the Son of God; or else a madman or something worse. You can shut him up for a fool; you can spit at him and kill him for a demon; or you can fall at his feet and call him Lord and God. But let us not come with any patronizing nonsense about his being a great human teacher. He has not left that open to us. He did not intend to."

The options are these: Jesus was crazy, and he may as well have said he was a staple remover; he was a liar, knew he was not God, and formed the most elaborately constructed lie ever; or Jesus was God in the flesh. Jesus obviously was not a lunatic, nor was he a liar, so the only option we have left is that he is Lord.

Some people say he was merely a good teacher, but this is not a possibility either. If he was just a good teacher, then he could not make the claims he made, have them be false, and still be a good person. We cannot put him in the category of "only a good teacher."

A final possibility is that Jesus' later followers made up his claims to deity. However, the apostles wrote the New Testament within a couple of generations of the events they recorded, which is not nearly enough time to distort a true story into a legend. This would be like someone today claiming that John F. Kennedy performed many miracles, claimed to be God, and rose from the dead. People would dismiss anyone who made claims like that as a fraud. But people living at the time of the New Testament were not able to refute Christianity's claims.

Jesus is unique in history in that he was fully God and man. He needed to be human to identify with us and live the life we are incapable of living. He needed to be God to pay for our sins.

The only way we can truly deal with our sin problem is to place our faith in Christ and trust Jesus to fix it for us. We must recognize that we are incapable of fixing our sin on our own. We must believe the facts of the gospel, acknowledge our sins, turn away from them, and then live a life following his teachings.

Trusting Jesus is more than just intellectual assent. This is like how we interact with a chair. We can know everything about a chair, describe it, and say that we believe it will hold us up. But we do not have faith that the chair will support us until we act and sit in it. Saving faith is a gift, but it requires us to trust and act.

If you want to know more about faith in Jesus, you should read the Bible and find a church that can guide you in your journey to know him. Look for a church that preaches from the Bible that Jesus is God and that he lived a perfect life, died for our sins, and rose again. You can also go to www.rcpbible.com for more information.

Made in the USA
Middletown, DE
29 December 2020